HISTORY BOOK

An Interactive Journey

MARCUS COWPER

The National Geographic Society is one of the world's largest nonprofit scientific and educational organizations. Founded in 1888 to "increase and diffuse geographic knowledge," the Society works to inspire people to care about the planet. It reaches more than 325 million people worldwide each month through its official journal, NATIONAL GEOGRAPHIC, and other magazines; National Geographic Channel; television documentaries; music; radio; films; books; DVDs; maps; exhibitions; school publishing programs; interactive media; and merchandise. National Geographic has funded more than 9,000 scientific research, conservation and exploration projects and supports an education program combating geographic illiteracy. For more information, visit nationalgeographic.com.

For more information, please call 1-800-NGS LINE (647-5463) or write to the following address:

National Geographic Society
1145 17th Street N.W.
Washington, D.C. 20036-4688 U.S.A.

Visit us online at www.nationalgeographic.com

For information about special discounts for bulk purchases, please contact National Geographic Books Special Sales: ngspecsales@ngs.org

For rights or permissions inquiries, please contact National Geographic Books Subsidiary Rights: ngbookrights@ngs.org

Published by the National Geographic Society

ISBN: 978-1-4262-0679-5
ISBN: 978-1-4262-0680-1 (Deluxe)

Printed in China

10/CAR/1

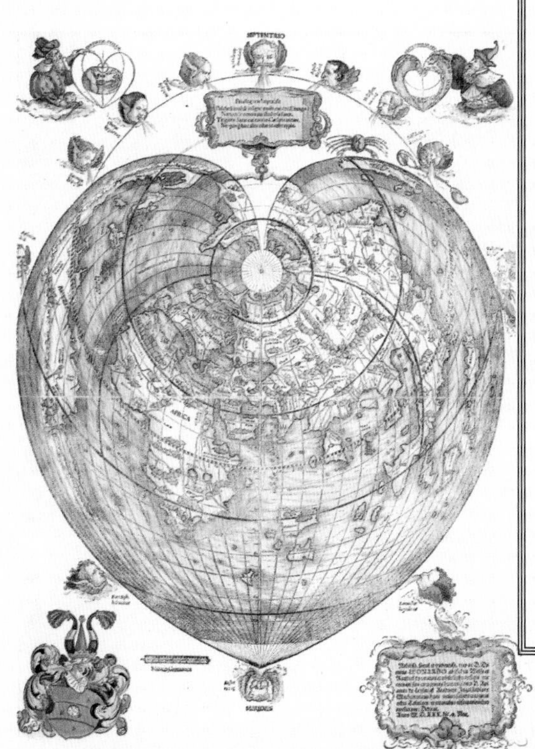

CONTENTS

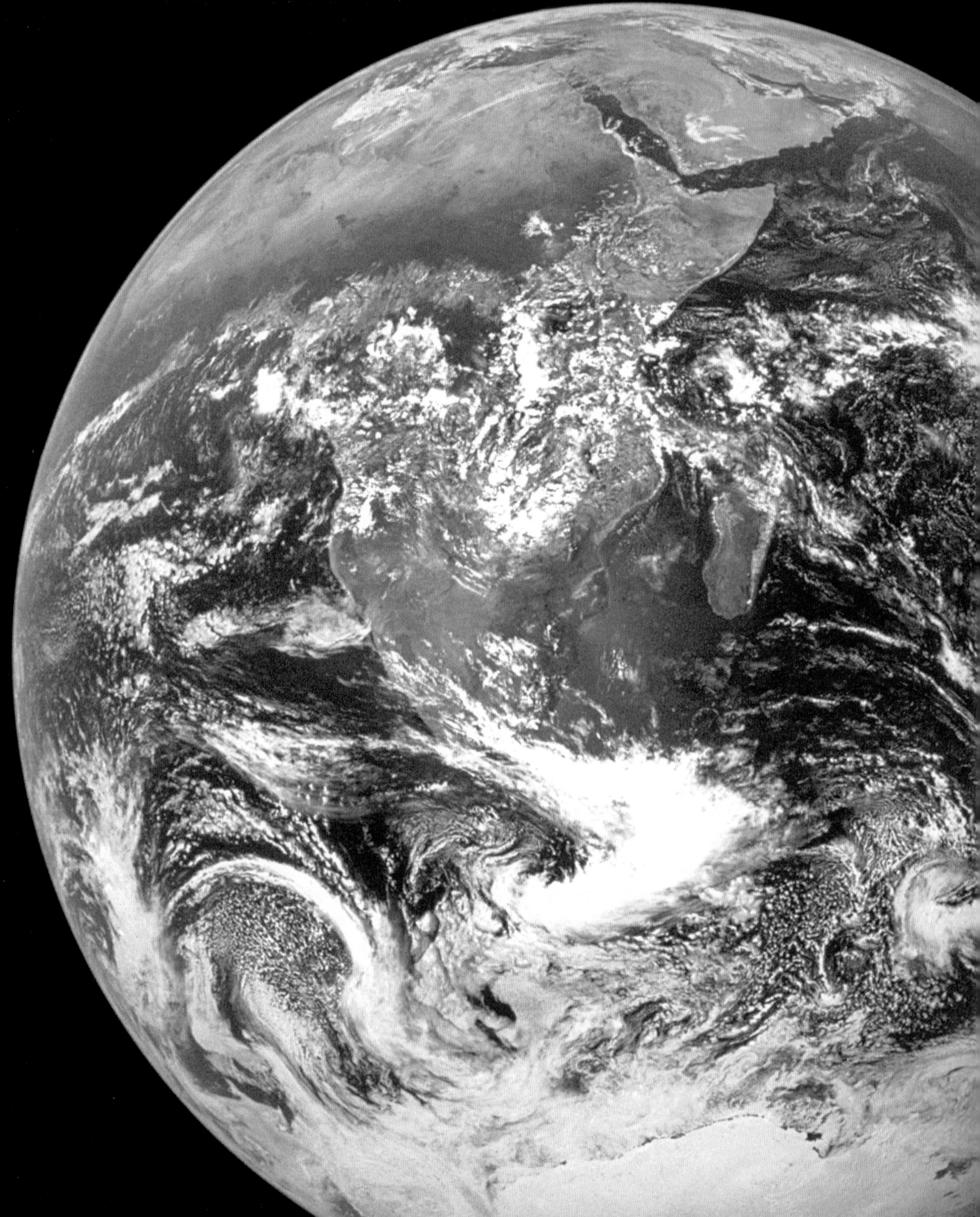

INTRODUCTION

A history of the world, whether by Herodotus or H. G. Wells, has always proved an ambitious undertaking, one that has buried many a historian under endless piles of research. Packing the events and people of more than 5,000 years into one volume becomes a matter of thematic selection. In preparing the current volume, the editors of National Geographic had two objectives in mind.

The first was to choose the people, periods, and events of the past that would have the most relevance and resonance with modern readers. The second was to present those selections in a tangible way, so that readers could have the feeling of actually reaching back through time and coming in contact with another world.

A brief word about selection. With the help of our resident experts and consultants, we picked 88 people, events, civilizations, time periods, and intellectual or cultural trends to highlight. Each of these 88 claims a separate spread. We follow a spread on the Roman Empire, for example, with one on Jesus of Nazareth. It was not enough to merely mention the Black Death along the way, so we gave the topic its own spread. Further along, we've highlighted Mozart, the Slave Trade, and Karl Marx. In the 20th century, there's Hollywood, Mao Zedong, and the World Wide Web. Each of these people and movements continues to have an important influence on the way we live.

Now to the fun part. To add luster to dusty topics and long-dead heroes and villains, we have literally packed our book with treasures. Turn the pages and you'll find documents, letters, journals, telegrams, posters, and artworks that you can pull out and examine. In the same way that historians approach their research, you can study the primary sources to see what really happened and who really did it. Pull out a copy of Shakespeare's will and see how he changed his mind about who got what. Examining a facsimile of the Zouche-Nuttall Codex gives you a sense of the turmoil of pre-Columbian Mexico. Interested in Napoleon's love life? Take a look at a steamy letter he wrote to his wife Josephine. Or, for a plunge into the grim realities of Nazi Germany, handle a British officer's on-site account of a concentration camp.

For added context, each spread includes informative time lines, rich illustrations, and related sidebars. A sidebar in the New World Colonies spread offers the most current information on Pocahontas. A different Captain Smith is the subject of a Titanic sidebar, offering the fascinating backstory on the "millionaires' captain." The Henry Ford spread has a sidebar on a newspaper, ironically Ford's own, that tainted the automaker's reputation by printing anti-Semitic articles.

The History Book: An Interactive Journey, then, is not an encyclopedia or a comprehensive survey; it is instead a storyboard of major characters, key plot points, and crucial details in the moving picture of human history. A portal through time, the book is also a collector's showcase of historical treasures and oddities, a between-the-covers museum of world history. We hope you'll refer to it often, that this scrapbook of the human family will become an old friend, and that learning firsthand will inspire you to investigate further on your own.

THE BEGINNINGS OF MAN

The solar system in which the Earth lies came into being 4.7–4.6 billion years ago out of the gas clouds and dust left over from the formation of the Sun. The Earth itself began to form 4.5–4.4 billion years ago, subject to heat and pressure so intense that it was at first a molten planet. The earliest stage of Earth's history is known as the pre-Cambrian period, divided into three separate sections: the Hadean, Archean, and Proterozoic.

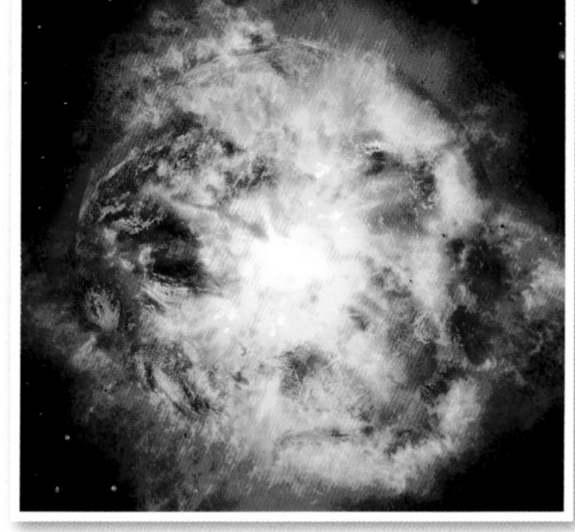

ABOVE: *A photographic simulation gives an idea of what the Big Bang might have looked like as the universe was formed out of gas clouds.*

LEFT: *The reconstructed skeleton of a* Tyrannosaurus rex, *which was the largest of the carnivorous dinosaurs.*

EARTH'S FORMATION

It was during the first period, the Hadean, that Earth was formed, began to cool, and fell into a regular orbit around the Sun. The cooling process gave rise to the Earth's first atmosphere, which consisted of gases produced by the constant eruptions on the surface, but did not contain any free oxygen. The cooling of the Earth's crust also produced vast clouds that gave out the enormous volume of rainwater required to create the oceans of the world. This led to the Archean period, from 4.0 to 2.5 billion years ago, which saw the first appearance of life on Earth, initially in the form of simple bacteria. By the beginning of the Proterozoic period, simple algae were beginning to photosynthesize and create oxygen; this period also saw the formation of the first super-continent, known as Rodinia, about 1.1 billion years ago.

LIFE FORMS

The end of the Proterozoic period and beginning of the Paleozoic era (542 to 251 million years ago) saw a massive upsurge in new forms of life, as shown in the fossil record. This "Cambrian explosion" led to the development of most of the major animal groups that survive today. While many of these species were to become extinct at the end of the Cambrian period, ca 488 million years ago, the Paleozoic period saw the increased specialization of organisms, with the

DEMISE OF THE DINOSAURS

Around 65.5 million years ago, many of the species that had developed during the "Cambrian explosion" were wiped out, including the dinosaurs. This event, known to scientists as the Cretaceous–Tertiary extinction event (or K-T Extinction, from the German), wiped out some 85 percent of the species alive on Earth. Its causes are uncertain, but one plausible theory is that a massive asteroid or comet hit the Earth, creating a mass cloud of vaporized rock and steam in the atmosphere, blocking out the Sun, and causing a catastrophic drop in temperature. This would have caused many plants to die out, disrupting the food chain and possibly causing the mass extinction.

KEY DATES OF THE BEGINNINGS OF MAN

4.5 BILLION YEARS AGO
Formation of planet Earth out of gas clouds and dust left over from the formation of the Sun

4.1 BILLION YEARS AGO
The surface of the Earth cools, forming a solid crust, and Earth begins to orbit the Sun

2.5 BILLION YEARS AGO
Beginning of photosynthesis, putting oxygen into the atmosphere and creating bacteria

1.2 BILLION YEARS AGO
The emergence of the first simple multicellular organisms

1.1 BILLION YEARS AGO
The continents begin to form and stabilize, beginning with Rodinia

separate development of fish, amphibians, and then mammals, birds, and reptiles.

It was this last group of creatures which was to provide the best-known life forms of the following period, the Mesozoic (250–65.5 million years ago). During it, reptiles developed into dinosaurs, the dominant species of the era, which came to an abrupt end with a mass extinction some 65.5 million years ago. It marked the end of the Paleozoic era and the commencement of the Cenozoic era, which continues to the present day. This period saw Earth's continents drift to the positions they currently occupy, while the disappearance of the dinosaurs led to the rise of the mammals—most notably our own species, *Homo sapiens*—as the dominant class of creatures.

LEFT: *A Cambrian trilobite fossil,* Moducia typicalis, *which was excavated from the Marjum formation of Utah, U.S.A.*
BELOW: *Maurice Wilson's painting of the life of* Homo habilis, *based on the finds of Dr. Leakey in the Olduvai Gorge, Tanzania.*

THE EARLIEST HUMANS

The human race belongs to the genus *Homo*, which first appeared around 2.5 million years ago. The earliest member of this genus, *Homo habilis*, developed in Africa and used simple tools. *Homo ergaster*, who existed some 1.65 million years ago, developed more complex tools, including axes and cleavers, and also spread beyond Africa for the first time. It was not, however, until the time of *Homo erectus*, some 1.8 to 1.5 million years ago, that man spread throughout Asia in any kind of numbers. The first known Europeans were *Homo antecessor* or *Homo heidelbergensis*, dating from some 800,000 years ago. Another species of *Homo*, the Neanderthals, also thrived in Europe from 200,000 to 25,000 years ago, when they finally became extinct, with their place being taken by *Homo sapiens*, modern humans.

225 MILLION YEARS AGO
The first dinosaurs develop from the earliest reptiles

65.5 MILLION YEARS AGO
The K–T extinction event wipes out much of life on Earth, including all the dinosaurs

2.2 MILLION YEARS AGO
The first hominid, *Homo habilis*, develops in Africa and uses simple tools

200,000 YEARS AGO
The first anatomically modern human, early *Homo sapiens*, emerges in Africa

25,000 YEARS AGO
Neanderthal man becomes extinct and *Homo sapiens* becomes the dominant species

THE SUMERIANS ≈ CA 3200–1700 B.C.

The Sumerian civilization flourished in the region that is now southern Iraq, and is one of the earliest known civilizations in world history. The land was very fertile, sitting between two great rivers, the Tigris and Euphrates (which gave the region its ancient name, Mesopotamia—"the land between the rivers"). The Sumerians achieved their success through intensive farming, with new agricultural techniques, such as irrigation and the specialization of labor, enabling farmers to cultivate fields year after year, forgoing the need to chase migrating herds or seek more fertile land.

This allowed the emergence of larger, more settled populations, with farming villages gradually growing into towns and cities. In turn, this facilitated exchange of ideas, culture, and learning, and the growth of trade, developments which led to the creation of writing (of a type known as cuneiform) around 3500 B.C. and many new inventions, including the wheel and the plough.

BELOW: A map of Mesopotamia drawn in 1458. The level of detail is evidence of enduring European interest in the region.

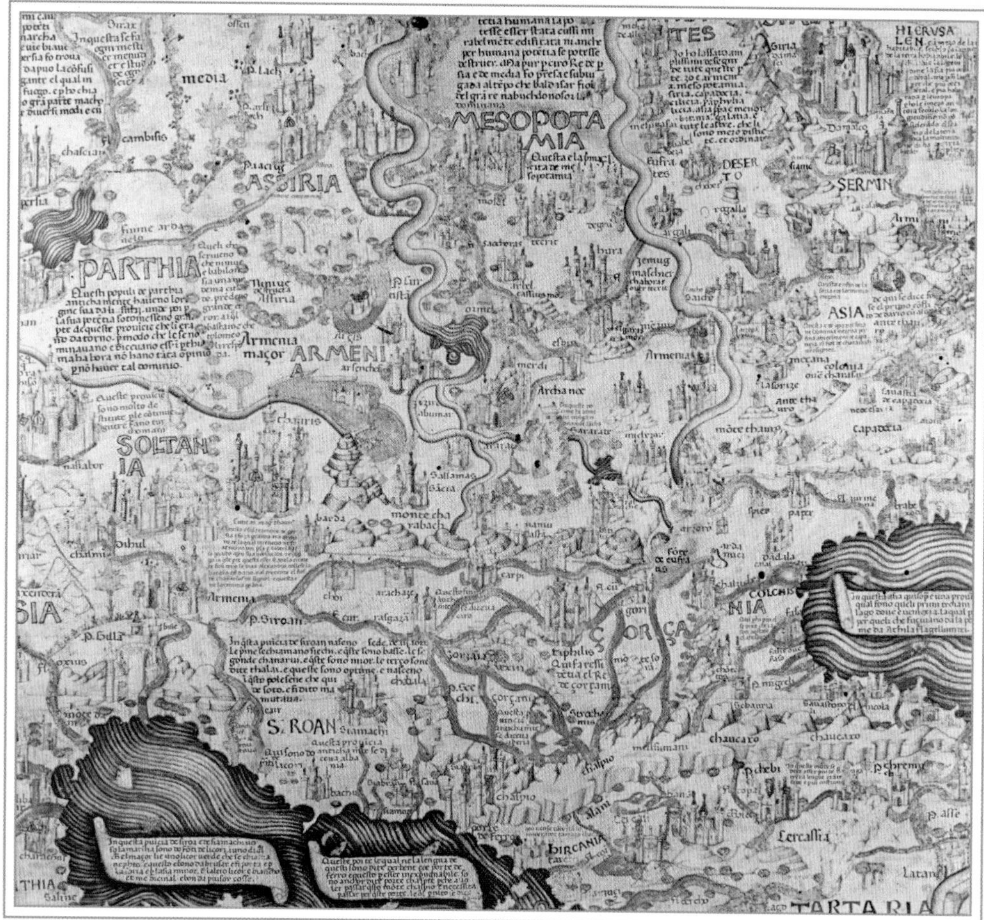

ABOVE: A cult vase of Entennena, Prince of Lagash, found at Tello in southern Mesopotamia. Made of silver and copper, and engraved to depict an eagle, it is thought to date from about 244 B.C.

CITY STATES

Cities were at the center of Sumerian life. Easily fortified, they allowed people to trade with one another in a centralized location. By 3200 B.C., Sumer was divided into several city states, which competed for political power. Each contained a temple dedicated to a patron god, the worship of whom was a central aspect of Sumerian life, with priests exercising great power within their city. Each city had its own religious

KEY DATES OF THE SUMERIAN CIVILIZATION

CA 3400–300 B.C.
Uruk IV Period, named after the Sumerian city of Uruk, flourishes in what is now southern Iraq

CA 2900–2334 B.C.
Early Dynastic period, in which successive dynasties rule Sumer

CA 2700 B.C.
Gilgamesh, the most famous of Sumerian kings, rules Sumer

CA 2500–2334 B.C.
Sumer dominated by ruling dynasty of the city state of Lagash

CA 2334–2218 B.C.
The Akkadian Empire, first empire in the region, rules Sumer

SUMERIAN WRITING

Sumerian writing is the oldest that has ever been discovered. It uses a mixture of hieroglyphs and symbols, with the latter representing spoken syllables. Surviving examples are found on clay tablets, and it appears that the writing was etched into the material using pointed reeds. This script is known as cuneiform (after its wedge-shaped forms). It was widely adapted across the ancient world, before eventually being replaced around 500 B.C. by the Aramaic writing system. A great many artifacts bearing Sumerian writing have survived, granting historians an extensive insight into Sumerian culture and way of life.

hierarchy, and each god's popularity was tied to the power of the city with which it was associated. Sumerian temples took the form of ziggurats, huge monuments built in the shape of a terraced pyramid. Several ziggurats still survive across the Middle East, most notably in Iraq. Sumerians believed the world to be a flat disk enclosed by a tin dome, and that after death the soul descended into an underworld and became a ghost.

CLIMATE PROBLEMS

The climate of Mesopotamia began to alter around 3000 B.C., making the land less fertile. This triggered mass migrations and frequent armed conflict as people struggled to adapt. From 2900 B.C., various of the competing city states managed briefly to unite Sumer under their rule, most notably Ur, Uruk, Umma, and Lagash. But in 2334 B.C., Sargon, a foreigner, formed the region's first empire, conquering all the disparate city states. His empire was short-lived, collapsing shortly after the death of Naram-Sin in 2218 B.C. as nomadic Gutians swept into Sumer from the east.

Failed harvests, famine, and decaying infrastructure meant difficult times for Sumer, but around 2110 B.C. this decline was briefly reversed under the 3rd dynasty of Ur, which presided over a "Sumerian Renaissance." This was a period of great cultural richness, but it was short-lived and, around 2000 B.C., pressure from nomadic Amorites and Elamites and revolts by some of Ur's subject city states led to its collapse.

LEFT: *Sumerian tablet with cuneiform script, etched with the wedge-shaped tip of a reed in rows running left to right. Early script comprised a stock of about 1,500 possible symbols, later reduced to around 600.*

BELOW LEFT: *The ziggurat at Ur was a massive stepped pyramid, part of the temple complex at the city's center. This photo was taken in the 1960s, before reconstruction of the staircase in the 1980s under Saddam Hussein.*

GILGAMESH
(DATES UNKNOWN)

Gilgamesh is the most famous of Sumerian kings. He was the fifth king of Uruk, according to the Sumerian King List, and ruled around the year 2700 B.C. Little is known about the historical figure, and he is better known through the "Epic of Gilgamesh," a long poem describing his relationship with Enkidu, a friend with whom he undertakes many adventures. After Enkidu dies, Gilgamesh dwells upon his sense of loss, and begins a search for immortality. In the mythology of the Mesopotamian region, Gilgamesh is shown as being a god-like figure with incredible strength, who built a wall around the city of Uruk in order to defend his people.

CA 2218–2047 B.C.
Gutians rule Sumer after invading from outside its borders

CA 2100 B.C.
The Sumerian King List is written. It records all the kings and dynasties that ruled Sumer

CA 2110–CA 2004 B.C.
Sumerian Renaissance flourishes under the 3rd dynasty of Ur

21ST CENTURY B.C.
The ziggurat of Ur built during reign of Ur-Nammu. It was reconstructed in the sixth century b.c.

CA 1720 B.C.
Shift of Euphrates River and collapse of life at Nippur and other cities of Sumer

THE ANCIENT EGYPTIANS ca 2575–657 B.C.

For over two millennia, Ancient Egypt was the most advanced and influential power in the Mediterranean region. Its legacy—in mathematics, astronomy, medicine, and architecture—profoundly influenced the great cultures that came after it. The Ancient Egyptians left extensive written records, but did not themselves employ the conventional division of their history into 30 dynastic periods. This was devised by the third-century B.C. historian Manetho of Sabennytos, who drew on a range of contemporary Egyptian documentary sources, including their "King Lists."

ABOVE: *The mythological Papyrus of Meshsekeb, depicting gods and royalty.*
BELOW: *A mask of Anubis, the jackal-headed protector of the dead, from the 19th dynasty.*

Modern historians also generally use a division of Ancient Egyptian history into a number of broad epochs: the Early Dynastic (ca 3000–2575 B.C.), the Old Kingdom (ca 2575–2150 B.C.), the Middle Kingdom (ca 2000–1640 B.C.), and the New Kingdom (ca 1540–1070 B.C.), with Intermediate Periods between, when Egypt was disunited.

THE RULERS

From the first establishment of a unified Egyptian state around 3100 B.C., the pharaoh (or king) became an omnipotent figure. Pharaohs occupied an exalted position between god and mortal, and had a privileged role as mediator for humanity before the gods. A pharaoh's time was absorbed in ritual and ceremonial duties, most of it dedicated to ensuring the annual flooding of the Nile, which gave fertility to the land and guaranteed Egypt's prosperity. Much of the everyday running of the country was delegated to the powerful officials

RELIGION

The Ancient Egyptians worshipped a complex pantheon of up to 2,000 gods and goddesses. Some were believed to wield great powers of life and death and were revered across the land; others were less influential, regional or even personal deities. Amongst the most powerful gods of Ancient Egypt were Re, god of the sun; Osiris, the mummified king who ruled the underworld; his wife Isis, revered as a mother figure; and the jackal-headed Anubis, Osiris's predecessor as king of the underworld and the god responsible for guiding the dead on their journey there.

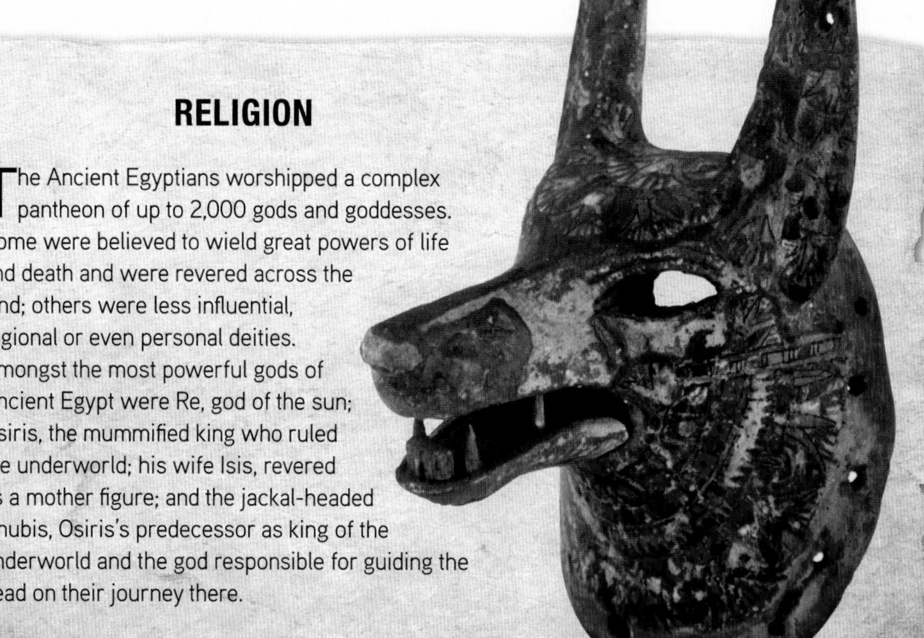

KEY DATES OF THE ANCIENT EGYPTIANS

CA 2575–2150 B.C.
Old Kingdom Egypt, comprising dynasties 3–6

CA 2530 B.C.
Construction of the Great Pyramid, one of the Seven Wonders of the Ancient World

CA 2150–2000 B.C.
First Intermediate Period extends through dynasties 7–11

CA 2000–1640 B.C.
Middle Kingdom Egypt, dynasties 11–13, sees renewed expansion and prosperity

CA 1640–1540 B.C.
Second Intermediate Period, incorporating dynasties 13–17, sees a phase of decline

who controlled Egypt's sophisticated bureaucracy, including the governors who ran the administrative regions (or *nomes*).

Today, Ancient Egypt is best remembered for its remarkable achievements in the architectural arena, chief amongst them the vast pyramids. The greatest of these, at Giza, were built for the pharaohs of the 4th dynasty between 2528 and 2472 B.C.. They are remarkable for the advanced engineering and architectural skills required to construct them.

Reflecting the Egyptian preoccupation with the afterlife, the bodies of pharaohs and other high officials were mummified (embalmed and wrapped in linen bandages) and placed in elaborately decorated tombs.

DECLINE & FALL

Egypt underwent several periods of decline, but always recovered. The Old Kingdom ended after the reign of Pepi II (2246–2152 B.C.), as famine caused central authority to collapse. But under Mentuhotep (2061–2010 B.C.), the first ruler of the 11th dynasty, Egypt saw a renewed period of prosperity that led to the Middle Kingdom. Egyptian armies conquered territory to the south, in Nubia, but by about 1650 B.C. pressure from the Hyksos (groups of raiders from Asia) caused the Middle Kingdom's collapse. Finally, under the New Kingdom, Ancient Egypt reached the peak of its prosperity and power, its armies campaigning as far as northern Syria. The long reign of Rameses II (1290–1224 B.C.) saw military success and the erection of huge monuments, but in truth Egypt was overstretched militarily and economically. During the 21st dynasty (from 1070 B.C.), a split developed between the country's pharaohs, who ruled from Tanis in the north, and its high priests, who gained control of the south and ruled from Thebes. Despite a brief reunion, the civil war left Egypt vulnerable to invasion from Nubia, its southern neighbor. The Nubian ruler Shabaqa first took over Thebes, establishing the 25th dynasty, before gaining full control of a reunited kingdom of Nubia and Egypt from around 720 B.C..

RIGHT: *Solid gold inlaid with semi-precious stones and glass paste, Tutankhamun's funeral mask stuns viewers with its opulence and beauty.*

BELOW: *Amenhotep III's colonnade at the Temple of Luxor (known as Thebes in ancient times). The temple was founded in ca 1400 B.C..*

TUTANKHAMUN (1332–1323 B.C.)

The reign of the boy-king Tutankhamun, 12th pharaoh of the 18th dynasty, lasted just nine years. Yet the discovery of his tomb by the British archaeologist Howard Carter in 1922 made him one of the most famous characters in the history of Ancient Egypt. Tutankhamun is thought to have inherited the throne at the age of eight or nine, when he began rebuilding temples damaged and destroyed during his father's reign. His tomb yielded an unprecedented range of artifacts, advancing modern understanding of life in Ancient Egypt, while his embalmed body betrayed signs of a violent death, suggesting that the young king may have been the victim of a hunting accident or of foul play.

CA 1540–1070 B.C.
New Kingdom Egypt, dynasties 18–20, the peak of Ancient Egyptian prosperity and power

CA 1370 B.C.
Birth of Nefertiti, wife of the pharaoh Akhenaten (whose religious reforms split the ruling elite)

CA 1332–1323 B.C.
Tutankhamun, legendary boy king and 12th pharaoh of the 18th dynasty, reigns

CA 1070–715 B.C.
Third Intermediate Period; Egypt divided into northern and southern regions

CA 720–657 B.C.
25th dynasty unites Egypt and Nubia (its neighbor to the south) under Nubian-based rule

THE BRONZE AGE ≈ CA 2600–1100 B.C.

ABOVE LEFT: *The reconstructed north entrance to the Palace of Minos at Knossos. It shows the typical Minoan-style red wooden columns and a reproduction of a fresco.*

THE PALACE OF KNOSSOS

Sir Arthur Evans (1851–1941) was the archaeologist primarily responsible for the excavation of the palace at Knossos and also for much of our understanding of Minoan culture. In fact, it was Evans himself who came up with the name "Minoan" to describe the cultural era he was exploring. Evans purchased the site from the newly independent Cretan government in 1900 and immediately started excavating the site. He uncovered—and controversially restored—the elements of the palatial structure that can be seen to this day. The dig also uncovered some 3,000 clay tablets in scripts known as Linear A, which remains undeciphered, and Linear B, which was fully deciphered in 1953 and is closely associated with the Mycenaean culture.

The Bronze Age civilizations that developed first on Crete and later throughout the Aegean are some of the earliest recorded in Europe, and their palaces and citadels still remain as monuments to their power and artistic achievements.

MINOAN CULTURE

The earliest record of the palace civilization that developed on the island of Crete comes around 2700 B.C.. This culture is known as "Minoan," named after the mythical Cretan King Minos, whom the archaeologist Sir Arthur Evans associated with the site of Knossos, the foremost of the Minoan palaces. This palace culture spread throughout the island of Crete and beyond, with archaeological remains found on Rhodes and throughout the Cyclades. Minoan culture appears to have been largely mercantile, with little military element to it. Its inscriptions—in a script known as Linear A—and the language they contain have not as yet been deciphered, so much

RIGHT: *Known as* The Blue Ladies, *this Minoan wall painting dates from ca 1600 B.C..*

KEY DATES OF THE MINOANS AND MYCENAEANS

CA 2600 B.C.
Development of Bronze Age culture on Mediterranean island of Crete

CA 1700 B.C.
Start of the construction of the palace at Knossos, Crete, following its initial destruction by fire

CA 1600 B.C.
Eruption of Thera (Santorini), a possible reason for the decline of Minoan culture

CA 1420 B.C.
Occupation of Minoan palace sites by Mycenaeans from southern Greece

CA 1380 B.C.
Destruction of the Minoan palace at Knossos

ABOVE: *Probably the most well-known feature of the site, the Lion Gate is one of the still-extant remnants of the ancient city of Mycenae.*

about Minoan civilization is yet to be discovered. However, the remains left in the palaces reveal a highly developed artistic and material culture.

Around the middle of the second millennium B.C., Minoan culture fell into decline, perhaps as a result of the catastrophic volcanic explosion on the island of Thera (modern-day Santorini) around 1600 B.C., and many of its sites were subsequently taken over by a people from the north, the Mycenaeans.

MYCENAE

The Mycenaeans are named for one of their principal fortified sites—the city of Mycenae in the Peloponnese, the southern peninsula of mainland Greece—and they came to dominate much of the Aegean world from around 1400 B.C.. The successful deciphering of their script, Linear B, has meant that much more is known about them than the Minoans. They were dominated by powerful warrior-kings known as *wanax*, who controlled a landed aristocracy, which in turn ruled over the population beneath them. These leaders were based in a series of strong fortifications throughout Greece, most notably Mycenae, Tiryns, and Pylos. The names of some of them have been immortalized by the poems of Homer: Agamemnon, Menelaus, Ajax, Achilles, and Nestor. The poetic descriptions of the Trojan War are possibly based upon historical events from around 1260–1250 B.C., at the height of Mycenaean dominance. It is also from this period that the most impressive Mycenaean structures date, such as the Treasury of Atreus and the Lion Gate, both at Mycenae.

From the 12th century B.C., Mycenaean society went into a rapid decline. By 1100 B.C., all of Greece, and much of the Eastern Mediterranean, had fallen into a "dark age" that lasted for almost 500 years. The causes of this decline are unknown, and many theories have been proposed, ranging from climate change to catastrophic foreign intervention. All that is clear is that the fortifications collapsed and were never rebuilt, and large areas of the Peloponnese were depopulated during this period.

RIGHT: *The typical armor of an Achaean soldier, dating from the 15th century B.C., which was discovered in a tomb at Dendra.*

ABOVE: *A drinking vessel, called a* rhyton, *in the shape of a bull's head, which would have been used for ceremonial purposes. This was discovered at the Little Palace of Knossos.*

THE TROJAN WAR

Immortalized in the epic poems the *Iliad* and the *Odyssey* by Homer, the events of the Trojan War and its aftermath provide some of literature's most iconic moments. It is extremely difficult to unearth the historical truth behind these tales, but excavation work carried out since the 19th century, most notably by the German archaeologist Heinrich Schliemann, has identified the mound of Hisarlik in northwest Turkey, overlooking the Aegean Sea and close to the Dardanelles, as the probable site of Homer's Troy. Schliemann also excavated the city of Mycenae itself.

CA 1300 B.C.
Treasury of Atreus at Mycenae is constructed, a highly impressive Mycenaean structure

1260–1250 B.C.
Destruction of "Troy VIh," the probable site of Homer's Troy

CA 1250 B.C.
The Lion Gate at Mycenae is constructed at the entrance to the city

1200–1180 B.C.
Destruction or collapse of many Mycenaean fortifications

CA 1100 B.C.
Widespread decline of Bronze Age culture in the eastern Mediterranean

MESOPOTAMIAN EMPIRES ~ CA 1700–600 B.C.

Following the decline of Sumerian dominance in the ancient Near East, a series of powers rose and fell in the region, each in turn exercising hegemony over what was culturally and materially the most advanced part of the world at the time. Two of the most important of these were the Babylonian and Assyrian empires.

THE BABYLONIANS

The Babylonian Empire was the earliest of the two, coming to prominence in the 18th century B.C. with the conquest by Hammurabi of the independent city-states and kingdoms that made up Mesopotamia. Yet the empire rapidly found itself under threat from the growing Hittite menace to the north, as well as from the Kassites to the east. The Hittites actually managed to sack Babylon in 1595 B.C., and in the chaos that followed the Kassites took control of the empire, holding it until 1155 B.C., when the Elamites seized power, followed shortly afterwards by the rise of a local dynasty under Nebuchadnezzar I.

While Babylonia was experiencing a period of decline, another power was rising in the region, that of Assyria. Based around the cities of Nineveh, Ashur, and Arbil, the first Assyrian state arose about 2000 B.C., but then came under the sway of the Mitanni kingdom from the 15th to the 14th century B.C.

THE ASSYRIANS

Following the collapse of the Mitanni under Hittite pressure, the Assyrians once more established their independence and started to expand their territory, occupying Babylonian land to the south and Hittite territory to the north. Under Tiglath-Pileser I (reigned 1114–1076 B.C.), the Assyrian Empire pushed to the Mediterranean coast and possibly as far as the Black Sea, but his murder in 1076 B.C. caused it to contract to its ancestral heartlands, under assault by the Arameans, a group of nomadic tribesmen.

LEFT: *The ruins of Ashur, the capital of what was Assyria, which can be found in present-day northern Iraq.*
ABOVE RIGHT: *The black stela, now in the Louvre Museum in Paris, France, on which Hammurabi's Code was inscribed.*

HAMMURABI
(?–1750 B.C.)

Hammurabi, who ruled from 1792 to 1750 B.C., was the sixth king of Babylon, and first ruler of the Babylonian Empire, extending his rule over all of Mesopotamia. Although his military conquests increased his authority, he is most famous for his code of laws, introduced in 1780 B.C. Hammurabi's Code is preserved on a black stone stela found in 1901 in Iran by a French Egyptologist and now preserved in the Louvre Museum, in Paris, France. The code contains a series of 282 separate laws covering all aspects of human behavior and dealing harshly with any transgressions; the death sentence is a frequently prescribed punishment. Hammurabi's reputation as a lawgiver has seen him represented on a number of United States government buildings.

KEY DATES OF THE MESOPOTAMIAN EMPIRES

CA 1764 B.C.
Elamites, ruled by the Eparti dynasty, conquered by Hammurabi of Babylon

CA 1725 B.C.
Babylonian Empire dominant over all of Mesopotamia and running along the whole of the Euphrates River

CA 1525 B.C.
Fall of the Babylonian Empire to the Kassites, who rename Babylon Karanduniash

CA 1360 B.C.
Beginning of the rise of the Assyrians, following the collapse of the Mitanni kingdom

CA 1200 B.C.
Start of the Iron Age in the Middle East after iron-smelting techniques are used in Anatolia

ABOVE: *A carved relief depicting the Assyrian ruler Ashurbanipal on a hunting expedition for lions.*
RIGHT: *A mural of Tiglath-Pileser III, the ruler of Assyria, in which he is shown granting an audience.*

This period of weakness continued through till 911 B.C. and the accession of Adad-Nirari II, founder of what has become known as the Neo-Assyrian Empire. This empire flourished under a number of dynamic rulers, none more so than Tiglath-Pileser III (reigned 745–727 B.C.), who expanded it to cover practically all of the Near East, extending his influence throughout Babylonia, Syria, and Palestine. Successive Assyrian rulers continued this enlargement, until in 663 B.C., Ashurbanipal (reigned 668–627 B.C.) extended the empire into Egypt. However, after he died in 627 B.C., Assyrian control rapidly collapsed amid a series of internal revolts and rebellions, together with external pressure from Scythian tribes on the border. Babylonia, having won its independence once more, laid waste to the Assyrian capital of Nineveh in 612 B.C., finally destroying Assyria as a power and heralding the rise of the Babylonian Empire once more.

TIGLATH-PILESER III

Tiglath-Pileser III ruled Assyria from 745 to 727 B.C. and his reign saw the expansion of the empire in all directions. He came to the throne following a bloody palace coup, largely brought about because a lack of strong, central direction had caused instability and led to external pressure on the borders. The new king sought to dispel this pressure through a series of campaigns. Having conducted a wide-ranging reform of the Assyrian army, he launched his troops to the south against Babylonia, and then northwards against Urartu. He then moved westwards into modern Syria and Israel, seeking to control the lucrative trade routes along the eastern coast of the Mediterranean. By the time of his death in 727 B.C., he had pushed the boundaries of the empire to the south of Gaza and assumed the throne of Babylonia.

1116–1093 B.C.
Assyria becomes the dominant power in the region

745–727 B.C.
Reign of Tiglath-Pileser III, peak of the Late Assyrian Empire

663 B.C.
Conquest of Egypt sees Assyrian Empire at its largest extent

627 B.C.
Death of Ashurbanipal leads Assyrian power to decline rapidly under external and internal pressure

612 B.C.
Capture of Nineveh by the Babylonians. Assyrian Empire divided between Babylonians and Medes

THE PEOPLE OF THE INDUS ~ CA 3000–1300 B.C.

Just over 5,000 years ago a Bronze Age civilization emerged in what is now northern India and Pakistan. Just as in the contemporary cultures of the Middle East, the development of new metallurgical techniques served as an impetus for improvements in agriculture, the development of trade, and the creation of a complex society. The civilization first appeared around 3000 B.C. in the valley of the River Indus, and archaeologists believe it reached its peak around four centuries later. This Bronze Age society survived until around 1300 B.C., although the reasons for its final collapse are unclear.

BELOW: *Sculpture of a priest-king from the Bronze Age settlement of Mohenjo-Daro or Moenjodaro, in modern-day Pakistan, dating from ca 2500 B.C.*

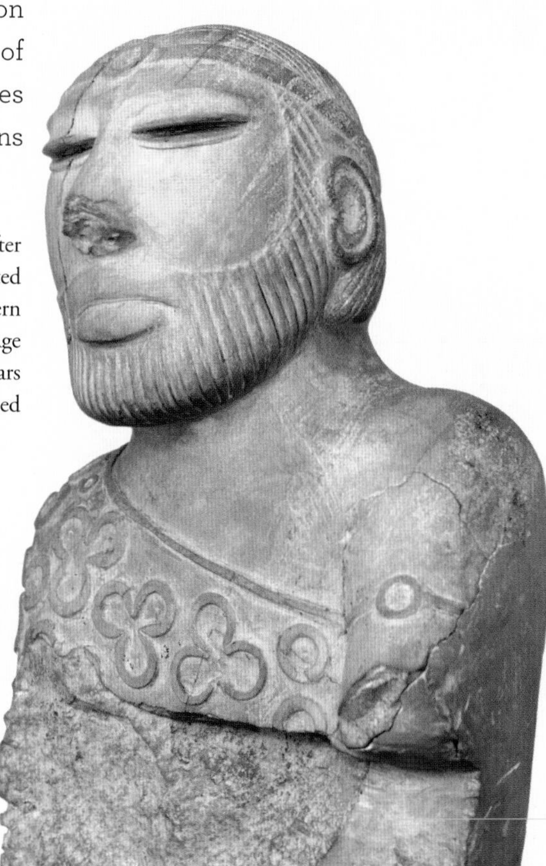

The Indus Valley was inhabited from at least 7000 B.C., and for nearly 4,000 years Neolithic farmers there exploited the relatively fertile land of the region and herded animals. This Mergarh culture—named after an important Neolithic site in modern Pakistan—was agrarian, and there are no signs that its people grouped themselves into towns. The introduction of bronze-working technology allowed the development of a more complex civilization and the creation of larger urban centers. This Bronze Age phase in the Indus Valley has been labeled the Harappa Culture, after the ruins of a well-defended city which was excavated in the 1920s in Punjab (in what is now northeastern Pakistan). The remains of another large Bronze Age center—Mohenjo-Daro—were discovered a few years later, and subsequent townships have been unearthed elsewhere in the Indus Valley.

URBAN DEVELOPMENT

The excavations of these large urban centers have shown that, at the same time as Bronze Age cultures were thriving in Mesopotamia, Egypt, or Crete, these bustling fortified cities were major centers of trade and commerce. Archaeologists discovered that the Indus Valley cities were planned, with sophisticated sewerage systems, commercial,

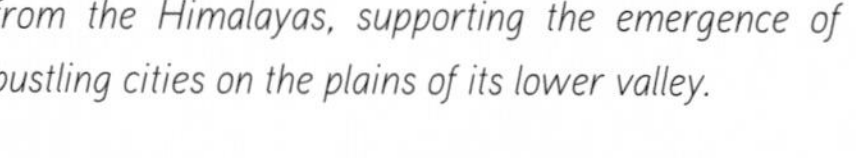

LEFT: *The River Indus carries a fresh water supply from the Himalayas, supporting the emergence of bustling cities on the plains of its lower valley.*

OUT OF INDIA

In India the Harappan civilization is sometimes called the Indus-Sarasvati or Ghaggar-Hakra civilization, and is the subject of political as well as archaeological debate. It has been proposed that Indus Valley religion was a precursor of Hinduism, Harappan writing was an early form of Sanskrit, and the Harrapans were an indigenous Aryan people rather than one which migrated to the Indian subcontinent from elsewhere in Asia. Justification for this is based on the *Rigveda*, a 3,000-year-old collection of sacred texts written in Sanskrit, which suggests that this Indo-European language had its roots in Harappan culture. This is known as the "Out of India" theory.

KEY DATES OF THE INDUS CIVILIZATION

CA 7000 B.C.
First indications of Neolithic settlement in the Indus Valley

5500–3300 B.C.
The growth of Neolithic settlement in the Indus Valley

3300–2600 B.C.
The Early Harappan Period—the development of the Indus culture

CA 2800 BC
An era of cultural transition, as large urban centers develop in the Indus Valley

2600–1900 B.C.
The Mature Harappan Period, and the flowering of Bronze Age India

INDUS SCRIPT

Also known as Harappan script, this takes the form of short strings of symbols rather than recognizable letters. Developed around 2600 B.C., its meaning has long been forgotten, although numerous attempts have been made to decipher it. It has been seen as a precursor of Sanskrit or Brahmi script, both of which developed in India in the Iron Age. A stumbling block is that the spoken language referred to is unknown, although again numerous theories have been proposed. Scholars are divided as to whether it is an early Indo-European language, or a version of proto-Dravidian and so the ancestor of south Indian languages.

domestic, and civic areas, and centrally located religious sites. It has been estimated that, at its peak around 2000 B.C., Harappa had a population of up to 40,000, making it one of the largest cities in the world at the time.

The culture of the Bronze Age Indus Valley was clearly a complex one, whose prosperity was underpinned by agriculture and trade. Pottery finds prove that caravan trade routes linked the Indus Valley cities with Mesopotamia, Persia, Central Asia, and the rest of the Indian subcontinent. The development of the Indus script, around 2,000 B.C., assisted the governance of these cities, although the exact nature of this system—whether it was an actual script or symbolic pictograms—is still a matter of debate.

DECLINE AND FALL

The Harappan civilization underwent a decline around 1900 B.C., and within two centuries the great cities were abandoned. The reason for this is unclear, but climate change is considered the most likely theory, reducing the available area of arable land, and so making it harder to feed the population of the great urban centers. However, traces of the civilization developed during the Harappan period can still be found for another millennium in the Indus Valley, suggesting a gradual rather than a catastrophic decline in the once-sophisticated society. The importance of this great lost civilization is still being evaluated.

ABOVE RIGHT: *Pictographic writing and a carved animal on a stone tablet from Mohenjo-Daro (Moenjodaro), Pakistan.*
RIGHT: *Ruins of the city of Harappa, in modern Pakistan; in the foreground are the remains of the granaries.*

CA 2600 B.C.
The development of the still-undeciphered Indus script

CA 2300 B.C.
The start of the Bronze Age in Europe, a millennium after the Indian subcontinent

1900–1300 B.C.
The Late Harappan Period, and the decline of the Indus civilizations

CA 1700 B.C.
The Harappan cities of the Indus are abandoned

CA 1300 B.C.
The beginning of the Iron Age in the Indian subcontinent

THE SHANG DYNASTY ~ CA 1554–1045 B.C.

The Shang dynasty ruled China from circa 1554 to 1045 B.C., and was, by tradition, the second dynasty to rule the country after the earlier Xia dynasty was violently overthrown. Its control was centered around the Yellow River valley, in the northeast of inner China. The Shang faced grave threats from warlike groups to the north of their borders, a threat which would continue for centuries, eventually resulting in the construction of the Great Wall in the fifth century B.C.

ANCESTRAL WORSHIP

Under the Shang, power was divided between the king, aristocrats, and a priestly class. Shang nobles pledged their support to the king's military campaigns in return for lands and patronage. The priests fulfilled the role of record keepers and interpreters of the gods' will. Religion at this time was based upon ancestor worship; Taoism, Buddhism, and Confucianism were all systems of belief which developed much later. The king himself was the high priest, presiding over the most important religious ceremonies and believed to have the most direct contact with the gods. Divination using "oracle bones" was frequently practiced to predict crop harvests or military success.

BELOW: *The valley of the Yellow River, the second-longest river in China. Also the sixth-longest river in the world, the Yellow River's length is estimated at 3,395 miles. Its color comes from the silt continually carried in it.*

WRITING SYSTEMS

The Chinese writing system at this time was well developed, and examples have been found on various bronze objects, as well as pottery, jade, and ivory. The most significant artifacts displaying writing are the oracle bones that bear the results of divinations, among them the earliest examples of Chinese writing (written in "oracle-bone script"). Using these records, historians have managed to piece together the various rulers who held power throughout the Shang dynasty, resulting in a complete record of dynastic power in this period. Together with the large number of artifacts recovered from royal tombs, we have some idea of political developments during the Shang dynasty.

Industry and agriculture flourished under the Shang, the most important crops being wheat and barley. Large numbers of bronze artifacts and tools have been found, indicating a degree of sophistication in metallurgy and an advanced industrial economy, too. Most of the bronze was used to make ritual vessels for this aristocratic society's many ceremonies. It was also employed for military purposes, as the material for spoked chariot wheels and hand weapons. Excavated tombs show that Shang kings were buried with grave goods of great value, presumably for use in the afterlife. Hundreds of other bodies (which could have been slaves) have also been found buried together in one Shang royal burial so they could continue to serve their master after death.

THE END OF AN ERA

The Shang dynasty came to an end when the Zhou, who occupied territory to the west, conquered it

KEY DATES OF THE SHANG DYNASTY

2100–1600 B.C.
The Xia dynasty rules, the earliest known dynasty to hold power in China

1900–1350 B.C.
The Erlitou culture begins the industrial casting of bronze vessels

CA 1554 B.C.
The Shang dynasty is founded, and flourishes for the next five centuries

CA 1398 B.C.
The Shang capital is moved from Zhengzhou to Yinxu

1250–1200 B.C.
Early Chinese script is written on oracle bones, providing a wealth of information about Shang society and its rulers

SHANG MILITARY POWER

The extensive use of bronze in Shang society also allowed its armies to be equipped with the best-quality weapons available before the discovery of iron. Though they also used stone, it was their bronze spears, axe-heads, and arrowheads that allowed Shang troops to dominate their rivals, especially the marauding barbarians to the north and west of the Shang heartland. We know that the Shang also used chariots in combat, though probably only rarely. They were more often seen as symbols of elite power and as a means of transportation. The vast majority of troops came from the common people, who were generally conscripted into the military.

LEFT: *In 2005, Chinese archaeologists work on newly discovered horse-drawn chariots in the ruins of Yin (Anyang).*

around 1045 B.C. The last Shang king, Di Xin, committed suicide by gathering his treasures around him and burning his palace down after his armies were defeated. The Zhou were the first Chinese dynasty to claim a divine right to rule, invoking the "Mandate of Heaven" which gave them the right to govern, and gave the decrees of their rulers a semi-divine status. Subsequent dynasties which seized power legitimized their actions by claiming that the Mandate of Heaven had simply now transferred to them.

RIGHT: *Bronze axe-head from the Anyang period (ca 1300–1030 B.C.), from Shandong province. Although lacking the sophistication of later pieces, even this early bronzework is decorated far beyond the basic requirements of utility.*

ABOVE: *A ding, or three-legged pot, from the 15th–14th century B.C. Its surface is intricately decorated but has no script.*

CA 1250 B.C.
The Zhou people settle in the Wei River valley

CA 1200 B.C.
Royal consort and warrior Fu Hao is buried in her tomb at Yinxu. This is excavated in 1976 and provides a wealth of archaeological evidence about the Shang dynasty

CA 1200 B.C.
Chariots using bronze-spoked wheels come into widespread use

CA 1122 B.C.
Zhou dynasty established in peripheral Shang areas

CA 1045 B.C.
The Zhou people conquer the areas ruled by the Shang dynasty. Di Xin commits suicide

ALEXANDER'S EMPIRE 323–146 B.C.

Following the death of Alexander the Great in 323 B.C., the great empire that he had built was divided between his military commanders, known as the *diadochi* ("the successors"). Legend has it that, on his deathbed, Alexander willed his lands to "the strongest," a lack of clarity which set off a bitter round of fighting between his leading generals and eventually led to the emergence of three major kingdoms. Egypt and the Middle East, the richest of the three, came under the control of Ptolemy and his successors; Syria and the remains of the Persian Empire went to Seleucus, while Macedonia, Thrace, and some of Asia Minor fell to Antigonus and his son Demetrius.

The 200 years that followed witnessed a complex series of wars and alliances, as the three kingdoms struggled to retain their identities and to defend their borders from one another and from outsiders, most notably the Romans. The period has come to be known as Hellenistic, a term derived from the Greek word "Hellene," meaning Greek. During it, Hellenistic culture and ideas spread beyond the traditional heartlands of Greece itself and into the new territories that had been absorbed into Alexander's empire.

THE ROYAL LIBRARY OF ALEXANDRIA

Founded during the reign of Ptolemy I Soter (323 B.C.–ca 283 B.C.) or his son Ptolemy II (ruled 283 B.C. to 246 B.C.), the Royal Library of Alexandria was the greatest library of the ancient world. At its peak, it housed 400,000–700,000 papyrus scrolls. Among the most famous scholars to work in the library was Aristophanes of Byzantium, a great Homeric researcher and the man credited with compiling one of the world's earliest grammars. It was at the Royal Library of Alexandria that Homer's *Odyssey* and *Iliad* were first edited to produce the canonical texts that we know today.

ABOVE LEFT: *Roman mosaic depicting the death of the Greek mathematician and physicist Archimedes (ca 287–212 B.C.).*
ABOVE: *A 19th-century German engraving of the reconstruction of a hall in the great Library of Alexandria.*

KEY DATES OF ALEXANDER'S EMPIRE

323 B.C.
Death of Alexander the Great leaves his extensive empire to be struggled over by his generals

294 B.C.
Demetrius, son of Alexander's general Antigonus, seizes Macedonian throne

285–247 B.C.
Lighthouse of Alexandria, Egypt, built by Sostratus of Cnidus

267–262 B.C.
Greek cities revolt and lose their independence in the Chremonidian War

CA 255 B.C.
Antigonus defeats Egyptian fleet at Cos to control Aegean Islands

ALEXANDER THE GREAT

(356–323 B.C.)

Inheriting the kingdom of Macedonia from his father, Philip II, at the age of just 20, Alexander the Great changed the course of ancient history. His death in 323 B.C. is normally taken to mark the end of the Classical Greek period and the beginning of the Hellenistic Age. A military commander of undisputed genius, Alexander founded over 70 cities and campaigned in Egypt, Babylonia, Persia, Media, the Punjab, and the valley of the Indus. His territorial legacy was vast, yet within 250 years of his death, most of his great empire had fallen into the hands of Rome or had been recaptured by new Persian rulers.

HELLENISTIC CULTURE

Often dismissed as being of less cultural importance than the Classical Greek period that preceded it, the Hellenistic Age was a time of significant developments in Greek culture, architecture, art, and philosophy. Where art and literature during the Classical period had been preoccupied with the ideal, Hellenistic works were more concerned with the "real," relating the exploits of gods, heroes, and common mortals to everyday life and familiar emotions, although with an occasional tendency to excessive erudition and florid language. Portrayals of figures on coins became more "lifelike," while in sculpture the work of the fifth-century master Polykleitos remained very influential. New architectural styles emerged, most notably including the Corinthian Order, first seen on the exterior of the Temple of Olympian Zeus in Athens. Public buildings and monuments were constructed on a larger scale in more complexity, and included the Lighthouse or Pharos of Alexandria, one of the Seven Wonders of the Ancient World and for centuries one of the tallest manmade structures.

Throughout the Hellenistic era, Athens remained the most prestigious seat of higher education in Ancient Greece, although its libraries were a pale shadow of the Royal Library of Alexandria. Among the brilliant thinkers of the era were the poets Kallimachus and Apollonius of Rhodes, as well as the geometrician Euclid and the mathematician Archimedes of Syracuse.

The traditional Greek powers of Sparta, Athens, and Thebes never really reasserted their political authority in the third century, and after the Athenians' defeat at the hands of the Antigonids in 262 B.C., Macedonian dominance was almost complete. It was only disturbed, and the power of Greece itself threatened, by the rise of Rome. The Romans became interested in Greek affairs because of the alliance in 205 B.C. between Philip V of Macedonia and Rome's bitter enemy Carthage. A series of political maneuvers led ultimately to a declaration of war between Rome and Macedonia in 172 B.C., a conflict that ended in crushing defeat for the Macedonians. Finally, in 146 B.C., the Greek peninsula became a Roman protectorate, and the days of Greek independence were effectively over.

ABOVE: *A 19th-century engraving of the Lighthouse or Pharos of Alexandria, Egypt, built by Sostratus of Cnidus.*
LEFT: *A marble sculpture of the head of Ptolemy I Soter (367–283 B.C.), which is said to be from El-Faiyum.*

217 B.C.
Peace of Naupactus unites Macedon and Greek leagues under Philip V

218–201 B.C.
Second Punic War fought between Carthage and the Roman Republic

146 B.C.
Greek peninsula conquered by the Romans and becomes a Roman protectorate

31 B.C.
Anthony and Cleopatra defeated at Actium; fall of Ptolemaic dynasty

27 B.C.
Greek peninsula becomes known as the Roman province of Achaea

QIN SHI HUANG ~ 259–210 B.C.

As the first emperor of a unified China, Qin Shi Huang (259–210 B.C.) is one of the key figures in Chinese history. Among his legacies was the forerunner of the Great Wall of China, which evolved into an enduring wonder of the world. However, as well as being one of history's great builders, he was also a tyrant who laid the foundations for almost two centuries of autocratic imperial rule in China.

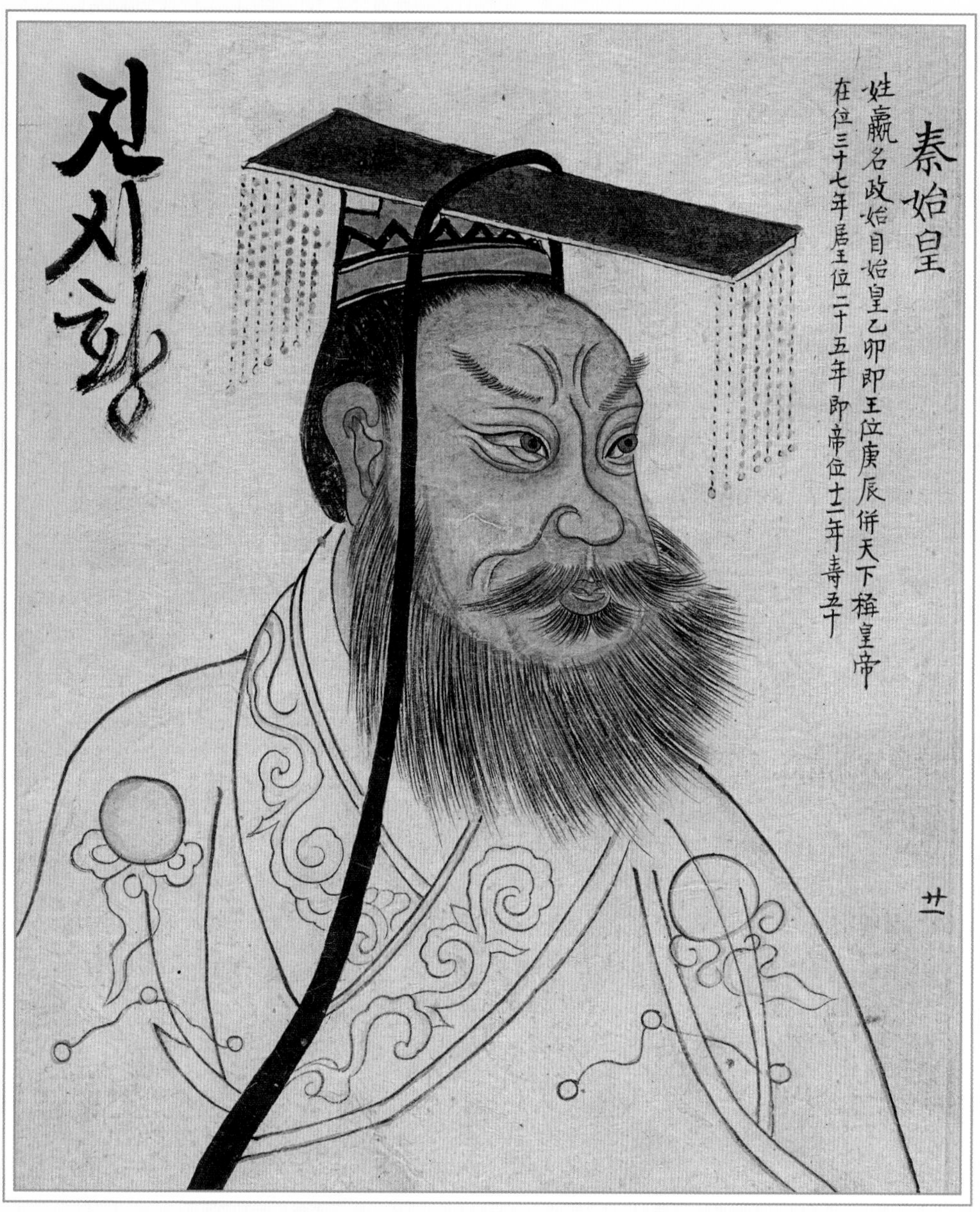

END OF THE WARRING STATES

Qin Shi Huang's origins have been mythologized, but according to the second-century historian Sima Qian, he was a prince of Qin, an ancient Chinese state. His given name was Ying Zheng. During the "Warring States Period" (475–221 B.C.) China was divided into seven embattled regions, and by the time the teenage Zheng ascended the Qin throne in 246 B.C., his state was a well-organized military power.

Assuming full control of Qin after the death of the regent in 238 B.C., the young ruler set about building up his military forces, then unleashed them in a campaign of conquest. By 230 B.C. he had subdued neighboring Han. The following year a major earthquake disrupted the state of Zhao, and so the Qin general Wang Jian seized the opportunity to invade and conquer the country. Next to fall was Wei in 225 B.C. That left the small Yan, and the kingdom of Chu in southern China, the most powerful of all the warring states.

In 225 B.C. Ying Zheng's army invaded Chu, but was defeated. Wang Jian led a second invasion the following year, and this time the Qin were victorious. By 221 B.C. Chu was completely conquered, and soon afterwards the last independent state, Qi, surrendered. With all the warring states overcome, China was

ABOVE: *The mausoleum of General Wang Jian, near Chengdu in Sichuan province. Wang Jian was considered one of the four most prestigious generals from the Warring States Period.*

LEFT: *Illustration of Qing Shi Huang from a 19th-century Korean album. The Emperor's legacy was felt throughout the Far East.*

KEY DATES IN THE EMPIRE OF QIN SHI HUANG

246 B.C.
Aged just 13, Ying Zheng becomes king of the Qin, under a regent for the first eight years

230 B.C.
Start of Ying Zheng's wars of unification, defeat of the rival state of Han

229 B.C.
Subjugation of the state of Zhao by Qin forces, expanding their realm

221 B.C.
Conquest of the kingdom of Chu by Qin army; Ying Zheng of Qin proclaimed Qin Shi Huang

220 B.C.
Construction of the Qin boundary wall, precursor to the Great Wall of China, starts

THE TERRACOTTA WARRIORS

Before his death, Qin Shi Huang ordered the building of a vast mausoleum on a hillside outside Xian (Chang'an), the capital of Shaanxi province. The tomb was guarded by an army of more than 8,000 life-size statues constructed from terracotta. This "terracotta army" included recognizable generals, soldiers, musicians, horses, chariots, and clerks—everything Qin Shi Huang needed to continue his conquests in the afterlife—and each face was different from the others. They were placed as if to guard the first emperor's tomb and the sprawling necropolis surrounding it. Today, the Terracotta Army is regarded as one of great archaeological treasures of the world.

ABOVE RIGHT: *The massed ranks of terracotta soldiers, with horses and chariots, in the burial pits of Emperor Qin Shi Huang near Xian, China.*

RIGHT: *The Great Wall of China as it is today, at Badaling, northwest of Beijing, China.*

finally unified. In 221 B.C. Zheng proclaimed himself emperor, and took the name Qin Shi Huang (or Qin Shi Huangdi), meaning "First Sovereign Qin Emperor." He continued to rule his new empire for a further 11 years, until his death in 210 B.C.

THE UNIFIED LEGACY

During this time Qin Shi Huang embarked on several ambitious building projects, among them construction of the forerunner of the Great Wall of China, to keep troublesome raiders at bay. Work began in 220 B.C., and the wall was still unfinished when the emperor died ten years later. Another major construction project was the Lingqu Canal, linking the Chang Jiang (Yangtze River) with the Pearl River near Guangzhou (Canton), over 350 miles to the south.

Qin Shi Huang was an autocrat, and ruled China harshly. He penalized free philosophical thought, as a means of espousing "legalism"—a dogma centered on imperial governance and rule of law. In 213 B.C. he ordered the burning of thousands of books, and burned alive scholars who refused to surrender their libraries. Although few mourned his passing, he left behind a strong imperial state, under a single regime for the first time.

THE GREAT WALL OF CHINA

One of the great historical structures, the "Long wall of 10,000 *li*" was built on the orders of Qin Shi Huang, largely as a demonstration of Chinese unity, and to define the northern and western borders of his empire. It also served to protect northern China from raids by the nomadic peoples of the Gobi Desert. Local stone was used, augmented by earthen banks, and today very few sections of the original Qin-dynasty walls survive. The Great Wall was rebuilt by subsequent Chinese dynasties, and extended, so creating the massive 5,500-mile stone wall that is still extant today.

215 B.C.
Work begins on Qin Shi Huang's mausoleum and the Terracotta Army

214 B.C.
Work starts on construction of the lengthy Lingqu Canal

213 B.C.
Qin Shi Huang orders extensive burning of books, to control free thought

210 B.C.
Death of the first emperor, Qin Shi Huang, and succession of his son, Qin Er Shi

1974
Terracotta Army discovered in Xian, China; public imagination is captured worldwide

THE ROMAN EMPIRE ~ 753 B.C.–A.D. 476

At the time of its foundation (thought to be in 753 B.C.), Rome was no more than a village. Over the course of ten centuries, it grew into a city and then into a kingdom, becoming the nerve center of the greatest empire the world had ever known. Rome's first rulers were kings, probably of Etruscan descent, but in 509 B.C. this line of hereditary kings was overthrown when the Roman people rebelled. That, as tradition has it, followed the rape of the beautiful noblewoman Lucretia by the son of King Tarquin the Proud.

THE ROMAN REPUBLIC

From then until the establishment of the empire under Augustus (Octavian) in A.D. 27, Rome was ruled as a republic, with two annually elected consuls governing on behalf of a broader senate.

BELOW LEFT: *A four-tiered Roman aqueduct near Nerja in Andalucia, Spain.*

RIGHT: *Silver denarius coin from 44 B.C. showing the head of Emperor Julius Caesar.*

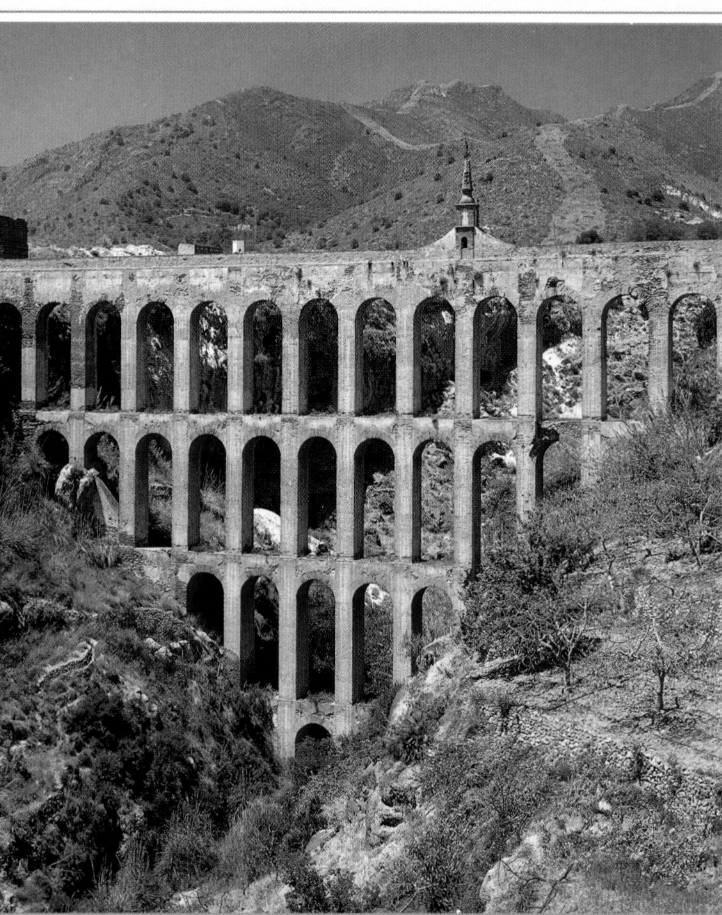

Rome's first military ventures brought mixed successes, with Roman troops taking the Etruscan city of Veii in 396 B.C. following a ten-year siege, but soon finding themselves targeted for attack when the Gauls sacked Rome in 390 B.C. It took some time for Rome to recover, but by 343 B.C. the Romans had begun to expand their territory again, and by 275 B.C. they controlled almost all of the Italian peninsula. With the defeat of the Carthaginians in the First Punic War in 241 B.C., Sicily became Rome's first overseas possession. In the Second Punic War (218–201 B.C.) Roman forces under Scipio Africanus defeated Hannibal and took a large part of North Africa. With the defeat of Perseus of Macedonia, in 168 B.C., his kingdom also came under Roman rule.

THE ART OF WAR

Rome's military successes were owed in large part to a willingness to adopt and adapt the best military technology and tactics of its enemies. This willingness to assimilate extended to Roman culture, with Rome's gods becoming closely identified with figures of Greek

JULIUS CAESAR

(100–44 B.C.)

A great politician and an inspired military commander, Julius Caesar held posts including the governorships of Spain and Roman Gaul, and was responsible for conquering much of central Europe. He was the first Roman general to cross the English Channel, leading two expeditions to Britain in 55 and 54 B.C. but not establishing a permanent base there. At home, he defeated his rival general, Pompey, in a prolonged civil war before being elected consul and, finally, taking the title of Dictator for Life in February, 44 B.C. His dictatorship proved short, however. On the Ides (15th) of March of the same year, he was murdered by 60 conspirators led by Cassius and Brutus, who feared he might make himself king. His death sparked the final round of civil wars that ended the Roman Republic.

KEY DATES OF THE ROMAN EMPIRE

753 B.C.
City of Rome said to have been founded by Romulus and Remus on Palatine Hill

509 B.C.
Beginning of Roman Republic, after popular rebellion

451 B.C.
The Twelve Tables developed—the first Roman law code, which would have lasting influence across Europe

390 B.C.
Gauls sack Rome, led by Brennus, a chieftain from central France

312 B.C.
Construction begins of first aqueduct and first major road in the Roman Empire

See the poster of a Pompeii frieze in Envelope I

mythology. Much later on, Christianity became an official religion in Rome, following its official toleration by the Emperor Constantine in A.D. 312 (and his subsequent active promotion of it).

A series of civil wars in the middle of the first century B.C., in which the general and statesman Julius Caesar (who died in 44 B.C.) played a prominent role, led to the fatal destabilization of the Roman Republic. In a renewed civil war, Caesar's adoptive son Octavian emerged victorious. He gathered supreme power to himself, becoming the first emperor in 27 B.C., under the name Augustus. During his reign and that of his successors, Roman territorial expansion continued, taking in Britain and Dacia (modern Romania), as well as Egypt and Mauretania in North Africa, and pushing eastwards in Mesopotamia and Syria.

The glory days of the Roman Empire resulted in the construction of some architectural masterpieces, including the Colosseum in Rome and Hadrian's Wall in Britain, while early Imperial Rome also saw the flourishing of Latin literature, with poets such as Ovid and Virgil, and the works of historians such as Livy.

From the late second century A.D., barbarian tribes began to press against Rome's borders along the Rhine and the Danube, and by the fourth century the pressure of new groups such as the Alamans, Franks, and, most especially, the Goths had become intolerable. After smashing the eastern Roman army at Adrianople in A.D. 378, the Goths invaded the Italian peninsula and sacked Rome in A.D. 410. Meanwhile, distant territories such as Britain, Gaul, and Spain slipped beyond Rome's control, and the Vandals took North Africa in A.D. 439. Power was gradually yielded to Germanic tribes, until Rome's last Western emperor, Romulus Augustus, abdicated in A.D. 476.

ABOVE LEFT: *An aerial view of the Colosseum in Rome, constructed in A.D. 70–80. The largest amphitheater in the Roman Empire, it was used for gladiatorial games and other public spectacles.*

BELOW: *The* Capitoline Wolf, *a bronze statue, date unknown, of the she-wolf nursing the infants Romulus and Remus.*

THE BIRTH OF ROME

Legend has it that Rome was founded on April 21, 753 B.C., and archaeological evidence supports the idea that the original settlement on the Palatine Hill dates from around that time. According to popular mythology, the city's origins can be traced back to the Trojan War hero Aeneas. His son Ascanius (also called Julus) founded the city of Alba Longa, and the twins Romulus and Remus were his descendants. Cast out from the city by their usurping uncle, they were nursed by a she-wolf and raised by a shepherd and his wife. Learning of their true heritage, the boys raised an army to overthrow their uncle, and went on to found the city of Rome—named for Romulus—on the Palatine Hill.

107 B.C.
Gaius Marius reforms the Roman army, encouraging more people to join up

27 B.C.
Octavian becomes Rome's first emperor, taking the name Augustus

A.D. 312
Constantine decrees official toleration of Christianity, paving the way for its later adoption by the empire

A.D. 410
Sack of Rome by the Goths, led by Alaric

A.D. 476
Emperor Romulus Augustus abdicates to Germanic rule

JESUS OF NAZARETH ~ CA 5 B.C.—A.D. 33

Revered by Christians as the Son of God, recognized within Islam as a prophet, and considered a false messiah by Jews, the figure of Jesus Christ has influenced the course and shape of human history to an extent that is almost unrivaled. From the seventh century, the dating system used in Europe and spread by Europeans worldwide depended on an acknowledgment of the historicity of Jesus, with events divided into two broad eras, B.C. or "Before Christ" and A.D.—Anno Domini or "in the Year of our Lord"—counted from the supposed date of Jesus's birth.

ACCORDING TO THE GOSPELS

No records of Jesus's teachings and activities written within his lifetime survive. Our knowledge of the historical Jesus is instead drawn largely from accounts completed in the century that followed his death. These were subsequently collected together in the *New Testament*, including the Gospels of Matthew, Mark, Luke, and John, and the writings of Paul. While these early reports vary in certain particulars, historians of the period typically accept that the healer known as Jesus was born in Bethlehem (near Jerusalem, in modern-day Israel) between 6 and 4 B.C. during the reign of Herod the Great in Judaea; was baptized by his cousin, the prophet John the Baptist, in or around A.D. 26; and was sentenced to death by crucifixion by the Roman prefect Pontius Pilate in Jerusalem in circa A.D. 30–33.

The narrative of the Christian New Testament can be fitted around these historical points. Christians celebrate Jesus's birth to the Virgin Mary in a stable in Bethlehem on Christmas Day as the fulfillment of the Old Testament prophecy that a messiah would come to deliver the Jewish people from captivity. The young Jesus followed in his father's footsteps to become a carpenter until his ministry began, following his baptism at around the age of 30. The events described in the Gospels relate largely to the period of between one and three years following his baptism which culminated in his death and—his followers came to believe—subsequent resurrection.

LEFT: *The Christ Pantocrator icon from the Monastery of Aghiou Pavlou on Mount Athos, Greece.*

THE DISCIPLES

At the beginning of his ministry, according to accounts, Jesus chose 12 men known as his disciples —and after his death as apostles—to accompany him in his travels and assist him in his teachings. In Matthew 10: 2–4, the disciples are named as follows: "The first, Simon (who is called Peter) and his brother Andrew; James, the son of Zebedee, and his brother John; Philip and Bartholomew; Thomas and Matthew the tax collector; James, son of Alphaeus, and Thaddaeus; Simon the Zealot, and Judas Iscariot, who betrayed Him." Little is known about their backgrounds, although it is recorded that Peter, Andrew, James, and John were fishermen, while Andrew and one other may originally have been disciples of John the Baptist. Following Judas Iscariot's betrayal of Christ, it is possible that he may have been replaced by Matthias.

MIRACLES

Immediately after his baptism, Jesus endured 40 days and 40 nights of fasting in the desert, during which time the Devil sought unsuccessfully to tempt him. Three years of ministry in Galilee, Judaea, and Perea (modern-day Israel and Jordan) followed, a time when Jesus was accompanied by 12 disciples. He performed miracles and healings, including the raising of Lazarus from the dead and the miraculous multiplication of loaves and fishes to feed a crowd of 5,000 people. All the while, Jesus spread the word of God, often talking

KEY DATES IN THE LIFE OF JESUS OF NAZARETH

40 B.C. Herod the Great appointed king of Judaea, within the Roman Empire

6–4 B.C. John the Baptist and Jesus born in Judaea, about six months apart

4 B.C. Herod the Great dies, to be succeeded by his son, Herod Antipas

CA A.D. 26 Jesus baptized; period of his ministry across the region begins

CA A.D. 28 John the Baptist executed on the orders of Herod Antipas, who saw him as a threat

ABOVE: *In the Church of the Nativity in Bethlehem, a silver star marks the spot said to be the birthplace of Jesus.*

in metaphors or "parables" that set his theological teachings in familiar, everyday contexts.

Jesus was betrayed by Judas Iscariot, one of his disciples, arrested, and brought before the Roman prefect, Pontius Pilate, for sentencing. He handed the fate of the "King of the Jews"—as Jesus was accused of calling himself—to the Jewish people themselves, giving them the option of releasing either Jesus or a thief named Barabbas. The crowd chose to release Barabbas, and Jesus was crucified alongside two other thieves at a place known as Calvary (or Golgotha).

The date of Jesus's death is remembered in the Christian calendar as Good Friday. Three days later, on Easter Sunday, he is said to have risen from the dead. The Gospels record that Jesus remained on earth for 40 days more, before his ascension to heaven to sit alongside God on the day now known as Ascension Day.

ABOVE RIGHT: Jesus Raises Lazarus from the Dead, *painted by Jacopo Palma the Elder (ca 1480–1528).*

BELOW: *A manuscript illustration of Christ being judged before Pilate, ca 1420–30.*

PONTIUS PILATE
(DATES UNKNOWN)

Prefect (governor) of Judaea from A.D. 26 to 36, Pontius Pilate was the man responsible for the sentencing and death of Jesus Christ. Portrayed in the Bible as an indecisive character, Pilate is best known for having "washed his hands" of Jesus's fate, perhaps influenced by a prophetic dream of his wife's, after which she advised him to have nothing to do with Jesus. History, nevertheless, indicates that Pilate was a man of action, a soldier rather than a diplomat, yet even so a man who took seriously his task of cementing relations between his Roman superiors and the Jewish people over whom he ruled.

A.D. 30–33
Crucifixion and, three days later, alleged resurrection of Jesus

CA A.D. 47
First recorded use of the term "Christian," in Antioch (near the modern Syrian-Turkish border)

CA A.D. 49
Paul's Epistle to the Thessalonians—earliest known *New Testament* writing—appears

CA A.D. 70
Gospel of Mark, one of the four main components of the *New Testament*, composed

A.D. 80–100
New Testament Gospels of Luke and Matthew composed

CONSTANTINE THE GREAT ≈ CA A.D. 274–337

While the Romans were generally tolerant of other religions, Christianity was one exception. The Romans regarded their own religion as a means of unifying their society, while early Christianity, with its emphasis on a single deity and its repudiation of the traditional Roman pantheon, undermined this link between faith and the Roman state.

ABOVE: *A gold coin depicting Constantine, A.D. 335.*
LEFT: Christ Pantocrator Between Emperor Constantine IX Monamachus and Empress Zoe, *a Byzantine wall mosaic from the cathedral of Hagia Sophia, Istanbul, dating from the 11th–12th century.*

PERSECUTION

Just as significantly, many of the later Roman emperors were regarded as deities, and so Christian refusal to acknowledge the divine status of their secular overlord was viewed as tantamount to treason.

Emperor Nero blamed the Christians for the burning of Rome in A.D. 64, and for the next 250 years persecution of Christians received intermittent imperial support. While it was at times both sporadic and regional, this persecution reached a height around A.D. 303–05 during the reign of the Emperor Diocletian (A.D. 284–305). Christian churches were destroyed and their congregations arrested, tortured, or killed. Draconian edicts banning Christian teaching and worship were enforced through much of the empire.

In A.D. 286 Diocletian divided the empire in two, ruling its eastern portion while the former general Maximian ruled in the west. In A.D. 305, Diocletian

THE EDICT OF MILAN

This was a joint declaration, signed by both the Emperor Constantine and his Eastern Roman counterpart Licinius, which proclaimed a tolerance of Christian beliefs throughout the Roman world. Earlier edicts of tolerance had paved the way for this ground-breaking ruling, which in effect marked the legalization of Christianity. The two emperors signed the declaration during a summit convened on the occasion of Licinius's marriage to Constantine's sister to restore peace throughout the Roman world after a damaging spate of rebellions and civil wars. Licinius would later renege on his declaration, but the Constantinian shift towards Christianity was both heartfelt and irreversible.

KEY DATES IN THE LIFE OF CONSTANTINE I AND ROMAN CHRISTIANITY

A.D. 286
Division of the Eastern and Western Roman Empires

A.D. 303
Beginning of the persecution of Christians under Emperor Diocletian

A.D. 305
Emperor Diocletian retires, as does his Western Roman counterpart Maximian

A.D. 306
Constantine proclaimed Western Roman Emperor

A.D. 311
The Edict of Toleration signed by the Eastern Roman Emperor Galerius

and Maximian both stood down, and Galerius and Constantius assumed control of the eastern and western portions of the empire respectively. Constantius died the following year, and his son Constantine laid claim to his father's office as senior Roman emperor in the west.

While both Diocletian and Galerius persecuted Christians, Constantius and Constantine were more tolerant, and Constantine ended persecution in the western half of the empire. However, domestic policies were overshadowed by civil war, as Constantine's power was challenged by Maximian (Diocletian's former co-emperor) and his son Maxentius. Two years of warfare were finally brought to an end in A.D. 312, when Constantine defeated Maxentius at the Battle of the Milvian Bridge, north of Rome.

TOLERATION

In A.D. 311, Galerius reversed his policy while on his deathbed, and issued an Edict of Toleration ending the persecution of Christians within the eastern provinces of the Roman Empire. He died soon afterwards, and so in A.D. 313 his successor Licinius and Constantine jointly signed a new document—known as the Edict of Milan—which removed any bar on the declaration of Christian beliefs. Licinius later reneged on this edict, and resumed the persecution of Christians within the Eastern Empire. When Licinius was deposed in A.D. 324, Constantine became the sole emperor of both east and west. One of his first acts was to found the city of Constantinople as a symbol of this reunification.

Emperor Constantine "the Great" was tolerant of religious beliefs, and he only openly embraced Christianity after A.D. 324. In A.D. 325, he summoned the Council of Nicaea, an ecclesiastical assembly that set about establishing an agreed set of Christian doctrines. In effect, it laid the foundations for the established Christian Church. By the time Constantine died in A.D. 332, Christianity had become the dominant religion within the Roman Empire, supported by its own orthodox structure, and by the power of the Roman state.

ABOVE LEFT: *The Arch of Constantine in Rome, constructed in A.D. 312–315 in memory of the Battle of the Milvian Bridge.*
BELOW: *The* Battle of Constantine and Maxentius, *painted by the great Flemish artist Peter Paul Rubens in* ca *1620.*

THE BATTLE OF THE MILVIAN BRIDGE (A.D. 312)

According to the Roman historian Lactantius, Constantine had a dream on the eve of the battle, telling him to mark the shields of his soldiers with a Christian symbol. He did so, and the following day a cross was seen in the sky over the battlefield. Despite being heavily outnumbered, Constantine's army emerged victorious, decisively crushing the opposing force. Maxentius was killed, and Constantine emerged as the undisputed ruler of the western half of the empire. Although Constantine only embraced the Christian faith some time afterwards, the battle was seen as a turning point in the official recognition of Christianity within the Roman world.

A.D. 312
Battle of the Milvian Bridge—acceptance of Christian beliefs by Constantine

A.D. 313
The Edict of Milan legalizes Christianity within the Roman world

A.D. 324
Constantine defeats and deposes Licinius, leaving him as sole Roman Emperor

A.D. 325
The Council of Nicea establishes orthodox set of beliefs for the Christian Church

A.D. 337
Death of Emperor Constantine I, leaving Christianity dominant across the Roman Empire

THE MAYA EMPIRE ~ CA 200 B.C.–A.D. 1200

Extending across modern-day southern Mexico, areas of the Yucatán Peninsula, Guatemala, Belize, El Salvador, and Honduras, the Mayan region represented the largest area of Mesoamerica. Politically and administratively, it was divided into a multitude of smaller territories, which in turn can be grouped into three main zones: the southern highlands incorporating parts of Guatemala; the southern or central lowlands just beneath them; and the northern lowlands covering the Puuc hills.

URBANIZATION

The Classic Period of Mayan civilization—generally regarded as lasting from around A.D. 200 or 300 until the culture's collapse circa A.D. 900—saw a flourishing of Mayan society and the production of many of the artifacts, buildings, and writings from which our understanding of the Maya is derived. A period of urbanization marked the beginning of the Classic Period, with populations coalescing around towns and cities, each presided over by rulers who were often believed to have been descended from the gods. These city states existed in a state of constant warfare, with various of them coming to exert a hegemony over the others under particularly effective rulers, such as Bird Jaguar IV of Palenque (A.D. 752–68).

RIGHT: *A Mayan ceramic figure of a nobleman on a throne.*
BELOW: *An 18th-century engraving of a Mayan or Aztec pyramid which was used for human sacrifices.*

THE FOOD OF THE GODS

Highly prized in Mayan society, chocolate (known as *xocoatl*) was regarded as a gift from the gods to the Mayan race. Cocoa beans were employed as currency, traded for commodities such as jade, cloth, or feathers, and used in religious rituals. They were also used to make the chocolate drink that was, until around 1600, reserved for consumption by the most prestigious members of society. The significance of cocoa and chocolate within Mayan life can be seen in the wealth of references to the making and consumption of chocolate in hieroglyphs, artifacts, and ancient Mayan texts.

KEY DATES OF THE MAYA EMPIRE

3114 B.C.
Mayan date for the beginning of the world, according to their long-count calendar

CA 1000 B.C.
Earliest evidence of Mayan architecture having existed

CA 250 B.C.
Earliest evidence of Mayan script having been in use

36 B.C.
Evidence of awareness of the concept of zero among Mayan mathematicians

CA A.D. 200
Classic Period of Mayan civilization begins, marked by growing urbanization

Royal palaces, pyramids, and temples on a grand scale dominated these settlements, many of which survive at sites such as Tikal, Palenque, and Chichén Itzá. These provide evidence of a people preoccupied with ritual and ceremony. Human sacrifice formed an integral part of Mayan religious rituals in the worship of a pantheon of gods related to the natural phenomena that made up their known world. One of the foremost figures among their gods was Kukulkan, the Mayan name for the feathered snake deity known to the Aztecs as Quetzalcoatl.

Mayan culture was highly sophisticated. The Maya were responsible for creating the first fully developed written language of Mesoamerica, and they also developed an advanced system of mathematics, which by 36 B.C. included the concept of zero. Keen astronomers, the Maya built great observatories and produced remarkably accurate charts depicting the movement of the moon and planets. Their calculation of the length of the solar year was also highly accurate, although this was not used in the production of their calendars, which worked on both a 365-day year and a 260-day cycle, coinciding every 52 years to produce the Mayan equivalent of our century (known to historians as the "Calendar Round").

MAYAN INFLUENCE

Throughout the Classic Period, Mayan influence extended far beyond the broad geographic area that they occupied. Evidence suggests that their international trading relations brought them into contact with peoples up to 1,600 miles away in central Mexico, Panama, and the Caribbean.

No firm explanation exists for the collapse of Mayan civilization in the southern lowlands around A.D. 822–900, but we do know that large-scale architectural construction and the production of hieroglyphic writings ceased at around this time. Popular theories can be divided into the ecological, suggesting the cause as a major drought or an epidemic disease, and the non-ecological, including overpopulation, foreign invasion, or the collapse of key trade routes. Nevertheless, Mayan culture survived in the northern population centers. By 1250, the central Itza Maya, Ko'woj and Yalain groups had reconstituted themselves to form competing city states. Even the arrival of the Spanish in Mesoamerica in the 16th century could not stamp out the Mayan culture entirely, and it continues to survive in some regions to this day.

RIGHT: *The Pyramid of Kukulkan, the Mayan snake deity, in Chichén-Itzá in Yucatán, Mexico. The pyramid is known as El Castillo (meaning "the castle") in Spanish.*

BELOW: *A Mayan relief of hieroglyphic script from Quirigua, Guatemala, sculpted ca A.D. 775.*

MAYAN SCRIPTS

The Ancient Maya boasted the only fully developed written language of the pre-Columbian Americas, with evidence of their writings dating from around 250 B.C. The first bishop of Yucatán compiled a phonetic key to reading the Mayan language as early as 1566, but it was not until the 1950s that any major breakthroughs were made in the deciphering of meaning within Mayan texts. A logosyllabic script made up of hundreds of logograms (representing whole words), as well as glyphs for individual syllables and place names, Mayan writing usually appeared in paired vertical columns to be read from left to right. Examples of Mayan texts have been found on stone, bark, wood, and ceramics, as well as on a few surviving manuscripts.

CA A.D. 675
Construction of Temple of Inscriptions at Palenque (in modern southern Mexico) begun

A.D. 800–900
Collapse of southern Mayan civilization, especially in lowlands

CA A.D. 1250
Central Itza Maya, Ko'woj, and Yalain groups form competing city states

A.D. 1517
Spanish explorer Francisco Hernández de Córdoba arrives at Yucatán

A.D. 2005
Rabinal Achí, a play written in a Mayan language, is celebrated by UNESCO

THE UNIFICATION OF CHINA ~ A.D. 581–604

Following the collapse of the Han dynasty in A.D. 220, China began to fragment. It was the Sui dynasty which reunited China after a lengthy split between the north and south, a period known as the Southern and Northern dynasties, which lasted from A.D. 316 to 589. The northern ruler Wen Di of Sui conquered the south of China in A.D. 589 and united the country once more. He claimed that he possessed the Mandate of Heaven, which granted him the divine favor of the gods and qualified him to rule China.

CENTRALIZATION

The Sui dynasty was short-lived (collapsing in A.D. 618), but it achieved much in that time, most significantly the consolidation of centralized power. The land was made more secure and prosperous with the completion of infrastructure projects, such as the extension of the Grand Canal, and the construction of granaries that stored surplus food in large settlements.

The centralization of power that characterized this dynasty was driven by a new bureaucratic system, which would go on to provide China with an effective means of administration for most of its history. Aspiring officials were made to undergo extensive examinations in order to qualify for their roles. There were several levels of seniority, each one requiring rigorous study and dedication in order to qualify. Examinations could last for tens of hours at a time, while the aspiring official sat in an enclosed box-like room. This system developed from Confucian methods of education, which were officially adopted by Emperor Yang Di (the son of Wen Di) in A.D. 605.

THE GREAT WALL

The Sui dynasty saw the rebuilding and strengthening of the Great Wall. It is often called the "wall of bones" in China after the practice of burying the bodies of the many millions who lost their lives during its construction within the wall itself. Sui military endeavors were not purely defensive, however, and Emperor Yang Di undertook several expeditions in the hope of conquering nearby territories. One of these, the attempt to take Champa (roughly equivalent to modern-day Vietnam), ended in disaster when many of the northern Chinese troops

LEFT: *An 18th-century Chinese portrait of Sui Emperor Wen Di, who reigned A.D. 581–604.*

BELOW: *A pottery figure from the Northern Qi dynasty (one of the Northern dynasties), ca 563, of the Buddhist bodhisattva Avalokitesvara. A bodhisattva is a being who has attained enlightenment but delays entering nirvana in order to help other people find salvation.*

BUDDHISM

In the late Han period (A.D. 88–220), Buddhism had spread from India throughout China, and by the time of the Sui dynasty it had attained widespread popularity. There was little in the way of a state religion, and not much centralized control, and so Buddhism was free to flourish. It served as a unifying cultural influence and helped bind the disparate peoples of China under a common heritage. Recognizing the significance Buddhism held for many of his subjects, Emperor Wen Di converted to the religion, and styled himself as a Cakravartin ruler—a kind of ideal religious king, responsible for defending the peoples of his faith.

KEY DATES IN THE SUI DYNASTY

A.D. 581–604
Rule of Emperor Wen Di of the Sui dynasty

A.D. 598
First Goguryeo war begins in what is now Korea. Millions of Sui Chinese are mobilized

A.D. 601
Emperor Wen Di has Buddhist relics distributed to temples throughout China

A.D. 604–18
Rule of Emperor Yang Di, the son of Wen Di

A.D. 605
The imperial examination system is founded, beginning a long tradition of bureaucratic examination

contracted tropical diseases, such as malaria, to which they had no immunity. A series of attacks on the Korean kingdom of Goguryeo between the years A.D. 598 and 614 also incurred huge losses for very little success.

The great loss of life caused by the huge building projects of the Sui dynasty, together with the numerous and costly wars, were an enormous drain on China's economy and population. It was not long before the dynasty began to collapse in the face of popular revolt and discontent. The emperor tried to escape the turmoil by moving the capital south to Yangzhou, but the rebellion was widespread, and in A.D. 618 Yang Di was murdered by Yuwe Huaji, a senior general. The throne was soon taken over by Li Yuan, a former Sui general, who became Emperor Tang Gao Zu, the first ruler of the Tang dynasty. Although the Sui dynasty ended in violence and chaos, it had been instrumental in unifying the country and bringing it under the authority of a single ruler, achievements that would lead to China becoming one of the world's most powerful civilizations in the centuries to follow.

LEFT: *A late Sui/early Tang dynasty pottery figure of a warrior, from ca 581–650.*

BELOW: *Emperors Yang Di and Wen Di with attendants, detail from Portraits of Thirteen Emperors, attributed to Yen Li Pen (d. 673), the greatest artist of the early Tang dynasty.*

GRAND CANAL

The Grand Canal is one of the greatest engineering achievements of the pre-modern world. Stretching from Beijing in the north to Hangzhou in the east, it was a vital trade link across China's vast territory for centuries. Although construction began as far back as the fifth century B.C., it was expanded and reached its final form during the Sui dynasty, at the cost of several hundred thousand deaths. It is about 1,100 miles long, and remains the longest canal in the world. Its significance to the Sui was that armies in the north no longer had to live off the land; they could instead rely on the supply of food shipped up the canal.

A.D. 609
The Grand Canal is completed, linking the cities of Hangzhou and Beijing

A.D. 611
The Four Gates Pagoda is completed in the modern-day province of Shandong

A.D. 612
Second Goguryeo war begins, with over one million Sui troops

A.D. 613–14
Third and Fourth Goguryeo wars. Emperor Yang Di eventually accepts a peace offer and retreats

A.D. 618
The rebel Li Yuan takes over the throne and becomes Tang Gao Zu, beginning the Tang dynasty

THE PROPHET MOHAMMED ~ A.D. 570–632

Mohammed, the Islamic prophet, the messenger of God, and the founder of the Islamic faith, was born in A.D. 570 in Mecca (in modern Saudi Arabia). As an orphan he was brought up by an uncle—Abu Talib—and reputedly worked as a trader within the city. Unfortunately, the historical details are scanty, and have since become interwoven with later Islamic traditions.

He reputedly married when he was 25, but he soon became disillusioned with the secular world, and took to occasional withdrawals from society, seeking solace and spiritual guidance in a mountain cave. Islamic tradition has it that around A.D. 610, during one of these periods of retreat on Mount Hira, the archangel Jibril (Gabriel) appeared before him, and he received the first of many revelations from Allah (God).

PREACHING

In A.D. 613, after three years of meditation, Mohammed began publicly preaching the word of God. More revelations followed, and these formed the basis of the Koran—"the recitation," detailing Allah's guidance for mankind, as revealed directly to Mohammed. The revelations would continue until Mohammed's death in A.D. 632. At first the revelations were memorized by Mohammed, but soon his followers were able to recite them word for word, and helped to spread the message. A written record followed, but the verses were only collated into a single volume after the death of the prophet.

At first, Mohammed was persecuted for his preaching, although the number of his followers grew steadily. Some were hounded from the city, and sought refuge on the far side of the Red Sea in Abyssinia (Ethiopia). The death of his wife and uncle in A.D. 619—the "year of sorrow"—

RIGHT: *A 16th-century miniature showing Mohammed's vision on Mount Hira, from* Siyer-i Nebi, *a Turkish epic on the life of Mohammed.*

BELOW: *This 1,200-year-old copy of the Koran is displayed for the Muharram festival in Srinagar, Kashmir, India.*

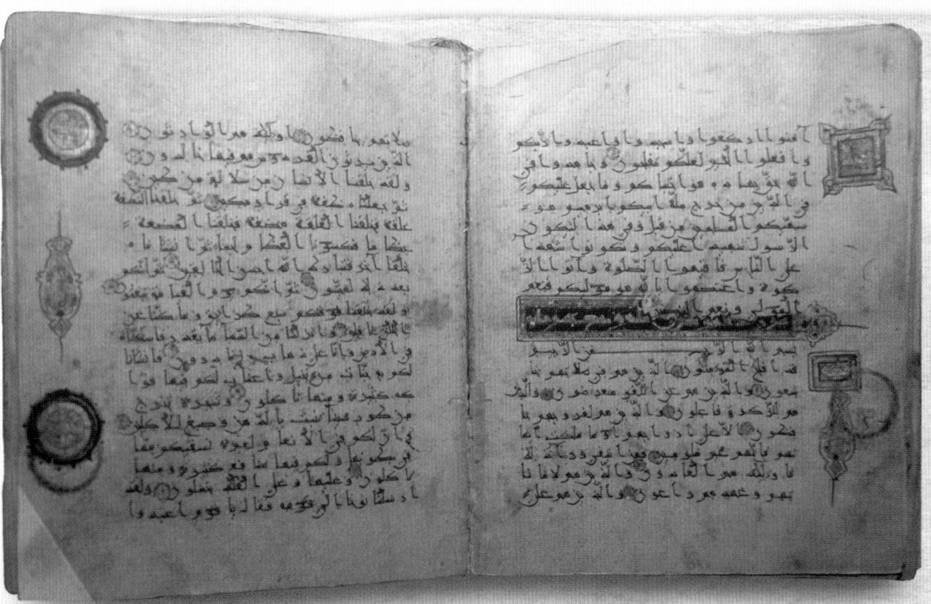

THE ORIGINS OF THE KORAN

It is assumed that the Koran was recorded by the followers of Mohammed immediately after each revelation, as dictated to them by the prophet. Shortly after his death these writings were gathered together into a single volume. The main theme of these revelations were monotheism, resurrection, reward for the faithful, the penalty of non-belief, and the governing of Islamic life. According to tradition, the first to believe Mohammed was a true prophet were his wife, Khadija; Mohammed's young cousin, Ali ibn al Abi Talib; and Ali's friend, Abu Bakr. The two youngsters would become the first scribes of the Koran.

KEY DATES IN THE LIFE OF MOHAMMED

A.D. 570
Birth of Mohammed, in Mecca (in modern Saudi Arabia)

A.D. 610
The first revelation to Mohammed from Allah (God) on Mount Hira

A.D. 613
Mohammed begins preaching the word of Allah after revelations and meditation

A.D. 621
Mohammed experiences the *Isra* and *Mi'raj*

A.D. 622
The *Hijra*—the Muslim emigration from Mecca to Medina

THE NIGHT JOURNEY

In 621, Islamic tradition holds that Mohammed experienced a revelation known as the *Isra* and *Mi'raj*, or the Night Journey. In it, Jibril brought Mohammed the winged steed Buraq who transported him to "the furthest mosque," which is generally assumed to be Jerusalem. There, Mohammed led other Abrahamic prophets in prayer before remounting Buraq, who took him on a tour of heaven, where Mohammed was presented to Allah. The prophet was instructed in piety before being returned to earth on his winged steed. While some Muslim scholars consider this a literal journey, most regard it as a miraculous vision.

ABOVE: *Pilgrims rest outside the Prophet Mohammed Mosque, burial place of the prophet, in the holy city of Medina al-Monawarah, Saudi Arabia.*
BELOW RIGHT: *More than 1,300 pilgrims surround the Kaaba, Islam's most sacred site, for sunset prayers at the Grand Mosque in Mecca, Saudi Arabia, during the* hajj *pilgrimage in 2007.*

placed Mohammed in a vulnerable position, as Abu Talib had protected the prophet from his opponents. Mohammed and his followers fled from Mecca in A.D. 622, and re-established themselves in Medina (also in modern Saudi Arabia), a long-time rival of Mecca. There, the prophet soothed the feuding between competing Arab tribes, converting many of them to the new faith of Islam ("submission"), which was based on the revelations he had received. As a result, he gained a secure base for himself and his followers to propagate the tenets of their new religion.

WAR

Soon Mecca and Medina were at war; Mohammed's Muslims joined the fight, and helped secure victory after the Battles of Badr and Uhud, and the siege of Medina (A.D. 627). These permitted the Muslims to go over onto the offensive, and in A.D. 630 they conquered Mecca, allowing Mohammed to return to his native city and expunge all traces of the old polytheist Meccan religion. Soon Muslim rule extended throughout the Arabian Peninsula, and the Arab tribes united under the banner of Islam. In A.D. 632, Mohammed commenced his great pilgrimage—his *hajj*, a farewell procession to Mecca where he addressed the faithful in a final sermon. He died just months after his return to Medina, and was buried in his adopted city. His legacy was immense: no less than the foundation of one of the world's great religions.

A.D. 624
Battle of Badr: Muslims help the Medinans defeat the army of Mecca

A.D. 630
The conquest of Mecca by Medina, supported by Muslims

A.D. 631
Muslim rule extends over most of the Arabian Peninsula, uniting Arab tribes

A.D. 632
The prophet's farewell *hajj* (pilgrimage to Mecca)

A.D. 632
The death of Mohammed, in Medina

EMPEROR CHARLEMAGNE ≈ A.D. 768–814

Son of the Frankish king Pepin the Short and Bertrada of Laon, the man known today as Charlemagne was born near Liège (in modern Belgium) in A.D. 742. His given name was Charles, the name by which he is more normally referred to (Charlemagne) being derived from Carolus Magnus, meaning Charles the Great.

ABOVE: *Charlemagne departing for the Spanish Crusade with Roland and Archbishop Turpin of Reims, depicted in 13th-century stained glass from the Charlemagne lancet window in Chartres Cathedral, France.*

RIGHT: *A gothic reliquary bust of Charlemagne dating from the mid-14th century—one of the treasures of Aachen Cathedral, Germany, Charlemagne's burial place.*

FRATERNAL CONFLICT

Upon the death of Pepin in A.D. 768, Charles and his brother Carloman ascended jointly to the Frankish throne, with Charles ruling the outer lands in western and northern France, Frisia, and the eastern territories in Germany, and Carloman ruling southern and eastern France, Burgundy, and southeastern Germany. Relations between the brothers were strained, and Carloman refused to assist Charles in suppressing an uprising in Aquitaine and Gascony in A.D. 769.

In A.D. 770, Charles married the Lombard princess Desiderata as part of a bid to surround his brother with his own allies, but within a year he repudiated his bride in order to marry the 13-year-old Swabian Hildegard. This presented Carloman with an ideal opportunity to join forces with Desiderata's slighted father and move against his brother, but Carloman himself died in A.D. 771, and thus Pepin's kingdom passed to Charlemagne in its entirety.

A series of bloody military encounters saw Charlemagne expand his territories into Italy, Bohemia, and the Danube basin. In A.D. 773–74 he invaded Lombardy in support of Pope Hadrian I, who was being threatened by the Lombard ruler Desiderius, and overcame his erstwhile father-in-law, claiming the title of king of the Lombards for himself. Between A.D. 780 and 800, Charlemagne added Bavaria and some Slavic territories to his empire, and by A.D. 804 he had completely subdued the Saxons, following a gruelling campaign which lasted more than three decades. As a Christian, Charlemagne could not accept the Saxons' pagan practices. Throughout the A.D. 780s he and his followers practiced forced conversion in the Saxon territories.

CHARLEMAGNE (CA 742–814)

The *Vita Karoli Magni*, Einhard's definitive biography of Charlemagne, is believed to have been written within a decade of the great man's death. In it he describes the emperor in vivid detail: "He was heavily built, sturdy, and of considerable stature… He had a round head, large and lively eyes, a slightly larger nose than usual, white but still attractive hair, a bright and cheerful expression, a short and fat neck, and a slightly protruding stomach. His voice was clear, but a little higher than one would have expected for a man of his build."

KEY DATES IN THE LIFE OF EMPEROR CHARLEMAGNE

A.D. 742
Charlemagne born in Herstal, near Liège in modern-day Belgium

A.D. 754
Charlemagne and brother Carloman anointed by Pope Stephen III

AD 768
Ascent to the throne: joint rule with brother Carloman, with whom his relationship is strained

A.D. 769
Charlemagne subdues Aquitaine and Gascony; Carloman refuses to help

A.D. 771
Carloman dies. His wife, Gerberga, flees to Desiderius's court with her sons for protection

RONCESVALLES

Perhaps the most famous of Charlemagne's exploits is that memorialized in the *Chanson de Roland*: the Battle of the Roncesvalles Pass, which ended in defeat for the Franks. In A.D. 778, Charlemagne embarked upon a brief campaign into Spain, to liberate the north of that country from the Muslims. Victory at Pamplona was followed by defeat at Saragossa, and Charlemagne's army was in retreat at the Roncesvalles Pass when Basques or Gascons set upon the rear guard, killing many, including Roland, one of its commanders.

In A.D. 800, Charlemagne marched again to Italy in support of Pope Leo III. In recognition of Charlemagne's support, the Pope crowned him emperor on Christmas Day of that year. Legitimizing his rule over his Italian territories, the title that he assumed, "Charles, most serene Augustus, crowned by God, great and pacific emperor, governing the Roman empire," clearly prefigured the formal establishment of the Holy Roman Empire the following century.

Charlemagne had intended to split his territories between his sons upon his death, but by A.D. 814 only his youngest son, Louis the Pious, remained living. Louis ruled his father's empire in its entirety—despite several bitter civil wars caused by his sons' attempts to enhance their future inheritances—until his death in A.D. 840, but after this time Charlemagne's conquests began to fragment and fall apart.

BELOW: *Sword and scabbard belonging to Charlemagne. The emperor always carried a sword, typically with a gold or silver hilt, but he generally avoided excessive ornamentation.*

BELOW: *The coronation of Emperor Charlemagne by Pope Leo III at St. Peter's, Rome, on Christmas Day, A.D. 800, from a 14th-century illuminated manuscript.*

THE CAROLINGIAN RENAISSANCE

Learning flourished under Charlemagne, as the emperor, himself apparently illiterate, placed great value on the liberal arts. Charlemagne was at pains to ensure that his children and grandchildren were well educated, and he himself studied grammar, rhetoric, dialectic, and astronomy, taking a particular interest in the stars. The period of his rule is referred to as the Carolingian Renaissance, a reference to the boom in scholarship, literature, art, and architecture that he supported and encouraged. A large number of ancient Latin texts were transcribed during Charlemagne's reign, and in many cases these remain the earliest surviving examples of these classics.

A.D. 778
Battle of the Roncesvalles Pass brings numerous losses, including several important aristocrats

A.D. 800
Charlemagne endorsed as emperor by the Pope in Rome on Christmas Day

A.D. 804
Charlemagne finally subdues the Saxons after three decades of fighting

A.D. 813
Charlemagne's son Louis the Pious is crowned co-emperor

A.D. 814
Charlemagne dies, and is buried in Aachen Cathedral (in modern-day Germany)

THE INCA ≈ CA 1150–1532

The Inca Empire at its height occupied some 400,000 square miles stretching 2,500 miles from modern-day Ecuador to Chile, and it is estimated that four to nine million people inhabited it. Over 100 distinct Inca societies cultivated and farmed diverse lands, ranging from the coast to the mountains and the pampas to the forest, making the Inca the largest pre-Hispanic society in South America.

LEFT: *The Inca citadel of Machu Picchu, in modern Peru, lies 8,000 feet above sea level and remained undiscovered by the modern world until 1911. Dating from ca 1450, it features dry stone walls of classic Inca style.*

RIGHT: *A Peruvian ceramic figure from ca 1430–1532 of a man carrying a typical Andean backpack or* anyballus. *Such containers are still common in South America today.*

A GROWING EMPIRE

The empire was ruled and administered from its capital at Cusco (in modern Peru), which was founded around 1200, and where Inca architecture provides the foundations for many buildings that survive today. Inca legend claimed that the Inca people were descended from the inhabitants of Tiwanaku on Lake Titicaca, although modern historians consider that the majority of Inca probably came from the remnants of the Wari empire in Chokepukio, some 450 miles to the northwest of Tiwanaku.

Inca territorial expansion began as early as 1250, with Inca warriors conducting a program of conquest. The greatest period of expansion came during the 55 years that followed Pachacuti's ascent to power in 1438. Pachacuti took his name, meaning "transformer of the Earth," after he usurped the rightful ruler of the empire following the defeat of the Chanca people. Pachacuti and his more famous son Tupac Inca (1471–93) conquered great swathes of territory.

Much of the Inca success in conquering and controlling land lay in the efficiency of their road network, with around 14,000 miles of roads providing arteries of transport, communication, and administration. The most famous surviving fragment of the Inca road system is the Inca Trail, which connected Cusco to the mountain settlement of Machu Picchu. As Inca society had no wheeled vehicles or horses, these roads were essentially well-maintained paths, used for running messengers, foot travellers, and llama trains bearing tribute to Cusco in the form of pottery, maize beer, or potatoes.

INCA SKULL SURGERY

The Inca were skilled in the art of trepanning or skull surgery, with archaeological evidence indicating that more than 30 percent of Inca may have received such surgery during their lifetimes. Study of Inca skulls from around 1000 onward shows that the Inca were expert both in scraping away bone to create an opening in the head, and in making circular incisions in the skull. The positioning of the trepanned holes in Inca skulls suggests that the technique may have been used primarily to alleviate fluid build-up and inflammation related to skull fracture wounds received in battle, although a small number of female skulls have also been found to have been trepanned.

KEY DATES IN THE INCA EMPIRE

A.D. 400
First mention of the Inca tribes in Peruvian mythology

1000
Inca surgeons are known to be practicing the art of trepanning

CA 1150
Inca arrive in Altiplano, Peru, renowned for its lake, Titicaca

CA 1200
Foundation of Cusco, from where Inca Empire was ruled and administered

1400–1500
Inca empire expands to cover around 400,000 square miles, partly thanks to its road system

THE SOCIAL HIERARCHY

Land within the Inca Empire was held by peasant farmers, and a form of serfdom existed whereby men would take turns in cultivating lands reserved for the Inca administration, building roads and bridges, and serving in the military. While heads of families took their turn to do labor for the state, some men and women were chosen to devote their whole lives to its service. In the case of women, this could involve religious duties, or the spinning and weaving of the textiles for which the Inca are remembered; for men, it often involved caring for the state-owned herds of llama. Together, these groups appear to have formed a kind of prototype civil service.

Today, the Inca are best remembered for architecture, some of the most splendid examples being dedicated to worship of Inti, the sun god. Inca structures were built of vast stone slabs, fitted together with astonishing precision.

The end of the Inca Empire came with the advent of the Spanish under Francisco Pizarro in 1532. Arriving in South America with a military force that was greatly outnumbered by the Inca army, Pizarro nevertheless quickly succeeded in subduing this ancient people. Today, Pizarro's astonishing success is attributed to a combination of four factors: his superior fire-power; the alliances that he formed with local enemies of the Inca; the fact that the Inca state was just emerging from a civil war; and the smallpox which his troops brought to South America and to which the Inca had no immunity.

QUIPU

The word *quipu* means knot. These knotted recording devices were used throughout Andean civilizations from the seventh to the 16th centuries, but are particularly associated with the Inca Empire. *Quipu* were constructed from a length of rope, to which other threads or ropes could be attached. Sometimes, further subsidiary threads were attached to these in turn. The length of the attached strings, their color, and the number and positioning of any knots tied into them, each conveyed a different meaning. A *quipu* could therefore record quantities of a particular commodity or details of a transaction, or could be used to record periods of time—for instance, the duration of the reign of a particular king.

ABOVE: *A* quipu *made in Peru ca 1430–1532. These apparently simple devices were used for recording a range of data, typically relating to population statistics or crops.*
RIGHT: *An engraving of the execution of an Inca by Pizarro. The Spanish conquest of the Inca Empire included the attempt to introduce Christianity, through a mixture of rough translation of its tenets and demonstration of its power.*

CA 1438
Defeat of Chanca people by Pachacuti triggers a period of further territorial expansion

1471
Tupac Inca becomes the first Inca ruler to be considered supernatural in his lifetime

1535
Inca society is overthrown by Pizarro, a Spanish conquistador and founder of Lima, the modern-day capital of Peru

1532
Atahuallpa defeats his brother Huáscar in civil war

1983
Machu Picchu declared a UNESCO World Heritage Site

THE CRUSADES ⁓ 1095–1291

The Crusades—a series of military expeditions by Christian armies against Muslim-held areas of the Eastern Mediterranean—were born out of an appeal by the Byzantine emperor Alexius I Comnenus to Pope Urban II in 1095 for help in reconquering territory lost to the Seljuk Turks in 1071. At the Council of Clermont later the same year, Urban preached the need for an armed pilgrimage to liberate the Holy Land (modern-day Israel, Palestine, and Jordan), most particularly the city of Jerusalem, from its Muslim rulers.

VICTORY AT A PRICE

All those who took part in such an enterprise were to have their sins remitted. The call attracted some 100,000 participants, of whom perhaps 60,000 reached Asia Minor in 1097 under the leadership of a coterie of European nobles. Taking advantage of internal Seljuk disunity, as well as an ongoing conflict between the Seljuks and the Fatimid rulers of Egypt, the Crusaders captured the cities of Antioch, Edessa, and, finally, Jerusalem in 1099, whose Muslim and Jewish inhabitants they massacred. The victorious Crusaders established four states: the County of Edessa; the Principality of Antioch; the County of Tripoli; and the Kingdom of Jerusalem.

The loss of Edessa in 1144 to a Muslim counter-attack provided the impetus for the Second Crusade in 1147, which attempted—and failed—to take the important center of Damascus.

The Muslim reconquest of the Crusader states continued throughout the 12th century and received a particular boost following the unification of much of the Middle East under Saladin's Ayyubid dynasty. This renowned Muslim leader, now with greater resources, launched attacks on the Kingdom of Jerusalem,

RICHARD I "LIONHEART"

(1157–99)

Born in Oxford, England, in 1157, Richard was the third son of Henry I and was not expected to become king. The early deaths of his brothers left him the heir apparent and he ascended the throne of England in 1189 after the death of his father. Richard had vowed to join a Crusade in 1187, following the fall of Jerusalem, and was one of the leaders of the Third Crusade, launched in 1189. He was instrumental in the conquest of Byzantine Cyprus, the successful siege of Acre, a major victory at Arsuf, and the negotiations with Saladin over the status of the city of Jerusalem.

ABOVE: *A medieval relief sculpture of Richard the Lionheart, created in 1289.*

LEFT: *European Crusader prisoners are brought before Saladin during the Battle of Hattin, which took place in 1187 near what is now Tiberias in Israel.*

KEY DATES OF THE CRUSADES

1096–99
First Crusade: Crusaders capture Edessa, Antioch, and finally Jerusalem, leading to the creation of the Crusader states

1148–49
Second Crusade: following the fall of Edessa, French and German crusaders under Conrad III and Louis VII attack Damascus

1187
The Battle of Hattin: the defeat of a Christian army by Saladin leads to the fall of Acre and the loss of Jerusalem

1189–92
Third Crusade: Richard I of England, Philip II of France, and Frederick Barbarossa attempt to recapture Jerusalem from Saladin

1201–04
Fourth Crusade: intending to assault Cairo, Crusaders under Louis I are diverted to Constantinople, which they sack in 1204

provoking its leaders into a disastrous defeat at the Battle of Hattin in 1187. This led to the loss of almost all the Crusader territory, and to the Third Crusade, under the leadership of Richard I of England, Philip II of France, and the Holy Roman Emperor, Frederick Barbarossa. A partial success, it failed to recapture Jerusalem, and the Crusader states became locked into a cycle of internal dissent and decay that continued until the fall of their stronghold, the city of Acre, in 1291.

LEFT: *An illustration from an illuminated 13th-century French manuscript which shows the siege and capture of Jerusalem during the First Crusade.*

BELOW LEFT: *A portrait of a Knight Templar. The initial group comprised just nine knights, who banded together to protect pilgrims.*

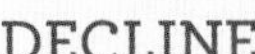

DECLINE

A number of other crusades had been launched, usually to try and neutralize the power of Egypt, but by the mid-13th century these had become national affairs, generally consisting of either French or German contingents, rather than genuinely international crusading efforts. Despite sporadic successes, such as the Holy Roman Emperor Frederick II's negotiated reoccupation of Jerusalem in 1229, the period overall was one of Crusader decline.

The Holy Land was not the only destination for Crusades during this period: Prussia and the Baltic region saw extensive crusades against their pagan indigenous peoples, spearheaded by the military order of the Teutonic Knights, while the Albigensian Crusade of 1209–29 was directed, mainly by the French, against the Cathars of southern France, Christian heretics who believed the physical world was created by an evil power.

THE MILITARY ORDERS

When Jerusalem fell to the Crusaders in 1099, the task of protecting the many pilgrims coming to the Holy Land was taken up by a new form of knightly force—the military orders. One of these bands was formed in 1119 and known as the Poor Knights of Christ after their vows of poverty, obedience, and chastity. They were to become more famous after being renamed the Knights of the Temple, or Knights Templar, following their occupation of the site of the Temple of Solomon. Other military orders such as the Knights of St. John (alternatively known as Knights Hospitallers) also played a key role in providing an elite force to defend the Crusader states.

1218–21
Fifth Crusade: a largely German and Hungarian force captures the Egyptian city of Damietta, before becoming overstretched during their march to Cairo

1228–1229
Sixth Crusade: the Holy Roman Emperor, Frederick II, manages to regain much of the Holy Land through negotiation

1248–1254
Seventh Crusade: the first crusade led by Saint Louis of France, aimed at Egypt

1270
Eighth Crusade: once again led by Saint Louis, this crusade attacks Tunis

1271–1272
Ninth Crusade: Prince Edward of England attempts to assist the dwindling kingdom of Jerusalem based at Acre

GENGHIS KHAN'S EMPIRE ⁓ 1206–27

Born in 1162 to a noble family, the man now remembered as Genghis Khan was first known as Temujin. Hailed by the Mongol nation as the greatest leader of all time, he conquered more square miles of territory than any other military leader before him, commanding an empire four times the size of that of Alexander the Great. His successors went on to maintain the largest contiguous empire in history.

His early life was fraught with hardships, with his father, Yesukhei, poisoned by Tatars shortly after Temujin's childhood betrothal to his future wife, Borte. While Temujin was still a young man, Borte was kidnapped and held hostage by a rival tribe, and the trauma of this experience perhaps provoked him to specifically include a passage prohibiting the capture of women when he came to compose his Yasa code of law. The rescue of Borte, aided by his father's old allies, Toghril and the Keraits, was among Temujin's earliest victories. Clashes with the Jadarans followed, and eventually with the Keraits as relations between Temujin and Toghril deterioriated. As Temujin emerged victorious from each encounter, his reputation as a great leader grew.

By 1206, Temujin had dominated all the tribes of Mongolia, and it was then that he took the title Genghis Khan, variously translated to mean Universal, Firm, or Resolute Ruler. From here, his career of international conquest began, fueled in part by a need for goods and riches that Mongolia couldn't provide.

ABOVE: *A Persian painting of Genghis Khan in battle, preceded by Gebe, one of his generals.*
LEFT: *Genghis Khan, Grand Mongol, a painting by Pierre Duflos of rue St. Victor, Paris, France.*

IMPERIAL EXPANSION

Genghis Khan's first major campaign was against Xi-Xia (Western Xia) in 1207. The Xi-Xia territories covered much of what is now northwestern China and Tibet, and the Mongols campaigned for three years before the Xi-Xia ruler finally submitted. The next

GENGHIS KHAN'S LAW

Best known for his military prowess and conquests, Genghis Khan was no less remarkable for the legal system, or Yasa, that he introduced throughout his territories. Believed to have been written in Uighur-Mongolian script on scrolls that have now been lost in their entirety, the Yasa was held in secret locations known only to Genghis Khan and his closest allies. Nevertheless, the regulations laid out within it were law throughout his empire. Enshrined within the Yasa were the principles of religious tolerance, together with details of crimes and their proper punishments, including the consequences of abducting women, stealing livestock, or defecting from the army. The most common punishment dictated by the Yasa was death.

KEY DATES IN THE LIFE OF GENGHIS KHAN

1162
Temujin (later to be known as Genghis Khan) born, near what is now Ulan Bator, capital of Mongolia

1171
Temujin's father, Yesukhei, fatally poisoned by neighboring Tatars

1184
Genghis Khan's wife, Borte, kidnapped but successfully rescued

1201
Victory over the Jadarans, local allies-turned-rivals

1203
Victory over the Nestorian Christain Keraits, former allies in the Mongolian region

MONGOL WARFARE

Mongol warriors owed much of their success in battle to their exemplary horsemanship and archery, skills honed through centuries of hunting on the steppe. Clad in lacquered leather armor, mounted on small, sturdy ponies native to the region, and armed with a number of bows made out of sinew, horn, and wood together with a range of specialist arrows, Mongol horsemen typically carried their rations and supplies with them, and traveled light. Genghis Khan's contribution to the evolution of Mongol warfare was the introduction of strict codes of discipline. Under his leadership, the Mongols refined their highly mobile tactics, perfecting the caracole technique and using it to great effect against their many enemies.

year, in 1211, following a great *guriltai* or campaign meeting, Genghis Khan and his generals resolved to tackle the Jin dynasty of northern China. Despite the fall of Beijing in 1215, however, the campaign proved inconclusive, as Genghis Khan's attention was diverted to focus on the Khwarezmid Empire, which ruled regions including Uzbekistan, Turkmenistan, Iran, Afghanistan, and Tajikistan.

The campaign against the Khwarezmids was triggered in 1219, when an expedition of Mongol traders was massacred in Otrar (in modern Kazakhstan). Genghis Khan initially sought a peaceful resolution, sending envoys to the Khwarezmid emperor Muhammad Khwarezmshah, but when his chief envoy was killed and others humiliated he had no option but to retaliate. Leaving one of his generals to continue the battle against the Jin, Genghis Khan led a Mongol army to Central Asia. After three years of relentless and strategically exemplary campaigning by Genghis Khan and four of his sons, the Kwarezmid defeat was complete and the Mongols returned to their old enemy, Xi-Xia.

CONSOLIDATION

It was Genghis Khan's practice to absorb warriors from conquered regions and allied tribes into his own armies, preventing such new recruits from forming factions and fomenting dissent. The conquered Xi-Xia had failed to provide troops to support the Mongols in their Asian campaigns, leaving Genghis Khan with a score to settle. He led his last campaign, against Xi-Xia, in 1226, meeting his end during the fighting; legend has it that he fell from his horse and died from internal injuries.

Genghis Khan was buried in a secret location. His legacy lived on, with his successors dominating the battlefields of Asia and central Europe until their empire stretched from the Pacific to the Adriatic.

TOP: *The Genghis Khan Mausoleum, in Inner Mongolia, China, houses relics of the great leader. The building is designed to be reminiscent of three yurts (Mongol tents).*

RIGHT: *A painting of two warriors fighting, from the 15th-century Persian Mongol school.*

1206
Temujin takes the title Genghis Khan, meaning Universal, Firm, or Resolute Ruler

1207–1210
Campaigns against the Western Xia (or Xi-Xia) in northwestern China and Tibet

1215
Fall of Yanjing (modern Beijing), capital of the Jin territory in northern China

1222
Conquest of the Khwarezmid Empire, which occupied much of today's Iran and Central Asia

1227
Genghis Khan dies, leaving an empire stretching in a single bloc from the Caspian Sea to the Pacific coast

MAGNA CARTA ~ 1215

The Magna Carta has been lauded as one of the most important legal documents in history, having a profound influence on British and American law along with that of many other nations. However, at the time, it was seen as a political bargaining chip between King John of England and his rebellious barons, and was not intended to have a lasting significance.

Following his accession to the throne of England in 1199, John became embroiled in a series of political disputes with both the French king and the papacy. The former led to conflict that culminated with the defeat of John's allies at the Battle of Bouvines in 1214 and the loss of his territories in France (principally Normandy and Brittany). His dispute with the pope led to England being placed under interdict, meaning that public worship could not be carried out, while John himself was excommunicated by Pope Innocent III in 1209. John's military failures and loss of revenue in France, coupled with the need to raise large sums to placate the angry pope, meant that he exploited his traditional sources of feudal revenue in England to an unprecedented extent, causing huge internal resentment and discontent amongst the nobility.

ABOVE: *King John reluctantly signs the Magna Carta at Runnymede, England, watched by his barons.*
RIGHT: *A depiction of King John from the* Historia Anglorum, *which is now in the British Library in London, England.*

REVOLT

This unhappiness erupted into revolt in 1215, when some of the leading barons entered London under arms, leading directly to a meeting with John at Runnymede near Windsor in the south of England in June. The result of this was the Magna Carta, issued under John's seal on June 15, 1215, with the barons renewing their oaths to John four days later. John's rejection of the charter almost immediately after it

KING JOHN
(1167–1216)

John was the youngest son of Henry II and came to the throne of England following the death of his more illustrious brother, Richard I, in 1199. Like his predecessors, he focussed much of his attention on the Angevin possessions in France, using his English revenues in an attempt to protect his territories in the face of French royal aggression. However, this, combined with a breach in relations with the papacy, was to lead to a breakdown in feudal relations that culminated in the Magna Carta.

KEY DATES OF THE REIGN OF KING JOHN & THE MAGNA CARTA

MAY 27, 1199
John is crowned King of England following the death of his brother, Richard I

MARCH 24, 1208
Papal interdict placed over England forbids priests from administering most sacraments or Christian burial

APRIL 21, 1214
Pope Innocent III accepts England as a papal fiefdom, ending his dispute with John

MAY 17, 1215
The rebel barons capture the Tower of London, greatly strengthening their position in their struggle with King John

JUNE 15, 1215
King John grants Magna Carta, only to reject it almost immediately

THE BARONS' WAR

John's failure to honor the pledges made in the Magna Carta led to the Barons' War in 1215, when the English barons sought support from Prince Louis of France. The death of John and accession of Henry III in 1216 did not end the conflict; it was the victories of William Marshal over Louis at the Second Battle of Lincoln in May 1217, followed by a series of naval defeats, that caused the French prince to renounce his claim to the throne of England in the Treaty of Lambeth, signed on September 11, 1217.

ABOVE: *The monument that was erected at Runnymede to commemorate the signing of the Magna Carta in 1215.*
RIGHT: *One of the three surviving examples of Magna Carta, which is now held in the British National Archives in London, England.*

had been produced, with Pope Innocent III's support, led to civil war in England. His successor, Henry III, however, accepted a modified version of the charter and it was regarded for centuries as a cornerstone of English law.

The original Magna Carta ("great charter") consisted of 63 clauses, largely dealing with the regulation and organization of the feudal relationship between crown and peerage. The most important clause for the barons was the sixty-first, which set up a committee of 25 barons who could at any time meet and overrule the will of the king, thereby fundamentally changing the nature of medieval kingship by limiting the authority of the monarch and placing him under the rule of the law.

HUMAN RIGHTS

Of the three clauses of the Magna Carta still in force in British law today, by far the most influential has been clause 39, which reads, "No free man shall be seized or imprisoned, or stripped of his rights or possessions… or deprived of his standing in any other way, nor will we proceed with force against him, or send others to do so, except by the lawful judgement of his equals or by the law of the land." This clause formed the basis of habeas corpus, the foundation for trial by jury in the United Kingdom, and it exerted a profound influence on the drafters of the American Constitution.

AUGUST 24, 1215
Pope Innocent III issues a papal bull declaring Magna Carta null and void

MAY 22, 1216
Prince Louis of France invades England and attracts substantial baronial support

JULY 12, 1216
King John loses his royal treasure in the Wash, an inlet of the North Sea

OCTOBER 18, 1216
King John dies at Newark, probably from dysentery. His nine-year-old son becomes King Henry III

SEPTEMBER 11, 1217
Treaty of Lambeth ends the Barons' War against French Prince Louis and the English barons

THE OTTOMAN EMPIRE ~ 1299–1326

Osman (ca 1259–1326), a tribal ruler from Asia Minor who founded an empire that would last for six centuries, was a man who came of age at a critical time in history. His father Ertuğrul was the leader of the Kayi tribe, a Turkic people who had migrated from Central Asia into Asia Minor in the 13th century.

From 1231, their tribal base was the village of Söğüt in Bithynia, on the Asian side of the Bosphorus. Ertuğrul held his land as a vassal of the Seljuks of Rum, who in turn had established control over central Asia Minor at the expense of the Byzantines, the successors of the Eastern Roman Empire. At the time of Osman's birth around 1258, the Seljuks were under pressure from the Mongols in the east—who captured Baghdad that year—and were riven by internal rivalries. Similarly, the Byzantines were militarily weak and over-dependent on foreign mercenaries, and lacked the political or financial power to re-assert their authority over Asia Minor.

A WARRIOR

Osman grew up at a time of a power vacuum, and like his father before him, he used this to his advantage. Osman succeeded his father in 1281, by which time he had already established a reputation as a warrior. He set about establishing a powerful army, using *ghazis*—militant but undisciplined Muslim holy warriors—as the core of his force. He began to expand his power base in western Anatolia (in modern Turkey), and in 1301 he defeated the Byzantines (Christians based at Constantinople, modern Istanbul) at the Battle of Baphaeon, fought outside Nicaea (İznik). The campaign came about as part of a Byzantine military response to Osmanli (or Ottoman) raids and incursions into Byzantine territory, culminating in the surrounding of Nicaea by the Osmanli army. The battle was fought in an unsuccessful attempt to relieve the city. In fact, Osman lacked the strength to exploit his victory by capturing either Nicaea or nearby Nicomedia (İzmit), but he did manage to achieve military dominance over the region, which allowed him to expand his power base significantly. Two years later, he captured the key Byzantine city of Hagios Theologos—the former Roman city of Ephesus—and

LEFT: *A portrait of Osman I.*

ABOVE RIGHT: *The ruins of the Celsus Library in the city Hagios Theologos (formerly Ephesus), which were pieced together by archaeologists.*

OSMAN'S DREAM

A late 13th-century Turkish poem attributed to the Sultan Osman I supposedly recounted the successes of the Ottomans in establishing their sprawling empire before it happened. In effect this poem, which recalls a dream by the young Osman, establishes a mythical basis for the establishment of Ottoman Turkish rule. In Turkish mythology it is known as "The Story of the Foundation." It follows the example of Muslim narrative poetry to emphasize both the Islamic piety of Osman and the divine nature of Ottoman rule. While the poem has some basis in fact, its origins remain contentious and vague.

KEY DATES OF THE RISE OF THE OTTOMAN EMPIRE

CA 1231
Establishment of Kayi control of Sögüt in Bithynia (in modern Turkey)

CA 1258
Osman is born in Sögüt, the son of Ertugrul, the leader of the Kayi tribe

1281
Osman succeeds his father as the Bey of Sögüt

1299
Osman declares himself Sultan, and founds the Osmanli (or Ottoman) Empire

1301
Osman's victory at Baphaeon, outside Nicaea

THE ADVICE OF OSMAN I

One of the most important documents of Sultan Osman I's life was a letter to his son Orhan, written shortly before his death in 1326. It stresses the vital nature of Islamic belief, the central importance of virtue, and the placing of religion at the heart of Ottoman policy. It also stresses the need to rule justly and fairly, to defend Ottoman borders, and to govern without cruelty. While Osman may have been the author, the document was probably drafted by Sheikh Edebali, the Sultan's religious advisor. It became a guiding tenet for successive generations of Ottoman rulers.

RIGHT: *A map of the Ottoman Empire from* Theatrum Orbis Terrarum, *which was published in 1570.*

BELOW: *The church of Hagia Sophia in Iznik, Turkey, a town which was formerly known as Nicaea.*

by 1308 he had ejected the Byzantines from their enclave on the southeastern shore of the Aegean Sea. The Byzantine fleet prevented any further expansion westwards, although a Byzantine military counter-offensive failed to drive back the Ottomans.

EXPANSION

Over the next two decades, Osman expanded his Ottoman lands to incorporate most of northwestern Anatolia, including territory on the peninsula of Gallipoli, on the western or European side of the Dardanelles. In 1326, Osman's army besieged and captured Brusa (Bursa), and Osman made this bustling city his new Ottoman capital. In the process, he demonstrated that his Ottoman Turks were no longer merely raiders and troublemakers—they had established a fledgling empire. He died shortly afterwards, and his son Orhan continued his father's policy of expansion and conquest, finally capturing Nicaea and Nicomedia in the late 1330s.

1303–07
Unsuccessful Byzantine campaign in northwestern Anatolia

1304
Ottoman Turks capture Hagios Theologos, the former Roman city of Ephesus

1326
Ottoman capture of Brusa, which becomes the first capital city of the Ottoman Empire

1326
Osman, the first ruler of the Ottoman Empire, dies in Sögüt

1326
Osman's son Orhan becomes Sultan, and continues his father's expansion of Ottoman territories

THE BLACK DEATH ≈ 1347–50

The Black Death ravaged Europe from 1347 to 1350, traveling rapidly across the landmass and killing up to one-third of the European population. Striking first in Italy, the plague soon spread through France, England, Germany, Denmark, Sweden, Poland, and Finland, reaching as far as Greenland.

RIGHT: *An illustration of the plague-carrying culprit, the rat, from* The Natural History of Animals *by Adam White, published in 1859.*
BELOW: *A 14th-century Flemish illumination depicting the burying of the dead during the Black Death in Tournai (in modern-day Belgium) in 1349.*

THE FIRST APPEARANCE

In Iberia, the plague struck first at Mallorca, in December 1347, soon moving to the mainland so that by May the next year religious processions were being organized in Barcelona in a futile attempt to stem its tide. In France, Marseilles acted as the epicenter of the first wave of the plague, from November 1347, and by August 1348 the Black Death had reached Paris. Everywhere, the onset of the disease was accompanied by social disorder, including riots and attacks on Jewish communities, as panicked populations sought any way, no matter how unlikely, to hold back the progress of the disease.

The plague hit England in 1348, striking in both its bubonic (flea-borne) and even more deadly pneumonic form. Sea ports were the first to suffer, but by 1350 the pestilence had traveled the length and breadth of the British Isles. Few settlements remained unaffected; some were wiped out entirely, while others suffered between 19 and 80 percent mortality rates.

THE SPREAD OF DISEASE

The Black Death was brought to Europe by infected oriental rat fleas. These fleas are thought to have originated in Africa or Asia, and were borne by the black rats that infested the boats traveling between the continents. Starting in southern Europe in 1347, by 1350 the plague had penetrated as far north as Greenland. Three forms of the Black Death ravaged Europe, with England being amongst the countries most severely affected. Of these three forms, the septicemic and bubonic plagues were transmitted directly by the fleas themselves, while the pneumonic variant of the plague was transmitted via the saliva of plague victims as they coughed and sneezed.

THE DEVASTATION

For plague victims, death came suddenly and sufferers rarely lived more than a week. Early symptoms of the onset of plague included headaches, chills and fever, vomiting, and nausea. Within a day or two, the "buboes" that gave the plague its name would begin to appear: painful lumps and swellings of the lymph nodes in the neck, under the arms, and on the inner

KEY DATES OF THE BLACK DEATH IN THE BRITISH ISLES

JUNE 1348
Black Death arrives in England, striking Melcombe Regis (Weymouth) on the south coast

NOVEMBER 1348
Black Death strikes London, spreading inexorably

JANUARY 1349
Parliament in London is postponed, to avoid further spreading the plague

SPRING 1349
Black Death spreads north and west, reaching Wales and the Midlands

JULY 1349
Black Death crosses the Irish Sea to reach its tentacles into Ireland

thighs. As these swellings grew, they turned black or purple with blood and pus, before eventually splitting open and beginning to ooze. Internal bleeding followed, bringing with it painful death. Some survived the bubonic plague, but the pneumonic version brought no buboes and had virtually no survivors as it attacked the lungs and victims coughed up blood. The septicemic incarnation of the plague caused the poisoning of the sufferer's blood, and was the swiftest killer of all.

Plague reached London at around the time of All Saints' Day (November 1), 1348. Living conditions in the capital were cramped and unsanitary, and provided an ideal environment for the plague to spread, allowing the rats that bore the infected fleas to flourish. Attempts to improve sanitation and hygiene were thwarted, as the London town council reported to the king in 1349 that all the street cleaners had died. The plague's effect on London was devastating. A contemporary reporter claimed that over 200 dead were buried each day in the city between February and April 1349, and new cemeteries were created to accommodate the accumulating corpses. Modern excavations show that the dead were stacked five deep in the graves of these new burial grounds.

Meanwhile, in northern Britain, the Scots interpreted the plague as God's wrath being unleashed upon the English, and tried to take advantage of the situation by attacking England in late 1349. Their plans were thwarted as the plague struck them, too. The disease spread to Wales and Ireland, and it is estimated that 30–45 percent of the total population of England, Ireland, Scotland, and Wales died between 1348 and 1350—a figure higher than the total British losses in the First World War. Nor did the plague end in 1350, as epidemics recurred throughout the remainder of the 1300s and into the 15th century.

RIGHT: *Plague physician "Dr. Schnabel," wearing protective clothing including a bird-like mask against the disease in a 17th-century German engraving by Paulus First.*

BELOW: *A fresco in St. Sebastian's Chapel in Lanslevillard, France, showing a physician lancing a bubo on a plague victim while another displays his armpit.*

PLAGUE DOCTORS

As the bubonic plague spread, the distinctive figure of the plague doctor became a common sight throughout Europe. Their duties were often limited to determining whether or not an individual actually had the plague. Clad in wide-brimmed black hats, primitive gas masks shaped like a bird's beak, and long, black overcoats to minimize skin exposure, they probably helped to spread the plague from house to house. Typically they were not medical doctors at all, but individuals willing to take the risk of entering premises potentially affected by plague in return for significant financial reward.

SPRING 1350
Major outbreak of plague in Scotland, despite Scottish belief that they might be spared

SEPTEMBER 1350
"First Pestilence" dies out, just over two years after its arrival

1361–64
"Second Pestilence," otherwise known as the "Plague of Children" as it killed a high number of children

1368–69
"Third Pestilence" strikes, no less brutal than its predecessors

1371–75
"Fourth Pestilence" sweeps Britain, again to devastating effect

THE RENAISSANCE ≈ CA 1400–1600

The Renaissance (from the French for "rebirth"), a period of cultural flowering in Europe that began in the 14th century (although there is some dispute over its precise dates and length), saw a resurgence of interest in classical civilization and a conscious effort to combine aspects of Greek and Roman art, writing, and architecture with more contemporary ideas. Renaissance painters represented Gospel scenes in Ancient Roman settings, while sculptors portrayed biblical figures in styles and poses previously reserved for the heroes of classical civilization.

BELOW LEFT: *Portrait of Lorenzo de' Medici painted by Girolamo Macchietti in the 16th century.*

BELOW: *Michelangelo's legendary sculpture of* David, *which he created from a single piece of marble between 1501 and 1504.Leonardo da Vinci was one of the committee members who decided where it would be placed in the city of Florence. It was eventually moved in 1873 from the Piazza della Signoria to its new home in the Accademia Gallery.*

LORENZO DE' MEDICI

(1449–92)

De facto ruler of the Florentine Republic during a large part of the Italian Renaissance, Lorenzo de' Medici was known as Lorenzo the Magnificent. A great humanist and a poet himself, Lorenzo was also a great collector of classic texts, and operated a workshop from which his books were copied and disseminated throughout Europe. It was thanks to his patronage that many of the greatest creative forces of the Renaissance were able to thrive. Lorenzo's court included artists such as Piero and Antonio del Pollaiuolo, Andrea del Verrocchio, Leonardo da Vinci, Sandro Botticelli, Domenico Ghirlandaio, and Michelangelo Buonarroti, who lived with the de' Medici family for many years.

FLORENCE

The Italian city of Florence emerged as a hub of creativity, where three friends, the architect Brunelleschi, the sculptor Donatello, and the painter Masaccio, are credited with establishing a new direction in art. Inspired by the dimensions of surviving classical buildings, Brunelleschi's work is best exemplified in the texture, color, and shapes of Florence's Pazzi chapel. He was the first to evolve a scientific theory of perspective, which inspired Masaccio to produce paintings with a new sense of depth and realism. Donatello, meanwhile, became the first sculptor of the Renaissance period to produce a free-standing sculpture with his giant marble *Saint Mark*, completed in around 1413.

The 1430s saw the style of the Renaissance travel to northern Europe, typified by Jan van

KEY DATES OF THE RENAISSANCE

CA 1413
Donatello's *St Mark*, the first free-standing Renaissance sculpture, is completed

1430
The Renaissance reaches northern Europe, as evidenced in Flemish and Dutch art

1470
Oil painting reaches Italy, giving rise to some glorious works of art

CA 1500
First etchings are printed in Augsburg, Germany: the rise of a new technique

1501
Michelangelo begins work on the statue of *David*, one of his greatest creations

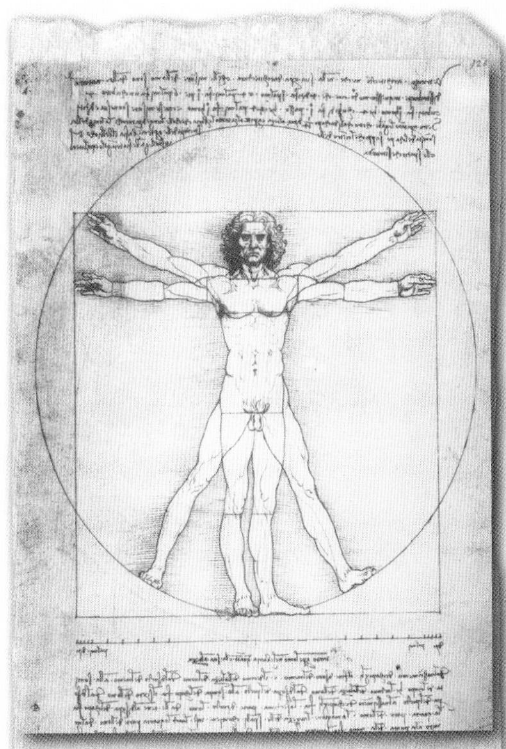

SCHOLARSHIP IN THE RENAISSANCE

The Renaissance represented a revival of classical learning for a new generation of scholars, and a new-found excitement at the re-reading of classical Greek and Roman texts within a humanistic and Christian context. Italian scholars were gripped by a hunger for classical texts, and many lost manuscripts were unearthed and familiar documents reinterpreted. Printing presses sprang up across Europe, and Greek type was struck to facilitate the wholesale reproduction of these documents, leading to the first printing of Virgil in 1470, Homer in 1488, Aristotle in 1498, and Plato in 1512.

Eyck's spectacular Ghent altarpiece of 1432. In the Netherlands, van Eyck, together with Robert Campin and Rogier van der Weyden, pioneered a new level of realism in portraiture, combining perspective with an ambitious drive to portray the sitter's personality through features and pose. In Italy and France, Fra Angelico, Jean Fouquet, Piero della Francesca, Botticelli, and Raphael all played their part in advancing artistic technique throughout the years that followed, each building upon the work of their predecessors to set new standards in the portrayal of realism and of emotion.

ART & SCIENCE

Around the turn of the 16th century came the emergence of the two artists most strongly associated with the term "Renaissance Man." Leonardo da Vinci was remarkable for his achievements in both experimental science and the visual arts, while Michelangelo excelled in sculpture, architecture, painting, and poetry. Best remembered for his *Mona Lisa*, Leonardo nevertheless saw himself primarily as an inventor and designer, sketching concepts such as flying machines and tanks that betrayed an ambition far ahead of his time. Among Michelangelo's greatest creations is his *David*, hewn from a slab of marble discarded by a fellow sculptor, as well as the frescoes he painted for the Sistine Chapel.

The Renaissance style of painting was slow to catch on in Venice, but by 1475 this had begun to change. Bellini, Giorgione, and Titian were amongst the great Venetian Renaissance painters to emerge, while Albrecht Dürer, perhaps the most original and influential artist of Renaissance Germany, drew inspiration from his travels to the city. Dürer's pioneering work included the adoption of etching, a new technique developed in around 1500, to which he brought a degree of informality and expression more commonly associated with pencil sketches.

RIGHT: *The dome of St. Peter's Basilica in the Vatican City, Rome, designed in 1546–64 and 1590.*

Renaissance scholarship reached a peak in the northern humanism of Erasmus, John Colet, and Thomas More, whose thinking and writings influenced works such as Machiavelli's *The Prince*, Shakespeare's *Hamlet*, and Spenser's *The Faerie Queen*. No fixed date marks the end of the period, but from the mid-16th century there was a gradual cultural shift towards greater realism, and by the 17th century, the Renaissance had drawn to its close.

LEFT: Vitruvian Man, *drawn by Leonardo da Vinci ca 1487, was named for the Roman architect Vitruvius, in recognition of his theories on proportion.*

CA 1505
Leonardo da Vinci begins the *Mona Lisa*, the painting for which he is best remembered

1513
Machiavelli begins *The Prince*, one of the first modern political treatises

1564
Death of artist and architect Michelangelo, aged 88, in Rome, Italy

1590
Edmund Spenser's epic poem *The Faerie Queen* is published in England

1603
William Shakespeare's play *Hamlet* is performed in England

THE GUTENBERG PRESS ≈ 1440

The printing press invented by Johannes Gutenberg completely changed the nature of book production in western Europe. Previously, the majority of books originated from specially designed *scriptoria,* rooms where highly educated monks spent long hours copying out manuscripts and documents by hand. With the advent of the Gutenberg press, it was possible for comparatively unskilled laborers to produce printed materials far more quickly than ever before.

THE FIRST PRESSES

Using as its basic principle multiple pieces of moveable type, Gutenberg's press was adapted from screw wine presses used in the Rhine Valley. Books had been printed in the East long before this date: the earliest known printed book, the *Diamond Sutra*, was printed in China in A.D. 868. However, the great number of characters in the Chinese written language, and the use of clay or bronze to create type from which to print, limited the effective practical value of these early printing ventures. Gutenberg's breakthrough was threefold: firstly, he drew upon his background as a metalworker to come up with a suitable metal

ABOVE: *An 18th-century colored engraving depicting Gutenberg examining the first proof of a page printed on his new press.*

RIGHT: *The printer Johannes Gutenberg, portrayed in a Flemish engraving from 1695.*

JOHANNES GUTENBERG
(1398–1468)

Johannes Gensfleisch zur Laden zum Gutenberg was born to a patrician family in Mainz, Germany, in 1398, where he would die in relative poverty at the age of 70. Despite the significance of his invention, relatively little is known about the man himself. His family moved to Strasbourg in around 1428 following a dispute with the guilds in Mainz, and Gutenberg experimented with early careers in metalwork, gem-cutting, and teaching, before his breakthrough invention in 1440. The invention of the Gutenberg press was funded by loans, first from Andreas Dritzehn, and later from Johannes Fust. As Gutenberg's relationships with both of his sponsors soured, court cases ensued and Gutenberg was left destitute.

KEY DATES OF PRINTING AND THE GUTENBERG PRESS

CA 200 B.C.
Woodblock printing is invented in China, as is paper

11TH CENTURY
Chinese inventor Bi Sheng produces the first moveable type, using wooden letters

1398
Johannes Gensfleisch zur Laden zum Gutenberg born in Mainz, Germany

1428
Gutenberg family moves to Strasbourg, because of a dispute with the local guild

1438
Gutenberg begins work on developing his printing press

See an extract of the Gutenberg Bible in Envelope I

from which to produce his typeface, forging an alloy of lead, tin, and antimony. Secondly, he developed a special matrix with which he could quickly create new type blocks from a pre-existing template. Finally, Gutenberg is credited with the creation of the first oil-based ink, which would prove more durable than the water-based inks before it.

Western printing in the days before Gutenberg's press had been restricted to woodblock technology, a complex and laborious process. By splitting text into its component parts and creating individual lower- and upper-case letters, punctuation marks, and abbreviations, Gutenberg brought a new flexibility to the printing process. Master letters were cut into the face of a block of steel to produce a precise reverse relief known as the punch. This was placed against a block of softer metal, such as copper, and struck with a hammer to produce a matrix. This in turn was trimmed down into a cube and filed to a uniform depth, and set with other cubes in a casting channel.

Gutenberg began work on his invention in 1438, entering into a partnership with Andreas Dritzehn and the papermill owner Andreas Heilmann. However, no written record of the project exists before 1439, when the details of a lawsuit against Gutenberg include references to his activities and materials. A second partnership saw Gutenberg acquiring further funds from Johannes Fust and establishing a print shop in Mainz, Germany, to house up to six printing presses. Here, his famous Bible was printed, as well as the *Ars Minor* (a Latin grammar by Aelius Donatus of which little evidence now remains) and, very probably, a large number of indulgences to be sold by the Catholic Church.

ABOVE: *Blocks of letters sit in casting channels. Although this method has been superseded by modern technology, it is still used to this day when composition by hand is required.*

BUILT TO LAST

Gutenberg's design proved so effective and efficient that it was not significantly bettered for three and a half centuries. It would not only transform the print process, but also, by making each copy of a book much cheaper than one copied by hand, allow books—and the knowledge they contained—to spread much more widely than had ever before been possible. This made the widespread dissemination of information a reality, and "definitive" versions of classic texts began to evolve. The print revolution took Europe by storm, and by 1500 over nine million printed books were in circulation. Town criers soon found themselves supplanted by printed handbills, and the first newspapers entered circulation in Germany in the early 17th century.

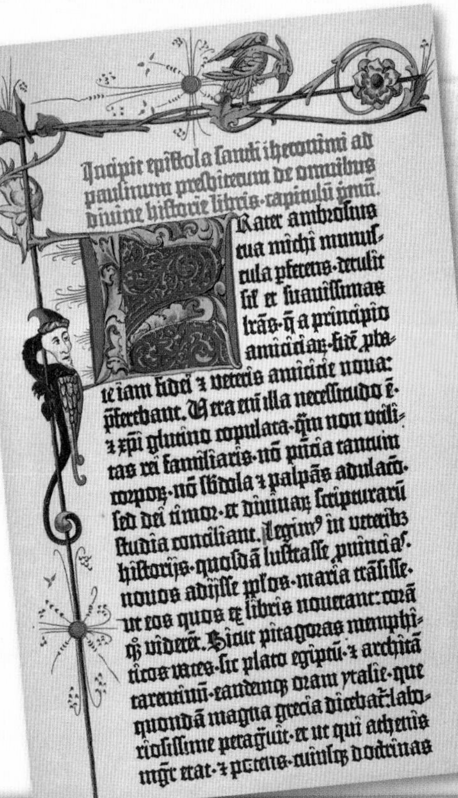

THE GUTENBERG BIBLE

The most famous product of Gutenberg's press is his Latin Bible, known as the "42-line Bible" because of the 42 lines of print on each page. A letter of March 12, 1455 from Enea Silvio Piccolomini, later Pope Pius II, tells of a great man promoting this Bible in Frankfurt, Germany, the previous year—in fact, every copy of Gutenberg's Bible was sold before printing was completed. The mass production of books presented marketing as well as technological challenges, and Gutenberg's decision to print the Bible assured him of a market throughout Western Europe.

ABOVE: *A simple printing press of the type developed by Johannes Gutenberg, which was based on the principle of a wine press with a screw mechanism.*

RIGHT: *A page from one of the 46 still-extant copies of the Gutenberg Bible printed at Mainz in 1450–56.*

1439
Lawsuit against Gutenberg makes the first known reference to his printing activities

1440
Gutenberg pioneers practical application of his printing press

1454
Gutenberg Bible project promoted in Frankfurt, Germany

1455
Gutenberg Bible, known as the "42-line Bible," is published in Germany

1468
Johannes Gutenberg dies in Mainz, Germany, having revolutionized communication

JOAN OF ARC ≈ 1412–31

The Hundred Years' War was a series of conflicts that lasted from 1337 to 1453, fought between the kings of England and France over the rights of the English monarchs to hold their ancestral lands in France free from any interference from the French crown. The early years of the war saw startling English victories at the Battles of Crécy in 1346 and Poitiers in 1356, leading to the Treaty of Brétigny in 1360, by which the French king acknowledged English rule in parts of France. The later years of the 14th century saw a French resurgence, then peace until the invasion of Normandy by Henry V of England in 1415.

AGINCOURT

This campaign culminated in a decisive English victory at Agincourt on October 25, after which Henry managed to conquer much of Normandy. He was then named heir to the throne of France by the Treaty of Troyes in 1420, but died in 1422, leaving his infant son, Henry VI, as heir to the thrones of both England and France.

The English held large areas of France for several years, but they found it difficult to garrison the major towns. Whenever they were forced to abandon territory, they employed scorched-earth tactics, ruining the land and thus the local agricultural production and economy. This constant turmoil had a devastating affect on France, with disease, famine, banditry, and general unrest causing as much damage as military conflict. By the mid-15th century the population of the country had been reduced by two-thirds.

THE BATTLE OF AGINCOURT

The Battle of Agincourt took place. on Friday, October 25, 1415, and was one of the most decisive battles of the Hundred Years' War. It was fought between an English army comprising a majority of longbowmen and a more mixed French force that contained a great many knights—French nobles in heavy plate armor and mounted on warhorses. The culminating moment of the battle came when the French knights charged the English lines, only to be decimated by massed longbow fire, which cut them down before they could close with the lightly armed English infantry. The triumph of English yeomanry over the French aristocracy was a blow to traditional concepts of chivalric combat and honor, and showed how warfare was changing to favor the use of ranged weapons over the traditional elite cavalry formations of earlier times.

ABOVE LEFT: *A procession of 15th-century French knights leaving a fortress, perhaps on the way to a tournament. From volume 4 of* The Chronicles *by Froissart.*

ABOVE: *A 19th-century watercolor of the Battle of Agincourt.*

KEY DATES IN THE LIFE OF JOAN OF ARC

AUGUST 26, 1346
Battle of Crécy: English longbowmen defeat French cavalry near the River Somme

1347
The Black Death reaches Europe, carried aboard ships from Asia

1377
Edward III dies. His grandson becomes King Richard II of England

CA 1412
Joan of Arc is born to peasant parents in rural Domrémy, France

OCTOBER 25, 1415
Battle of Agincourt: English longbowmen again prove instrumental in defeating French forces

RIGHT: *A 19th-century painting of* Joan of Arc's Entry into Orléans, Evening of the Liberation of the Town, May 8, 1429.
BELOW: *A contemporary illumination of* The Battle of Crécy Between the King of England and the King of France, *August 1346. The English longbows are evident on the right.*

THE MAID OF ORLÉANS

Yet amidst this troubled period for France, a young peasant girl called Joan became a symbol of French unification and resistance. Born around 1412, at an early age she began to experience visions which predicted the expulsion of the English and the restoration of the French crown. When she was 16, she petitioned King Charles VII of France to lead a relief force to the city of Orléans, which was under siege by English forces, claiming that God had shown her visions of eventual French victory. The demoralized and desperate French ruler granted Joan her wish, and she set off for the beleaguered city dressed in a set of white armor, arriving on April 29, 1429.

It is unclear what exactly Joan's role at Orléans was: whether she was a masterful tactician who helped take command of the French forces there, or simply an inspirational symbol. Whichever it was, her presence is credited with turning around the fortunes of the French troops, who now took the offensive, and soon lifted the siege. Charles VII's reinvigorated army then marched across the country, taking back many towns and cities that had fallen out of French control. On July 16, Charles's forces entered Reims, and he was crowned king in the cathedral the next day.

On May 23, 1430, Joan was captured during a skirmish with English and Burgundian troops at Compiègne. As her family lacked the money to pay her ransom, and funds to secure her release were not offered by Charles VII, she was eventually put on trial. The charge of heresy was motivated by an attempt to discredit Charles VII's legitimacy by undermining the religious orthodoxy of his rule. After a trial that was rigged against her and full of irregularities, she was burnt at the stake on May 30, 1431.

The Hundred Years' War continued for another 22 years, but Joan's impact was irreversible. The common people now saw the conflict as not just a squabble over dynastic possession but a fight for their very country. After a final French victory at Castillon in 1453, English territory in France was reduced to just a small area around Calais. Joan herself was beatified in 1909 and canonized in 1920. In France, she is revered as a freedom fighter and religious visionary, and has become a potent symbol of French nationalism.

THE AFTERMATH OF THE WAR

The Hundred Years' War was devastating to France, but also cost England dearly in its attempts to exert authority over a foreign country. In order to pay and supply the vast military forces (including mercenaries) necessary to fight its battles, England taxed its citizens heavily, contributing to the Peasants' Revolt of 1381. Though English forces plundered much wealth from France, the costs of the war proved to be too much to bear, and England gradually sought to reduce its commitments there. After such an extravagant foreign adventure, British influence in Europe was severely curtailed.

1422
Henry V of England dies on August 31, and Charles VI of France on October 21. Henry VI is crowned king of both England and France

1428
English forces besiege Orléans in France

1429
Joan of Arc helps defeat English forces at Orléans. Charles VII is crowned King of France at Reims

MAY 1430
Joan captured by Burgundians and sold to the English, who put her on trial and execute her

1453
English troops under John Talbot are defeated at the Battle of Castillon, which is generally seen as marking the end of the Hundred Years' War

THE FALL OF THE AZTECS ≈ 1517–20

Ninth elected ruler or *tlatoani* of the Mexica, Moctezuma II—also known as Moctezuma Xocoyotzin—is best remembered as the man who lost the Aztec Empire. Little is known of Moctezuma himself, and contemporary accounts of the fall of the Mexica are typically biased in favor of the Spanish conquerors.

What little evidence there is, however, paints a picture of a capable and well-respected ruler who was the victim of events beyond his control. The people known today as the Aztecs referred to themselves as the Mexica (pronounced Mesheeka), and were a sophisticated race. Their language was complex; their mathematics were advanced; they were religiously devout; and their military prowess was great, allowing them to conquer and rule the peoples around them.

A FLOURISHING EMPIRE

With his election as *tlatoani*, Moctezuma assumed the status not only of a king, but that of a semi-deity. Under his rule, the Aztec empire flourished, and he embarked upon ambitious building programs encompassing a palace, gardens, and even a zoo in the capital of Tenochtitlán. A shrewd politician and military commander, Moctezuma first received reports of the arrival of Spaniards on the coast of the Gulf of Mexico around 1517.

The expedition led by Hernan Cortés landed on Mexican soil in April 1519, and began forming alliances with vassals and enemies of the Mexica, notably the Tlaxcalteca. Moctezuma kept a close eye on the developing situation, sending gifts to Cortés in a gesture that may have been intended to assert Mexica superiority over both Spaniards and Tlaxcalteca. Cortés and Moctezuma finally met at Tenochtitlán in November of that year, and some—

ABOVE: *An Aztec mask from the 15th or 16th century made of cedro wood and covered in turquoise mosaic. Aztec art was mostly used to honor their gods.*

LEFT: *Moctezuma II, on whom opinions are divided: some see his reaction to the arrival of the Spanish as weak; others believe his politeness to the strangers was misinterpreted.*

BELOW: *Excavations of the ruins of a massive Aztec temple, the Templo Mayor, in Tenochtitlán.*

TENOCHTITLÁN

The ruins of the Aztec capital of Tenochtitlán lie beneath modern-day Mexico City. Founded in 1325, the site of Tenochtitlán—in the center of the vast Lake Texcoco—was chosen in accordance with a message believed to have been received by the Aztec chieftain from the god Huitzilopochtli. Tenochtitlán, once boasting a population of up to 200,000, flourished until the arrival of Hernan Cortés and the Spanish army in 1519. The Spanish destroyed the ancient Aztec city, reusing much of it as building material for their own colonial city. The first lost Aztec remains were unearthed in 1790, when excavations for water pipes uncovered two sculptures.

KEY DATES IN THE LIFE OF MOCTEZUMA AND THE FALL OF THE AZTECS

1466
Birth of Moctezuma, ninth elected ruler of the Mexica, in present-day Mexico

1485
Future explorer and governor Hernan Cortés born in Medellín, Spain

1502
Moctezuma elected *tlatoani* (ruler) of the Mexica people

1517
Moctezuma receives first reports of Spaniards' arrival on the Mexican coast

APRIL 1519
Cortés lands in Mexico at the head of a Spanish expedition

See pages from the Codex Zouche-Nuttall in Envelope I

including Cortés himself—believed that the Aztec emperor mistook Cortés for the embodiment of the great god Quetzalcoatl. Whether or not this was the case, it is certainly true that Cortés was most graciously received in the Aztec capital when he arrived with some 300 men at arms. Moctezuma quartered the Spanish invaders in his own palace, where he lived together with up to 200 noble Mexica families.

A SPANISH COUP

Within a week of the arrival of the Spanish, the tables had turned: through an ambitious coup orchestrated by Cortés, Moctezuma went from being host to becoming a prisoner in his own palace, ruling his empire in name alone. This situation continued for some months. Finally, in June 1520, tensions between Mexica and Spanish boiled over as one of Cortés's lieutenants led a massacre of Aztec nobles during a religious ceremony. Spanish accounts claimed that the attack was an attempt to prevent a human sacrifice; Mexica accounts attributed the attack to Spanish

ABOVE: *A Spanish interpretation of Moctezuma pleading with his people to surrender as they attack his palace. Some accounts say he was killed by a stray stone or arrow.*
RIGHT: *A portrait in oils of Hernán Cortés by an unknown 16th-century artist.*

greed for Mexica gold. Whatever the cause, Cortés returned from business outside the city to find the fortress besieged and a Mexica uprising underway.

The aftermath of this disaster spelled doom for Moctezuma. Upon his return, Cortés ordered the puppet emperor on to the roof or balcony of his palace, apparently to have him order the Mexica to abandon their assault. Some reports claim that he was fatally wounded by stones thrown by his own people; others that Cortés or his men murdered him. Whatever the truth of the matter, Moctezuma II died, and his empire did not long survive him. Cuauhtemoc, the last independent *tlatoani*, was captured, tortured, and finally hanged the following year.

HERNAN CORTÉS
(1485–1547)

Hernán Cortés Pizarro was born in Medellín, Spain, in 1485. After studying law at the University of Salamanca, he first set sail for the New World in 1504, where he acquired land in Hispaniola (Haiti and the Dominican Republic) before becoming mayor of Santiago. In 1519, he was tasked with leading an expedition to explore the newly discovered region of Mexico. Following his conquest, he became governor there until 1526, but went back briefly to Spain in 1528. In 1530, he returned to Mexico, or New Spain as it was then called, settling in Cuernavaca and pursuing a number of abortive expeditions along the Pacific coast. Cortés died of pleurisy in his native Spain in 1547.

NOVEMBER 8, 1519
Moctezuma meets Cortés, receiving him as a guest at Tenochtitlán

JUNE 1520
Cortés's men massacre Aztec nobles in their temple

JULY 1, 1520
Moctezuma dies violently on his palace balcony; at whose hands is not certain

MAY 31, 1521
Cuauhtemoc, the last independent *tlatoani*, captured (and killed the following year)

1547
Hernan Cortés dies of pleurisy, having returned home to Spain

EXPLORING THE AMERICAS ≈ 1492–

Before the rediscovery of the Americas by Christopher Columbus in 1492, North, Central, and South America were home to a rich variety of peoples. While the natives of Central and South America enjoyed well-developed forms of agriculture, sophisticated religions, and evolved political systems, those further north had generally not advanced much beyond the hunter-gatherer form of society.

For example, when the French explorer Jacques Cartier came into contact with the tribes of the East Woodland—a cultural group that extended from the Atlantic coast to the prairies of the Midwest in the 1530s—he found a society much less sophisticated than the ones his Spanish counterparts encountered in Central and South America, but which nonetheless featured the construction of elaborate tribal federations and alliances.

ABOVE: *A replica of John Cabot's ship* Matthew *in which he set sail from Bristol, England in 1497.*
RIGHT: *Jacques Cartier meets the Iroquois at the village of Hochelaga (present-day Montreal) in 1535.*

NORTH AMERICA

The Venetian explorer John Cabot (circa 1450–circa 1499) was the first of the Renaissance explorers to encounter the peoples of the North American mainland, and his voyage of 1497–98 under the flag of England took him to Newfoundland. In effect, he became the first European to make landfall in North America since the Vikings in the 11th century. His son Sebastian (ca 1481–1557) continued his father's exploration of what is now the Atlantic seaboard. This vast territory was

FIRST ENCOUNTER WITH THE IROQUOIS

During his exploration of the St. Lawrence River, Jacques Cartier penetrated deep into the American hinterland, encountering people whom no Europeans had contacted before—the Algonquin, Micmac, Iroquois Huron, and Montagnais. These predominantly Iroquoian-speaking societies had lived in the region since the Ice Age, and archaeological evidence suggests that they shared a single parent culture that existed over 3,000 years before Columbus, Cabot, and Cartier. Their societies were predominantly hunter-gatherer communities, but they also relied on fishing and agriculture for sustenance, and were grouped into well-defended villages of up to 4,000 inhabitants, which also served as tribal centers.

KEY DATES OF THE FIRST EXPLORATIONS OF NORTH AMERICA

1492
Columbus discovers the Americas, making landfall in the Bahamas

1497–98
Cabot discovers Newfoundland and explores the Atlantic seaboard

1498
Columbus discovers the South American mainland on his third voyage to the Americas

1500–01
Portuguese Gaspar and Miguel Corte-Real explore the coast to the north of Newfoundland

1513–14
Ponce de León explores Florida. He is killed there in 1521

THE TEMPLE MOUND PEOPLE

Unlike the loose tribal confederations encountered further north, the people encountered by the Spanish in Florida and what is now the Deep South shared a common language—Muskogean —but lacked political unity. Around A.D. 700 a culture which constructed large temple mounds developed in the lower Mississippi region, and by the time Juan Ponce de León arrived, this had spread throughout the southeast. The mound-builder culture had a strong emphasis on religion, and the temple mounds served as the focal point for these largely agrarian communities.

occupied by at least ten major indigenous peoples, from the Beothuk of Newfoundland to the Catawba people to the south of Cape Fear. In between lay the coastal lands of the Micmak, Abenaki, Massachuset, Narraganset, Susquenhannock, Delaware, and Powhatan.

TO THE SOUTH

The Italian explorer Giovanni da Verrazano (ca 1485–1528) explored the same coastline in the name of the King of France in 1524–25, and so helped lay the groundwork for subsequent French settlement and exploration in the Americas. Further south, the Spanish conquistador Juan Ponce de León (ca 1460–1521) used the springboard of Spanish settlements in the Caribbean basin to explore Florida in 1513, a land he assumed contained the legendary fountain of youth. Unlike many of his fellow Spaniards, Ponce de León sought to maintain a friendly relationship with the Calusa and Timucua people he encountered, and it is ironic that he died at their hands. Subsequent Spanish expeditions, such as those led by Hernando de Soto (1496–1542), were more campaigns of conquest than exploration, but they also revealed yet more undiscovered cultures—such as the Natchez and Karankawa peoples beyond the Mississippi River.

In 1534, the French explorer Jacques Cartier (1491–1557) reached Newfoundland, and then ventured further west into the Gulf of St. Lawrence. He was searching for the fabled "North-West Passage." While he never found it, he did encounter other North American cultures.

These first explorers saw North America as a garden of plenty and they were soon followed by European settlers. While settlement was problematic in the north, where tribal units was strong, further south the indigenous population was more vulnerable.

ABOVE: *A pair of wooden cat figures that were carved by the Calusa of southeastern America.*

LEFT: *A depiction of Hernando de Soto arriving at the Mississippi River in 1541, watched by local Native Americans.*

1525–29
Verrazano extensively charts the Atlantic seaboard of North America

1528–36
Spanish explorer de Vaca penetrates deep into the southwest of the continent

1534–36
Cartier charts the Gulf of St. Lawrence and explores the St. Lawrence River

1539–43
Hernando de Soto conducts an expedition through the southeast of the continent

1541
De Soto discovers the Mississippi River and claims the territory as part of New Spain

THE FATHER OF ASTRONOMY ≈ 1473–1543

Nicolaus Copernicus was born on February 19, 1473 in the city of Torun, Poland, the youngest of four children. When his father died in 1483, Nicolaus and his family were taken in by his uncle, Lucas Watzenrode, who became Bishop of Warmia in 1489. Under his uncle's direction, Copernicus studied hard and eventually became a student at the University of Kraków.

It was here that his interest in astronomy blossomed. In 1496, he went to the University of Bologna in Italy to study canon law, in preparation for a position as canon of the chapter of Frombork. In Bologna, Copernicus lived with the astronomy professor Domenico Maria da Novara and began making his first astronomical observations. Granted a leave of absence of two years by the chapter of Frombork, in 1501, Copernicus went to study medicine at the University of Padua, where he undertook the study of medical astrology (also known as iatromathematics). This required an understanding of astronomical and astrological theory, as it was then thought that the heavens had an impact upon a person's physical health on Earth.

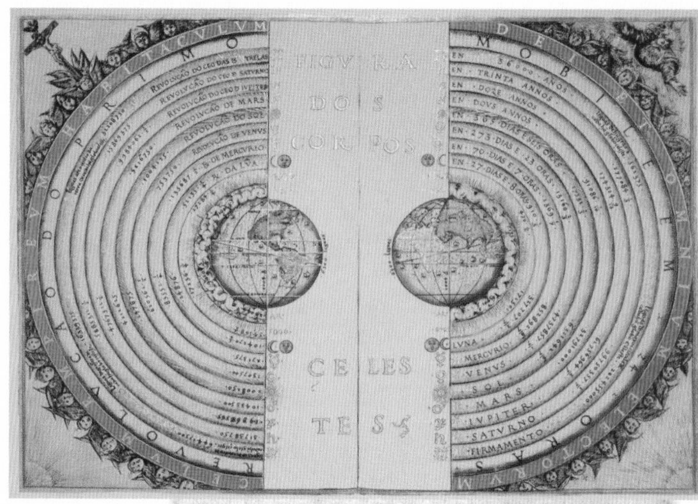

RIGHT: *The concentric spheres holding the celestial bodies, with the Earth at their common pivotal point, according to the world view that had held sway since Ancient Roman times.*

PRE-COPERNICAN ASTRONOMICAL THEORY

Copernicus's ideas were revolutionary. At the time, the most widely accepted astronomical theory in Europe was that of the Roman astronomer Ptolemy. His *Almagest* (published around 150 B.C.) held that the Earth was fixed at the center of the universe, and that stars were set in an outer sphere, which rotated. He said that the planets, the sun, and the moon occupied their own separate spheres. It was a view supported by the religious orthodox establishment of the time, as it placed God's creation—mankind and the Earth—at the center of all things. By proposing that the Earth, and so mankind, was in fact in a marginal position, Copernicus risked severe censure from religious authorities.

LEFT: *Jan Matejko's notable painting of Copernicus, surrounded by the instruments of his investigations, looking up to the heavens as if in conversation with God.*

KEY DATES IN THE LIFE OF COPERNICUS

FEBRUARY 19, 1473
Nicolaus Copernicus is born in Torun, Poland, the youngest of four children

1483
Copernicus's father dies, and the children's maternal uncle, Lucas Watzenrode, takes them under his protection

1491
Nicolaus Copernicus starts attending university in Kraków

1496
Copernicus goes to the University of Bologna to study canon law

1510
Copernicus leaves bishop's court at Lidzbark and moves to Frombork

See a poster of the solar system in Envelope I

DE REVOLUTIONIBUS ORBITUM COELESTIUM

Copernicus's most famous work was the culmination of years of research, study, and delay. While the "Commentariolus" essay was circulated among a limited number of fellow astronomers, as a way to test opinion regarding his new theory, *De Revolutionibus* was to be a full and public explanation of the heliocentric model. Copernicus's work as canon at Frombork constantly distracted him from completing the text, and the necessary astronomical observations and mathematical proofs also caused delays in the work's completion. When finished, it comprised six books, of which the first is the most famous as it outlined his heliocentric model. The other five books elaborated upon this theory and dealt with the motions of the various known celestial bodies.

NICOLAI CO
PERNICI TORINENSIS
DE REVOLVTIONIBVS ORBIum coelestium, Libri VI.

Habes in hoc opere iam recens nato, & ædito, studiose lector, Motus stellarum, tam fixarum, quàm erraticarum, cum ex ueteribus, tum etiam ex recentibus obseruationibus restitutos: & nouis insuper ac admirabilibus hypothesibus ornatos. Habes etiam Tabulas expeditissimas, ex quibus eosdem ad quoduis tempus quàm facillime calculare poteris. Igitur eme, lege, fruere.

Ἀγεωμέτρητος οὐδεὶς εἰσίτω.

Norimbergæ apud Ioh. Petreium,
Anno M. D. XLIII.

ABOVE LEFT: *The title page of* De Revolutionibus Orbitum Coelestium, *in six books, by Nicolaus Copernicus of Torun, published in Latin in Nuremberg, Germany, in 1543.*

ABOVE: *A woodcut from the Renaissance featuring Arab astronomers using the crude telescope and sights available at the time.*

"COMMENTARIOLUS"

Copernicus earned his doctorate in 1503, and spent the next seven years as his uncle's personal physician and secretary at Lidzbark before moving to Frombork in 1510 to take up his residence there. He devoted more and more time to astronomy. Although he was busy with his canonical duties, Copernicus found time to write an essay known as the "Commentariolus," a 40-page manuscript in which he first proposed the idea of a heliocentric universe, with the sun at the center and all other bodies—including the Earth—orbiting around it. This was in direct contrast to the orthodox model in the Middle Ages, which was geocentric, holding that the Earth was at the center of the universe. Copernicus sent copies of "Commentariolus" to several other astronomers, and began writing a fully developed theory of his ideas in a book entitled *De Revolutionibus Orbitum Coelestium* (*On the Revolutions of the Celestial Spheres*). He was convinced to publish the manuscript by Georg Joachim Rheticus, who had come to study with Copernicus in 1539. He had previously been reluctant to do so, fearful that he would be condemned for the unorthodox nature of his theory. The book was finally published in May 1543, just before Copernicus's death. It contained a dedication to Pope Paul III in an effort to mitigate any offence it might cause to the religious establishment. According to legend, Copernicus held the first printed copy of *De Revolutionibus* in his hands just hours before he expired, allowing him to die peacefully, satisfied with his accomplishment.

AN INSPIRATION

Copernicus is credited with heralding the start of the scientific revolution that would transform our understanding of the universe. His work encouraged further scientific investigation and inspired many other scientists and thinkers. *De Revolutionibus* caused relatively little controversy, but the ideas it contained had a profound effect in undermining the church's authority over scientific matters.

1522
Copernicus delivers his treatise on the minting of coinage at the Congress of the Estates of Royal Prussia at Grudziadz

CA 1532
Copernicus completes *De Revolutionibus Orbitum Coelestium*, but does not publish it

1539
Georg Joachim Rheticus (1514–74) from the University of Wittenberg comes to study with Copernicus

MAY 1543
De Revolutionibus Orbitum Coelestium is published

MAY 24, 1543
Copernicus dies, aged 70, having started a revolution in scientific thought

THE FALL OF CONSTANTINOPLE ≈ 1453

By 1453, the Byzantine Empire was in a state of terminal decline. A succession of crusades, civil wars, and conflicts with the Ottoman Turks had all taken their toll, so that almost all that was left of a once-great empire was its historic capital, Constantinople.

The Ottoman Empire, on the other hand, was in the ascendant, and its rulers coveted Constantinople's strategic location. Sultan Mehmed II laid siege to the city on April 5, 1453 with an army of over 80,000 men. Facing him was a garrison of only 8,000, consisting of some 5,000 Byzantines—mostly poorly trained militiamen—and around 2,000 foreigners and mercenaries.

BLOCKADE

The Byzantine defenders had placed large booms across the entrance to the Golden Horn (the sheltered inlet that gave access by sea to the city), making it impossible for any Turkish ships to mount an effective blockade. On April 20, four Genoese ships managed to enter the city, but soon afterwards the Turks finally succeeded in entering the Golden Horn by rolling their ships over logs and into the protected waters. The city was now completely blockaded.

The Ottomans put their supply of heavy cannon to good use by bombarding the walls of the city. The presence of large numbers of gunpowder siege weapons—among them one of the largest cannons of the time, with a barrel some 27 feet long, built by a Hungarian engineer—signaled that the era of medieval fortifications was drawing to a close. The great walls of Constantinople had not been designed to resist such powerful weapons, and several breaches were soon made.

The Ottoman forces launched a number of assaults against the walls, but each time were

ABOVE: *An example of the heavy bronze guns that were used by the Ottoman army of Mehmed II from the middle of the 15th century. None survives from the siege of Constantinople.*

LEFT: *A Turkish watercolor portrait of Sultan Mehmed II from ca 1453.*

MEHMED II
(1770–1827)

Also known as Mehmed "The Conqueror," the sultan was just 21 years old when he took Constantinople. During his short reign, he also went on to conquer areas of Anatolia and Eastern Europe, advancing as far as Belgrade. In 1480, he attempted to invade Italy, but although he initially met with some success by capturing the city of Otranto, it was retaken the following year (following Mehmed's death on May 3). The sultan was not only a strong military leader, but also a scholar. He became a patron of Ottoman literature and even wrote several poems himself under the pseudonym "Avni."

KEY DATES IN THE FALL OF CONSTANTINOPLE

- **APRIL 2, 1453** A chain is drawn across the Golden Horn. Mehmed II arrives near Constantinople
- **APRIL 5, 1453** The besieging Ottomans move to within a mile of the city walls, and the defenders take up positions
- **APRIL 12, 1453** The huge Ottoman cannon built by the Hungarian Urban fires its first shot
- **APRIL 20, 1453** Four ships break through the Ottoman fleet and into Constantinople
- **APRIL 28, 1453** Christian ships try to burn the Ottoman fleet in the Golden Horn, but fail

repulsed. Likewise, mining operations to destroy them from below were all detected and countered by the Byzantines. On May 24, a lunar eclipse occurred, taken to be an omen that the city would soon fall. Nevertheless, Emperor Constantine XI refused to surrender. Throughout the last week of May, morale amongst the defenders fell dramatically, as several portents indicated their doom: the icon of Mother God slipped from a platform during a procession, and a peculiar fog appeared over the church of Hagia Sofia.

BREACHING THE WALLS

On May 29, at 1:30 a.m., the final attack began. Within three hours, the Ottoman troops had broken through the city walls. As Turkish banners began to appear on the ramparts, the defense of the city collapsed. The death of Constantine XI has become a legend, although the veracity of the account is in doubt. He is said to have charged on to the beach, where he led his men in a last attack, and was cut down.

The fall of Constantinople is generally seen as marking the end of the Middle Ages and the start of the Renaissance. Many Greeks moved to Italy, taking their knowledge and heritage with them, providing an impetus to the development of humanist thinking. Additionally, European nations were now denied a land route to India and the Far East, and so began a the search for an alternative route by sea. This would lead in turn to the discovery of America, and a new era of colonization and overseas trade.

LEFT: *An aerial view of Hagia Sofia in Istanbul (formerly Constantinople), Turkey. It was opened as a museum in 1935.*
BELOW: *The siege of Constantinople with Christian defenders parading icons around the ramparts seeking heavenly help.*

CHRISTIAN REACTIONS TO CONSTANTINOPLE'S FALL

The fall of the Byzantine Empire caused great alarm among Christian nations in the West. Renaissance humanists lamented the fall of Greece, the seat of classical art and philosophy, to the "heathen" Turks, and the popular image of the Ottomans as a marauding and uncivilized people soon began to take root. Europeans also felt a new sense of vulnerability in the face of this new threat from the east, especially after the conquest of Hungary in the early 16th century. The fall of Constantinople resonated strongly for centuries, and in the early 1800s, Christians (including Lord Byron) would die fighting for Greek independence against the Ottomans.

MAY 24, 1453
Lunar eclipse causes consternation among the defenders

MAY 27, 1453
Mehmed II tours his positions and announces the final assault

MAY 29, 1453
Final assault on the city, which succeeds, breaking through in three hours

JUNE 1, 1453
Mehmed II orders that looting is stopped, and sends his army back to camp

JUNE 9, 1453
Ships arrive in Crete with news that the city of Constantinople has fallen

MARTIN LUTHER ≈ 1483–1546

In the early 16th century, a movement arose from within the Roman Catholic Church feeding on discontent at widespread clerical abuses, such as the sale of indulgences (which were said to ease the passage of a dead person's soul to heaven). Arguably, the leading figure of this movement—which became known as the Reformation—in Germany was Martin Luther.

THE HOLY BIBLE, Conteyning the Old Testament, AND THE NEW: Newly Translated out of the Originall tongues: & with the former Translations diligently compared and revised by his Maiesties speciall Comandment. Appointed to be read in Churches. Imprinted at London by Robert Barker, Printer to the Kings most Excellent Maiestie. ANNO DOM. 1611.

LEFT: *Martin Luther Translating the Bible, Wartburg Castle, 1521, painted in 1898 by Belgian Eugene Siberdt.* RIGHT: *The King James Bible of 1611 was written in English, making it accessible to ordinary people, as a consequence of Luther's stand.*

A LIFE OF DEVOTION

An intelligent young man of humble origins, Luther owed his university education at Erfurt, Germany to the small fortune his father had made in the mining industry. His initial studies were in the field of law, but following a brush with mortality in 1505, Luther resolved to devote his life to God.

Entering the Augustinian monastery in Erfurt, Luther was ordained a priest in 1507. Following his ordination, he devoted his time to a close study of the scriptures and grew acutely conscious of discrepancies between the writings he found in the Bible and the traditional practices of the Roman Catholic Church. He began to question the church's affirmation that the papacy was authorized to arbitrate in questions of forgiveness and salvation. Around 1516, Luther reached a turning point in his view of the church, declaring that man could find salvation through faith, rather than through deeds. His phrase *sola fide,* or "by faith alone," would later provide a rallying cry for his Reformist followers, and immediately set him at odds with the established church hierarchy.

OPPOSITION TO THE CHURCH

Luther's public opposition to the Catholic Church began with the nailing of his Ninety-Five Theses to the door of Wittenberg Cathedral on October 31, 1517. They were written in response to the special Jubilee Indulgence issued by Pope Leo X. Thanks to the recent advent of the printing press, the content of his theses spread like wildfire, polarizing Christians throughout the Catholic world and causing Luther to be called publicly to account. The first confrontation was with his own order at Heidelberg in April 1518, and this was followed in 1519 by a public debate at Leipzig between Luther and the theologian Johann Eck.

The following year, Luther developed his notion of a "Priesthood of All Believers," that all who believe should have an equal right to spread God's word and to read scripture in the vernacular. The implications of this were vast: without the hierarchy of the church, the governance of medieval Europe would be handed over entirely to the secular nobility. Incensed, Pope Leo

THE PRIESTHOOD OF ALL BELIEVERS

Finding nothing in the Bible to support the Roman Catholic assertion that the clergy alone could receive the word of God, Luther declared that all Believers were "priests," and that the term priest should properly be understood simply to denote one who believes. He reasoned that if, through Jesus Christ, each believer could come to possess the righteousness of God, each believer could therefore gain direct access to God without the need for an arbitrating clergy. Under the doctrine of the Priesthood of all Believers, five of the seven sacraments were void, in the face of the absence of scriptural justification for their existence. The remaining two, baptism and Eucharist, were opened up to the people of the church, and all enjoyed an equal right to perform the rituals of their religion.

KEY DATES IN THE LIFE OF MARTIN LUTHER

1483 Martin Luther born in Eisleben, Germany, son of a leaseholder of copper mines

1505 After a near-death experience in a thunderstorm, Luther devotes his life to God

1507 Luther is ordained into priesthood at Augustinian monastery at Erfurt

1512 Luther becomes professor of scripture at University of Wittenberg

1516 Luther's *Commentaries on Romans* develops his doctrine of justification by faith alone

Amore et studio elucidande veritatis, hec subscripta disputabuntur Wittenburge Presidente R. P. Martino Luther Eremitano Augustiniano Artium et S. Theologie Magistro, eiusdemque ibidem lectore Ordinario. Quare petit vt qui non possunt verbis presentes nobiscum disceptare / agant id literis absentes. In Nomine dñi nostri Ihesu Christi. Amen.

THE NINETY-FIVE THESES

The Ninety-Five Theses were 95 arguments against the rhetoric of indulgences. Underpinning the theses was Luther's deep-rooted belief that good works and the purchase of indulgences played no part in the route to salvation, and that the sale of indulgences, in particular, was nothing more than a mean and cynical trick devised to separate the poor from their hard-earned money. Initially, Luther distributed his theses amongst the faculty of Wittenberg University, before nailing them to the cathedral door on the day that has since become known as "The Day of the Reformation."

summoned Luther for trial in Rome. Fortunately, his protector, Frederick, the Elector of Saxony, persuaded the pope that Luther should present his views at the assembly of German princes, the Diet of Worms. This Luther did, but before the diet could sentence him as a heretic, Frederick sent him into hiding.

Frederick and many of the German princes were in accord with Luther's views, but this was because of his assertion that the ultimate authority as rulers should rest with them. By the time of Luther's death in February 1546, much of northern Europe supported his teachings, drawn to Lutheranism for the mixture of spiritual, political, and practical benefits it seemed to offer. The grip of Roman Catholicism in Europe was irrevocably weakened by this popular support for a man who had never hoped for anything more than unity for his church.

ABOVE: *The first page of Luther's Ninety-Five Theses (written in Latin), covering his first 87 points.*

RIGHT: *The door of Wittenberg Cathedral where Luther posted his theses.*

OCTOBER 31, 1517
Luther nails his Ninety-Five Theses to the door of the cathedral in Wittenberg

APRIL 1518
Luther successfully defends his theories to his own order in Heidelberg

1520
Luther develops his concept of the "Priesthood of all Believers"

APRIL 16, 1521
Luther arrives at the Diet of Worms, the assembly of German princes

1546
Luther dies, having suffered from ill health for some years

MEETING NATIVE AMERICANS ~ 1492–

In the United States, Columbus Day is celebrated to mark the discovery of North America, and by inference the first contact between Europeans and the indigenous peoples of the Americas. This first contact was actually made five centuries earlier. In around 1000, Leif Eriksson led an expedition from Greenland to Newfoundland, and made landfall on the northern tip of the island. The Norse Sagas record the first encounter with the locals—in 1006, Leif's brother Thorvald killed eight fishermen, probably of the local Beothuk tribe. Incensed, other Beothuk attacked the Norsemen, and Thorvald was killed.

LEFT: *A statue of Leif Eriksson which stands outside Hallgrimskirkja in Reykjavik, Iceland.*

RIGHT: *An engraving of a portrait of the Italian explorer Christopher Columbus.*

Relations with the native inhabitants briefly improved, and a Norse settlement was established—possibly the one discovered at L'Anse aux Meadows in northern Newfoundland in the 1960s. By 1009, the Norsemen were bartering with the local population, whom they called *skraelings*, trading milk and cloth for furs. Then, around 1010, relations deteriorated, and a trading party was attacked. Such hostilities prevented the further development of the Newfoundland colony, and the Norsemen soon left for Greenland, never to return to Newfoundland.

COLUMBUS'S FIRST VOYAGE

The next encounter took place in 1492, when Christopher Columbus, who had voyaged west from Europe in search of a route to Asia, made landfall in the Americas and claimed the land he discovered in the name of Spain. His meeting with local Arawak people was friendly, but Columbus took that as a sign of weakness, commenting how the native people would make good servants. Before he returned to Spain, Columbus ventured along the coast of Cuba and Hispaniola, where he captured several inhabitants to take back as curiosities. Other Europeans made contacts with local people elsewhere in the Americas. In the late 1490s, John Cabot sailed from England and had some dealings with the people of Newfoundland and Nova Scotia, but Gaspar

COLUMBUS'S FIRST CONTACT

On October 12, 1492, Columbus landed on an island in the Bahamas, where he encountered the local Arawak. Their friendliness was interpreted by Columbus as a sign of weakness:

"They ... brought us parrots and balls of cotton and spears and many other things, which they exchanged for the glass beads and hawks' bells. They willingly traded everything they owned.... They do not bear arms, and do not know them, for I showed them a sword, they took it by the edge and cut themselves out of ignorance.... They would make fine servants.... With 50 men we could subjugate them all and make them do whatever we want."

KEY DATES OF THE FIRST CONTACT WITH NATIVE AMERICANS

1000
Leif Eriksson and his Norse explorers make first contact with the North Americans

CA 1010
The Norsemen return to Greenland, and are never seen in North America again

1492
Columbus makes landfall in the Bahamas, and encounters the Arawak. The first European colony in the New World is established on Hispaniola

1498
Columbus discovers the northern coast of South America

LEFT: *An Arawak patterned gravestone found near the Three Rivers in Guadeloupe in the Lesser Antilles.*

BELOW: *The conquistador Pánfilo de Narváez waits on the shoreline with members of his crew after a disastrous storm near Florida in 1528.*

and Miguel Corte-Real encountered the Inuit of Labrador in 1500–01. These meetings were fleeting, as the Europeans made no attempt to establish settlements outside the Caribbean. There, however, the Spanish came to conquer.

HISPANIOLA

When Columbus and his successors returned to the Caribbean on subsequent voyages, they discovered that the peaceful Arawaks had been expelled from much of the Caribbean basin by the more warlike Caribs. These were less willing to accept Spanish colonization, and for two decades the islands of Cuba and Hispaniola became battlegrounds. By 1509, Hispaniola was subjugated, and in 1512 Pánfilo de Narváez began a brutal conquest of Cuba that would take seven years to complete.

In the wake of the conquistadors came the missionaries. On encountering the local population, these clergymen would read out "The Requirement," which demanded that the local people convert to Christianity, or risk severe consequences. These first contacts in the Caribbean did not bode well for the inhabitants of the North American mainland.

THE REQUIREMENT

On encountering Native Americans, Spanish missionaries read out a chilling statement called "The Requirement":

"I implore you to recognize the Church as a lady and in the name of the Pope take the King as lord of this land and obey his mandates. If you do not do it, I tell you that with the help of God I will make war.... I will subject you to the yoke and obedience to the Church and to his Majesty. I will take your women and children and make them slaves.... The deaths and injuries that you will receive from here on will be your own fault...."

1500
The Spanish explorer Pinzón discovers the mouth of the River Amazon

1501
The first shipment of African slaves reaches the New World

1502
Columbus sails on his fourth and last expedition, during which he is stranded in Jamaica for a year

1509
The population of Hispaniola is deemed to have been subjugated

1511
The conquistador Pánfilo de Narváez begins his brutal subjugation of Cuba

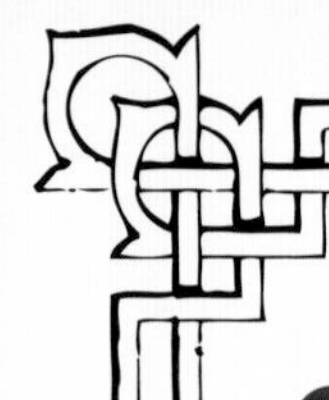

SULEIMAN I ~ CA 1494–1566

The exact date of birth of Suleiman I (later to be known as Suleiman "the Magnificent") is unclear, but it is believed to have been between April 1494 and November 1495. The only surviving son of Selim "the Grim," he served as a provincial governor of Kaffa, Crimea, before succeeding his father as tenth sultan of the Ottoman Empire in October 1520. He inherited a highly effective military force, including what was probably the most powerful train of artillery in the world.

Suleiman soon began using these military resources to expand his empire: he conquered the Christian strongholds of Belgrade in 1521 and Rhodes in 1522, and took control of much of the western Persian Empire in the 1530s. He captured Baghdad in 1534 and waged war against Emperor Charles V for Hungary and Austria during the 1540s.

ABOVE: *The siege of Vienna by Turkish troops under Suleiman I; a fresco attributed to Marcello Fogolino in Palazzo Lantieri, Gorizia, Italy.*

ABOVE RIGHT: *A portrait of Suleiman I by a Venetian painter from the circle of Titian, ca 1530.*

SULEIMAN'S ARMY

The key to Suleiman's military success was the size and quality of his army. Originally, the Ottomans relied on irregular horsemen, but by the reign of Suleiman the army had become the largest and most powerful military force in Europe and Asia. At its heart were the Janissaries, a corps of bodyguards recruited from young Christian slaves. They became feared infantrymen, and were fanatically loyal to the sultan. They were supported by Azabs—irregular infantry—and by a large corps of cavalry, which included the elite Sipahis, the equivalent of Western European knights. Like the Janisssaries, the Sipahis were supported by hordes of irregular cavalrymen. Then there was the Ottoman artillery, a powerful train of large guns, crewed by specially trained gunners. This fire-power, backed by such a large and professional army, meant that Suleiman had the tools to defeat any opponent he chose to fight.

KEY DATES IN THE REIGN OF SULEIMAN I

1520
Suleiman accedes to the throne as the Ottoman sultan

1521
Capture of the Christian stronghold of Belgrade by Suleiman I

1522
Defeat of the Knights of St. John of Rhodes and capture of the island

1526
Suleiman defeats and kills King Louis II of Hungary at the Battle of Mohács

1529
Unsuccessful Ottoman siege of Vienna marks furthest extent of Ottoman conquests in Europe

A BORN LEADER

Suleiman was not only a brilliant military tactician, but also had a talent for political and cultural organization. He initiated legislative changes in education, taxation, and criminal law. The overriding fount of the empire's legislation was sharia, which, as the divine law of Islam, was beyond the sultan's power to change. Suleiman found a way to circumvent this by working with a particular area of law known as the Kanuns, or Canonical Law, which could be adapted by the sultan as he saw fit. Suleiman had his experts assemble together all the legal decisions made by his predecessors, discard duplicate laws, and reconcile conflicting judgements, and then, using their work, promulgated a single Ottoman code of law, which remained true to the spirit of the basic laws of Islam. So great was his achievement that within the Ottoman empire he came to be known as Suleiman "the Lawgiver."

GRAND PLANS

Not content with military victory alone, Suleiman sought to make Istanbul the center of Islamic civilization. He began an unprecedented series of building projects, including bridges, mosques, and palaces. He employed an architect, Mimar Sinan, who is widely considered one of the most brilliant in history, and whose mosques are among the greatest architectural triumphs of Islam. The program of building was not limited to Istanbul, as Suleiman also restored the Dome of the Rock in Jerusalem and the walls of Jerusalem (the current walls of the old city). He renovated the Kaaba in Mecca and constructed a religious complex in Damascus.

Suleiman was also a keen educational reformer. He saw to it that schools attached to mosques and funded by religious foundations would provide free education to Muslim boys. He increased the number of primary schools, which taught children to read and write, as well as the principles of Islam. He opened new colleges for those who wished to further their studies and offered a wide range of courses in such diverse subjects as metaphysics, philosophy, geometry, astronomy, and astrology. Suleiman's reign was the golden age of the Ottoman Empire, representing the peak of the Ottoman Turks' military power and the pinnacle of their cultural and sociological achievements.

RIGHT: *A 16th-century Turkish manuscript illumination from the* Suleymanname *showing Suleiman the Magnificent receiving a French delegation at Belgrade in 1532.*

LEFT: *The Suleymaniye mosque, the second-largest in Istanbul, was designed by Mimar Sinan and completed in 1557. His designs brought a lighter and more symmetrical feel to Ottoman architecture.*

HÜRREM SULTAN
(CA 1510–58)

Suleiman became infatuated with Hürrem, a slave girl in his harem, the daughter of a Russian Orthodox priest from the Ukraine. Western diplomats called her "Roxolana." As their love blossomed, she became the inspiration for paintings, musical works, and novels. In the early 1530s, she became the Sultan's legal wife, and their legendary love affair lasted until her death in 1558. Suleiman even composed poetry to Hürrem, describing her as:

> *Throne of my lonely niche, my wealth,*
> *my love, my moonlight,*
> *My sincerest friend, my confidante—my*
> *very existence,*
> *My Sultan—my one and only love, the*
> *most beautiful amongst the beautiful.*

1532
War between the Ottoman and the Safavid Persian Empires

1534
Capture of Tibriz and Baghdad gives Suleiman de facto control of Persia

1551
Tripoli comes under Ottoman protection, giving Suleiman control of the Barbary Coast

1554
Suleiman passes laws protecting the Jewish population within his empire

1566
Suleiman dies, aged 71, while on campaign against the Hungarians

THE MUGHAL EMPIRE ≈ 1500–1850s

The Mughal Empire was an Islamic power that ruled much of the Indian subcontinent for more than three centuries. It was founded by the Timurid prince Babur, a Muslim ruler from Central Asia who invaded the subcontinent in the mid-1520s. The term Mughal (or Mogul) itself has been linked to "Mongol," underlining the Asiatic roots of the dynasty. Babur seized control of the lower valley of the River Indus, and in 1526 he defeated the Sultan of Delhi at the Battle of Panipat.

This effectively gave him control of the sultanate. Then, after defeating the Rajput Confederacy at the Battle of Khanwa (1527), he became master of the whole Indus valley, the most prosperous region of India.

AKBAR "THE GREAT"

When Babur died in 1530, he was succeeded by his son Humayun, who could not retain control over his father's dominions. He fled to Persia in 1540, but returned in 1555 and recaptured his father's capital of Delhi. His exile in Persia gave Humayun a taste for Persian learning and culture, but he died within a year of regaining his throne, before he could fulfill his dream of transforming Delhi into a great center of scholarship and the arts. Humayun was succeeded by his teenage son Akbar "the Great" (1556–1605), who was widely regarded as the greatest of the Mughal emperors. He was a wise ruler and a mighty warrior. During his long reign the empire's borders stretched from Persia in the west to Bengal and the mouth of the Indus in the east. He pushed southwards, too, capturing Gujarat and reaching Bombay. He was also known for his religious tolerance towards Hindus, which did much to remove a source of dissent within the empire.

ABOVE RIGHT: *An engraving of Akbar "the Great" (1542–1605), who stretched the empire's bounds and ruled it wisely.* BELOW: *The Red Fort in Old Delhi, built between 1638 and 1648, served as the Mughal capital until 1857.*

THE MUGHAL GOLDEN AGE

The reign of Shah Jahan (1628–58) was seen as the golden age of the Mughal Empire. While he was a reasonably successful military commander, Shah Jahan's most lasting legacy was architectural. He ordered the building of the Taj Mahal outside Agra between 1632 and 1652 as a memorial to his favorite wife Mumtaz Mahal. He was also responsible for the construction of the magnificent pearl mosques in Agra, Delhi, and Lahore, and the complex of palaces and mosques of Shahjahanabad in Delhi with the Red Fort at its heart. Roads and waterways linked the empire's towns and cities, and artistry flourished under imperial patronage. However, his military campaigns also drained the vast Mughal treasury, and when he fell ill in 1658, his son Aurangzeb seized power, and kept Shah Jahan prisoner in Agra until his father's death in 1666.

KEY DATES OF THE MUGHAL EMPIRE

1526 Foundation of the Mughal Empire by the Timurid prince Babur

1556 Accession of Akbar "the Great" at the age of 13

1628 Death of Jahangir, and accession of Shah Jahan, the fifth ruler of the Mughal Empire

1632 Work begins on the Taj Mahal, a memorial to Shah Jahan's favorite wife

1707 Death of Aurangzeb, the second-longest-reigning ruler of the empire, and start of Mughal decline

☛ See an extract from the Akbarnama in Envelope I

SCIENCE AND TECHNOLOGY

One of the great achievements of the Mughal dynasty was the marriage of Islamic scientific research with Indian scholarship. Many improvements in metallurgy came about through the development of Mughal military technology, and 17th-century India became one of the most advanced metallurgical centers in the world. Science, medicine, and astronomy benefitted from the patronage of the Mughal emperors. The observatory built by Humayun outside Delhi was one of the first facilities of its kind, and Indian astronomy was considered highly advanced during the Mughal Empire's heyday.

ABOVE: *The ethereal beauty of the Taj Mahal draws numerous tourists to Agra in India.*
RIGHT: *The first Mughal emperor, Babur (1483–1530), depicted at the spring of Khanja Sili Yaram in Kabul, Afghanistan.*

AN EXPANDING EMPIRE

For a century after the death of Akbar "the Great" in 1605, the borders of the empire continued to expand, as successive Mughal emperors—Jahangir (1605–27), Shah Jahan (1628–58), and Aurangzeb (1658–1707)—sought to conquer the Deccan plateau and southern India. Internal opposition from the Marathas, the Sikhs, and the Rajputs did little to weaken the empire until the death of Aurangzeb, when the Mughal dominions began to fall into decline through a combination of weak leadership and foreign invasions. At its height in 1707, the Mughal Empire had extended almost to the southern tip of India. Three decades later it was unable to defend its own capital. In 1739 the Persian emperor Nadir Shah sacked Delhi in 1739, and looted the Mughal "peacock throne," taking it back to Persia with him.

The growing power of the Hindu Maratha dynasty, its neighbor to the west, further weakened the Mughal Empire, as did dynastic strife, and in 1752 the Mughal emperor sought the protection of the Marathas. From that point onward, the Mughal emperor in Delhi became little more than a puppet ruler. In 1804, the ageing Emperor Shah Alam II accepted the protection of the British East India Company, which referred to him and his successors as kings rather than emperors. The last Mughal ruler was Bahadur Shah II (1837–57), who was exiled by the British in the wake of the Indian Mutiny of 1857, thereby bringing to an end three centuries of Muslim rule in the Indian subcontinent.

1717
Trading rights in Bengal granted to the British East India Company

1739
The Mughals are defeated at the Battle of Karnal by the Persians, who go on to sack Delhi

1752
Mughal Empire becomes a protectorate of the Maratha Empire

1804
Mughal Empire becomes a protectorate of the British East India Company

1857
The last Mughal emperor, Bahadur Shah II, is forced into exile

THE AGE OF ELIZABETH I ~ 1533–1603

From the execution of Mary, Queen of Scots to the defeat of the Spanish Armada; from the introduction to England of the humble potato to the ravages of the Black Death; and from the colonization of the New World to the creation of some of the greatest works in the English literary canon, the "golden age" of Queen Elizabeth I was a roller coaster of colorful characters and momentous events.

EARLY LIFE

Born to the ill-fated Anne Boleyn during her brief marriage to King Henry VIII, Elizabeth was denounced as illegitimate following her mother's beheading in 1536. Brought up far from the royal court, the young princess was nevertheless well educated and displayed a sharp intellect, proving herself a talented linguist, a keen sportswoman, and an avid supporter of the arts, drawing pleasure from music, dancing, and theater. Reinstated by her father in the line of succession in 1544, Elizabeth finally ascended to the throne in 1559, following the brief reigns of her half-brother Edward VI (1547–53), Lady Jane Grey, the "Nine-Day Queen," and finally her half-sister Mary I (1553–58), who had Elizabeth imprisoned in the Tower of London on suspicion of attempted treason.

Despite being linked romantically to Thomas

ABOVE: Elizabeth I, the Armada Portrait, *attributed to George Gower. The painting commemorates the famous naval victory over the Spanish, symbolic of the glory of her reign.*

WILLIAM SHAKESPEARE
(1564–1616)

The arts flourished during Elizabeth's "golden age," with writers such as Christopher Marlowe, John Donne, and William Shakespeare penning some of the best-known poetry and plays in the English language. Of Shakespeare himself, little is known. Few historical records exist to help us reconstruct the life of the Bard to whom we owe 37 of the world's most-performed plays. As a result, controversy haunts his work, with cases being made for the attribution of authorship of some of his works to figures as diverse as Christopher Marlowe, Francis Bacon, Edward de Vere, Earl of Oxford, and even Elizabeth I herself.

Mr. WILLIAM
SHAKESPEARES
COMEDIES,
HISTORIES, and
TRAGEDIES.
Published according to the True Originall Copies.

LONDON
Printed by Isaac Iaggard, and Ed. Blount. 1623.

KEY DATES IN THE AGE OF ELIZABETH I

SEPTEMBER 7, 1533
Princess Elizabeth born to Anne Boleyn and Henry VIII at Greenwich Palace

1536
Arrest and execution of Anne Boleyn, Elizabeth's mother

JANUARY 15, 1559
Coronation of Queen Elizabeth I in Westminster, London

1563
The Bubonic Plague or Black Death breaks out in London, and Elizabeth moves her court to Windsor

1564
Birth of Shakespeare in Stratford-upon-Avon, England

See Shakespeare's will in Envelope II

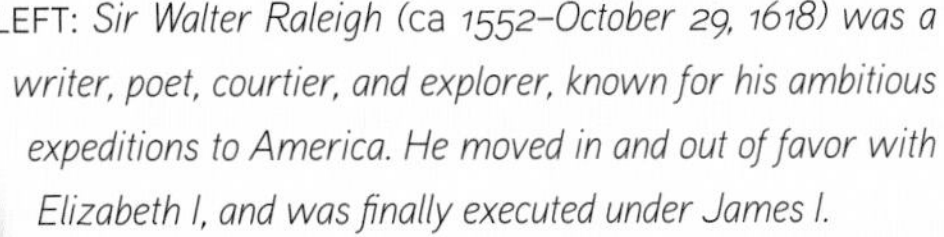

LEFT: *Sir Walter Raleigh (ca 1552–October 29, 1618) was a writer, poet, courtier, and explorer, known for his ambitious expeditions to America. He moved in and out of favor with Elizabeth I, and was finally executed under James I.*

Seymour, husband to her widowed stepmother Catherine Parr and a convicted traitor; Philip II of Spain, who sought her hand following the death of his wife, Mary I; Robert Dudley, Earl of Leicester; and two dukes of Anjou, Henri and Francis, Elizabeth never married. Whether her reasons were personal or political, driven by concerns over religious differences and loss of regal power, the "Virgin Queen" died childless as the last monarch of the Tudor dynasty.

POLITICS & RELIGION

Upon her coronation, Elizabeth cast out the Catholicism that had been in force during Mary's reign, returning England to the Protestant faith and laying the foundations for the modern-day Church of England. For much of Elizabeth's reign, her cousin Mary, Queen of Scots, posed a shadowy threat to the crown, exiled from her own country, where her son James VI was declared king in her place in 1567. The next year, Mary sought refuge in England, where for nearly 20 years Elizabeth held her prisoner until, in 1587, she authorized her cousin's execution on suspicion of involvement in the Babington plot.

Elizabeth proved herself an exceptionally able strategist, leading her country through a period of rapid territorial expansion and military conquest. Under her rule, an English fleet of some 200 vessels defeated Philip II's 130-strong Spanish Armada in 1588, while adventurers such as Sir Francis Drake, Sir Humphrey Gilbert, and Sir Walter Raleigh began the English colonization of the New World, with the first English colony at Roanoke Island and the naming and claiming of New Albion (California), Newfoundland, and Virginia. Her reign was a time of cultural achievement too, encompassing the work of playwrights such as Christopher Marlow, Ben Johnson, and, most notably, William Shakespeare, and of poets Edmund Spenser and Sir Philip Sidney.

Upon her death in 1603, Elizabeth was succeeded by her cousin's son James VI of Scotland, who as James I of England became the first king to unite the two countries under a single monarch.

ANNE BOLEYN
(CA 1507–1536)

Second wife to Henry VIII and mother to Elizabeth I, Anne Boleyn's tale is one of romance and tragedy. Her sister, Mary, had already had an affair with Henry by the time that Anne became involved with the king, and it was on account of his infatuation with Anne that Henry broke from the Catholic Church, having his marriage to Catherine of Aragon annulled. When Anne failed to produce the son that Henry longed for, however, the king's interest waned. In 1536, she was arrested on fabricated charges of adultery, incest, and even witchcraft; tried, found guilty, and beheaded, leaving Henry free to marry his latest mistress, Jane Seymour, mother to Edward VI.

LEFT: *The title page of Shakespeare's works, published in 1623, with an illustration of the author by Martin Droeshout.*
RIGHT: *A hand-tinted illustration of the fleet of the Spanish Armada just before its dramatic defeat in 1588.*

1577–80
Francis Drake circumnavigates the globe

1584
Walter Raleigh establishes Roanoke Island colony, Virginia

1587
Execution of Mary, Queen of Scots, at Fotheringay, England

1588
Defeat of Spanish Armada by English fleet led by Francis Drake

MARCH 24, 1603
Death of Elizabeth I and end of the spectacular Tudor dynasty

GALILEO GALILEI ~ 1564–1642

Galileo Galilei was born on February 15, 1564, the first of the six children of the musician Vincenzo Galilei. Raised near the Italian city of Pisa, he moved with his family to Florence when he was ten years old. Galileo became a student at the University of Pisa in 1580, where he initially studied medicine, later switching to philosophy and mathematics. In 1589, he was appointed Chair of Mathematics, and then in 1592 moved to the University of Padua, where he held the same position.

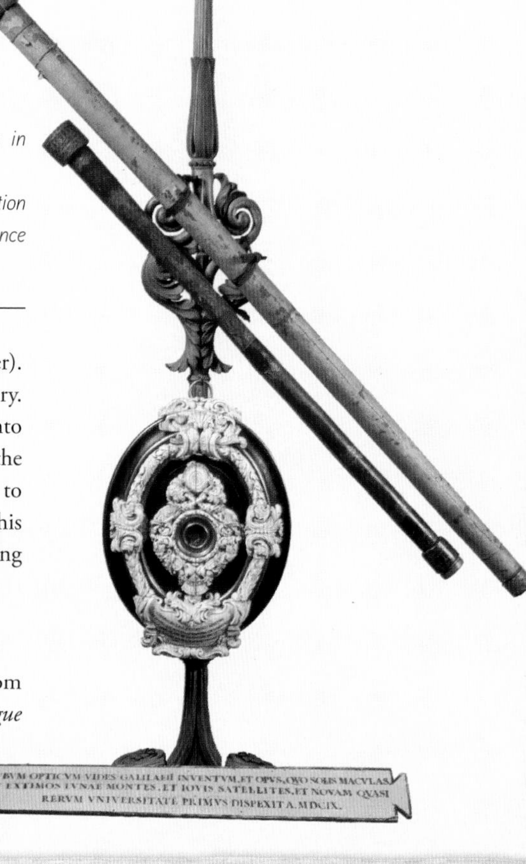

LEFT: *Galileo Galilei, painted by Giusto Sustermans in approximately 1636.*
RIGHT: *Two of Galileo's telescopes, now part of a collection displayed at the fascinating Museum of the History of Science in Florence, Italy.*

THE TELESCOPE

In 1609, Galileo heard of a new invention from Holland: the telescope. Without having seen an example, he constructed his own version, which was in fact superior to the original. With it, he made many unprecedented astronomical findings, the most famous of which is the discovery of Jupiter's four largest moons. These are now named the "Galilean Group" in his honor. He also observed the phases of the planet Venus, the phenomena of sunspots, and geographical features of the moon's surface.

During this time, astronomers did not, in general, publicly support the Copernican model of a heliocentric universe (with the sun at its center). However, Galileo was a vocal supporter of the theory. As a result, from 1612 he was increasingly drawn into disputes about Copernicanism, which many in the church deemed heretical. In 1616, Galileo went to Rome to try to persuade the church to tolerate his ideas, but he failed and was forbidden from teaching Copernican astronomical theory.

THE INQUISITION

For some years after this, Galileo stayed away from controversy, but in 1632 he published his *Dialogue Concerning the Two Chief World Systems.* Unwittingly, he framed the papal views in the voice of a character named Simplicio,

THE INQUISITION

The system under which Galileo was tried was known as the Roman Inquisition. This was a series of tribunals developed during the late 16th century, and was responsible for upholding the Catholic Church's orthodoxy. This largely meant prosecuting individuals suspected of committing the crime of heresy, but the Inquisition also persecuted those accused of witchcraft, blasphemy, and immorality. Additionally, it censored and denied the publication of many books. Originally designed to suppress the spread of Protestantism after the Reformation, it soon began to combat other perceived heresies.

KEY DATES IN THE LIFE OF GALILEO GALILEI

FEBRUARY 15, 1564
Galileo is born near Pisa, Italy, the eldest child of a musician

1577
Galileo and his family move to Florence, in Tuscany

1589–92
Galileo teaches mathematics at the University of Pisa. Legend has it that he dropped balls from the Tower of Pisa to show that objects fall at the same speed, regardless of mass

1592
Galileo obtains the Chair of Mathematics at the University of Padua

1609
Galileo constructs his own telescope, and soon puts it to use observing the sky

which implied that they were spoken by someone who was "simple." In 1633, Galileo was summoned to appear before the Inquisition in Rome to account for his apparently one-sided advocacy of the heliocentric theory. He was convicted of heresy, and ordered to recant his opinion that the sun was at the center of the universe. Sentenced to house arrest, his *Dialogue* was banned, along with all his other works. Legend has it that, after he publicly denied the idea that the Earth orbited the sun, he uttered the words, "*Eppur si muove,*" ("and yet it moves") in defiance of his prosecutors. He died on January 8, 1642—the same year that Isaac Newton was born.

Today, Galileo is seen as one of the most important figures in the history of science, and a champion of rational enquiry against the forces of religious orthodoxy. This, as well as his numerous scientific discoveries, has led to him being called "the father of modern science."

RIGHT: *The engraved frontispiece to Galileo's* Dialogue *(licensed by Ferdinand II, Grand Duke of Tuscany): Galileo (left) in discussion with Ptolemy (center) and Copernicus.*
BELOW: *Galileo stands trial for heresy before the Inquisition in Rome, in a painting by Robert-Fleury.*

DIALOGUE CONCERNING THE TWO CHIEF WORLD SYSTEMS

Written in 1632, Galileo's most famous publication was the *Dialogo sopra i due massimi sistemi del mondo* (*Dialogue Concerning the Two Chief World Systems*). This compared the Copernican system of astronomy with the more widely held Ptolemaic system, which taught that the Earth was the center of the universe and that other bodies revolved around it. The work was extremely popular at the time, and was translated into Latin by Matthias Bernegger, under the title *Systema Cosmicum*. It was soon banned by the Inquisition and placed on the Index of Forbidden Books. Only in 1835 was it permitted to be printed again.

1610
Galileo discovers the "Galilean" moons of Jupiter

1632
Dialogue Concerning the Two Chief World Systems is published

1633
The Catholic Church forces Galileo to recant his heliocentric view of the universe

JANUARY 8, 1642
Galileo dies, still under house arrest after his 1633 conviction for heresy

1992
Pope John Paul II issues an apology, and lifts the edict against Galileo

NEW WORLD COLONIES 1565–1638

Following the voyages of discovery of the 15th and early 16th centuries, the major European powers vied to steal a march on their rivals by colonizing the New World. The first major player in North America was Spain, which had already established colonies throughout the Caribbean and Central and South America.

THE SPANISH & THE FRENCH

The earliest Spanish attempts at colonization in what are now Florida, Georgia, and the Carolinas failed, but a punitive expedition against French Protestant settlers in Florida by the Spanish admiral Pedro Menéndez de Avilés led to the foundation of the colony of San Agustin in September 1565 on land owned by the Timucua Native Americans. Remaining in Spanish hands until 1763, it was acquired by Britain at the end of the Seven Years' War. It was the site of the first Catholic Mass celebrated in North America, the birthplace of the first colonial child in North America, and the only permanent European settlement for over 20 years.

The next European state to establish such a settlement on the mainland was France, with the establishment of Quebec in 1608 by Samuel de Champlain. In 1534, the explorer Jacques Cartier had taken possession of the area, which came to be called New France. He constructed a small fort in the region of Quebec in 1541, but the putative colony was abandoned two years later. However, following an exploratory expedition in 1603, Samuel de Champlain landed at Québec on July 3, 1608 and founded a *habitation* where the modern-day lower city lies. The site was gradually improved under de Champlain's dynamic direction, with a further fort being constructed on Cape Diamond that later became the official residence of the Governor-General of New France.

RIGHT: *Samuel de Champlain (1580–1635), French explorer, cartographer, and founder of Quebec City, who was also the first European to explore the Great Lakes.*

BELOW: *Pocahontas, painted in 1616, thoroughly European in appearance after her baptism into Christianity and marriage to Mr. Rolfe.*

POCAHONTAS

(ca 1595–1617)

The early European colonial settlers had mixed relations with the local Indians, who often felt, understandably, threatened by the establishment of permanent settlements on their ancestral lands. One of the most famous encounters between the English colonists and the Indians was that between Captain John Smith and Pocahontas, the young daughter of the Native American leader Powhatan. Smith, leader of the Jamestown colony, had been captured by Powhatan Indians and was threatened with execution when the young Pocahontas intervened and saved his life. This led to the start of a relationship between Pocahontas and the colonists that was to culminate with her marriage to an Englishman, John Rolfe, and travel to England in 1616, where she was presented to King James I.

KEY DATES IN THE COLONIZATION OF THE NEW WORLD

1565
Foundation of San Agustin by the Spanish under Admiral Pedro Menéndez de Avilés

1607
Virginia Company lands expedition at Jamestown

1608
Samuel de Champlain founds the *habitation* at Quebec

1614
Dutch colonization effort launched along the Hudson River

1620
Fort built at Cape Diamond, Québec, later official residence of the governor-general

THE ENGLISH & THE DUTCH

The English were not slow in following the French to North America and, following an abortive colony set up by Walter Raleigh at Roanoke in what is now North Carolina in 1585–87, a permanent settlement was established at Jamestown on the banks of the James River in modern Virginia. King James I granted the Virginia Company of London a charter in 1606, and the following year, an expedition of 105 men in three ships founded the colony. Despite early struggles, the appointment of Captain John Smith as Jamestown's leader in 1608 saw better relations with the local Powhatan Native Americans, and a further expedition in 1610 strengthened the post, which eventually became a royal colony in 1624.

In addition to England and France entertaining hopes of new territories in North America, both Sweden and Holland established settlements there. The Dutch launched an expedition under Adrian Block in 1614 which claimed the area of "New Netherland," lying between English Virginia and French Canada. The purchase of Manhattan from the local Native Americans in 1626 was followed by the construction of New Amsterdam (later New York), which became the capital of New Netherland. The English first captured the colony in 1664, which was ceded permanently to them following the end of the Third Anglo-Dutch War in 1674. In 1638, the Swedes settled further south, in Delaware Bay, but their colony only lasted until 1655, when it was captured by the Dutch.

BELOW LEFT: *Castillo de San Marcos, St. Augustine, Florida, built by the Spanish in 1672–95.*

BELOW: *A 1656 map of New Netherland, later to become part of New York and New Jersey.*

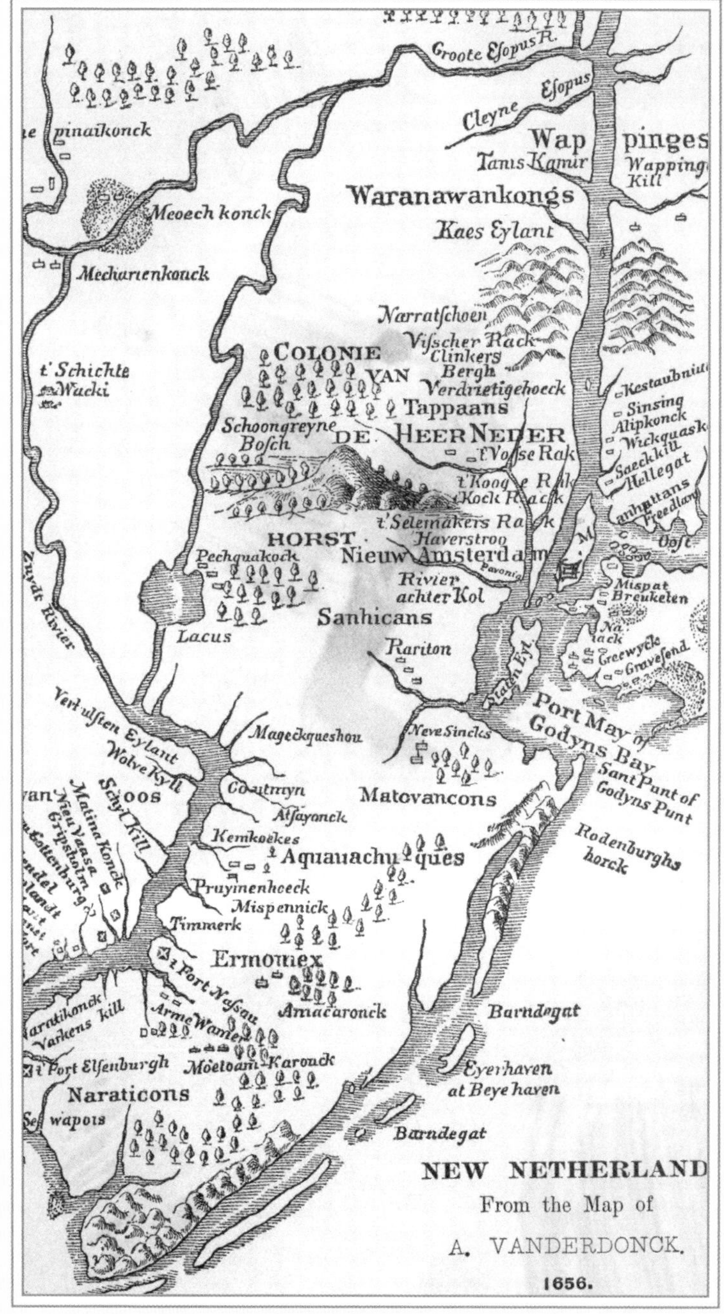

CASTILLO DE SAN MARCOS

The Castillo de San Marcos in Florida was constructed between 1672 and 1695 to replace the series of wooden fortifications that had defended the settlement of San Agustin since its occupation in 1565. It was one the first masonry fortifications built in North America, and was constructed in classic European style as a star-shaped fort. In 1702, it came under siege by English settlers from South Carolina. The fort did its job and the English were driven off. Castillo de San Marcos later saw action during the War of Jenkins's Ear (1739–48) and the Seven Years' War (1756–63), as well as the American Civil War (1861–65). It stands to this day as a national monument maintained by the U.S. National Park Service.

1626
Purchase of Manhattan from Native Americans by Peter Minuit sees foundation of New Amsterdam, later New York

1638
Swedish settlers land in Delaware Bay (modern Wilmington)

1655
Fall of Swedish colony to the Dutch under Peter Stuyvesant

1664
Capture of New Amsterdam by the English

1674
Treaty of Westminster sees New Amsterdam permanently ceded to England

SHAH ABBAS I ⁓ 1571–1629

Abbas I, Shah (king) of Persia from 1587 until his death four decades later, is one of the few world leaders to have earned the title "the great," and he has been described as the most successful ruler of Safavid Persia. Abbas was the third son of the weak-willed Shah Mohammed, whose reign was blighted by an invasion by the Ottoman Turks and their Uzbek allies. The Safavid Empire was also riven by internal dispute between rival Qizilbash groups, militant followers of the Shi'ite version of Islam, who had become the dominant military force.

In 1587, Shah Mohammed was deposed by the Shiite leader Murshid Qoli Khan, whose Qizilbash were trying to repel Turkish invaders while at the same time fighting their own war for dominance within Persia. The teenage Prince Abbas fell into the hands of Murshid, and in October 1587 the Qizilbash leader proclaimed him the new shah of Persia (modern Iran). Abbas, however, soon demonstrated that he would be no puppet ruler.

MANIPULATION OF POWER

In July 1589, he engineered the murder of Murshid, and seized control of what remained of his father's empire. His first step was to sign a humiliating peace treaty with the Ottoman Turks, ceding Karabakh, Azerbaijan, and other northern territories to the invaders. This left him free to deal with the militant Qizilbash. They formed the backbone of both the Persian army and the civil administration, but by promoting *ghulams* (a word meaning "slaves," although in this case it denoted outsiders who had converted to Islam) he was able to reduce Qizilbash influence. Recruiting *ghulams* allowed Shah Abbas to create an army that owed its allegiance to him rather than to tribal or religious factions. He further improved his position by

ABOVE: *Shah Abbas I "the Great" of Persia, depicted in an English stipple engraving from 1815.*
LEFT: *Ornate blue tiles cover the ceiling of the Imam Mosque in the town of Isfahan, Persia. Decorative patterned tiles like these are a feature of Islamic design.*

RELIGIOUS TOLERANCE

Shah Abbas I was a Shiite Muslim, and he was generally intolerant of Sunni Muslims, whom he saw as supporters of the Ottoman Turks, who were also Sunni. The shah generally tolerated Christians, although in 1604 he forcibly moved the Armenian Christians from their homeland as part of a policy of depopulating his frontier regions, and in 1614 he killed or forcibly moved the Georgian Christians, after they rebelled against Persian rule. However, the shah cultivated diplomatic links with the Christian states of Europe, seeing them as allies against the Turks, and he encouraged religious tolerance within his borders.

KEY DATES IN THE LIFE OF SHAH ABBAS I

1571
Abbas born in Herat, in the northwest of modern Afghanistan

1587
He becomes Shah Abbas I, following a Qizilbash coup against his father

1589
Shiite Qizilbash leader Murshid Qoli Khan is murdered

1590
Peace treaty signed between the Persians and Ottoman Turks

1598
Campaign against the Uzbeks, recapture of Herat. Establishment of new Persian capital at Isfahan

BELOW: *Sir Robert Shirley (1581–1628), English diplomat and traveler, who lived in Persia for many years and provided diplomatic liaison between Persia and the West.*

BELOW RIGHT: *A fresco from the Palace of Chihil Soutoun in Isfahan, Persia, showing Shah Abbas in battle against the Uzbeks in 1597.*

using troops to wrest back control of the provinces from semi-autonomous Qizilbash leaders. By the late 1590s, the empire was unified under Shah Abbas's leadership.

CLAIMING THE WIDER EMPIRE

In 1598, he reclaimed Mashhad (in modern Iran) from the Uzbeks, then led the Persian army to victory over the Uzbek khan outside the city of Herat (in modern Afghanistan), which his forces captured. By 1602, Shah Abbas felt strong enough to deal with the Ottoman Turks. He began by capturing Nahavand in northwest Persia, then in 1603 he seized Tabriz, the capital of Azerbaijan. The following year he conquered Armenia, and victory over the Turks at Lake Van in 1605 secured control of his newly reclaimed provinces. The war was renewed in 1618, when Shah Abbas defeated a Turkish army attempting to invade Azerbaijan. In 1624, he recaptured Baghdad and the rich province of Mesopotamia (modern Iraq), thus restoring the old frontiers of his father's empire. During his last years, Shah Abbas reclaimed the Persian Gulf island of Hormuz from the Portuguese, and Kandahar and Afghanistan from Mughal India. As well as being a great soldier and statesman, he was known for his civic achievements. He rebuilt Isfahan (in modern Iran), which became his capital in 1598, and continued to construct magnificent civil buildings and mosques in the city throughout the remainder of his reign.

THE SAFAVID PERSIAN ARMY

Before Shah Abbas remodeled the army in the 1590s, the rulers of Persia lacked a disciplined military force. Instead they relied on Qizilbash tribal leaders and their followers, whose allegiance was always questionable. The Ottoman Turks found these Persian tribal armies easy to defeat in battle. Shah Abbas created a loyal 3,000-strong bodyguard as well as a disciplined standing army of 40,000 men, the majority of whom were *ghulams*, trained by foreign military advisers, including two English brothers. This army was divided equally between cavalry and infantry, and supported by one of the strongest artillery corps in either Europe or Asia.

1602
Shah Abbas declares war against the Ottoman Turks once more

1605
Battle of Lake Van secures Persian conquests from the Turks

1618
Resumption of the Turko-Persian War, and defeat of the Turks

1625
Capture of Baghdad by Abbas's forces, recaliming the former Persian Empire

1629
Death of Shah Abbas I "the Great," in Mazandaran, a Persian province on the southern shores of the Caspian Sea

THE DUTCH TRADE BOOM ≈ 1602-1800

LEFT: *Andries van Eertvelt's dramatic view of the VOC's fleet returning to Amsterdam in 1599. The VOC built up a significant military force during its lifetime.*

THE EAST INDIAMAN

The success of the Dutch East India Company was in part due to a special type of armed merchant ship called, appropriately, an East Indiaman (*Oostindiëvaarder*). Because of the long voyages they were expected to undergo, with the corresponding dangers that could be expected, the ships were designed to be able to defend themselves against piracy, and even to bombard shore targets. This was in addition to carrying passengers and bulk cargo. The ability to maintain an armed presence along important trade routes was vital in protecting the VOC's interests at sea.

The Dutch East India Company or *Vereenigde Oost-Indische Compagnie* (VOC) was the world's first multinational corporation, and was also one of the very early joint-stock companies. It was founded in 1602 by the Dutch government in response to the creation of the British East India Company in 1600, and was granted a 21-year monopoly on all Dutch colonial trade in Asia.

COLONIAL POWER

During its 200-year-long period of dominance, it was so powerful that it acted as a colonial power in its own right, establishing colonies throughout Africa and Asia. Today, places such as Cape Town in South Africa and Jakarta in Indonesia (formerly the Dutch East Indies) can trace their founding to the VOC.

The 17th century was Holland's "golden age." Its power was built on an extensive trade network, which stretched from the Baltic and the North Sea all the way to the Pacific. The Dutch capital, Amsterdam, was a major commercial center, and acted as a center of banking and credit transactions throughout northern Europe. The success of the VOC drew on this prosperity, and contributed much to it during the company's trading heyday. The VOC revolutionized global commerce by opening up Asia to Western colonization and trade. A wide network of its own factories, ports, and settlements exerted and consolidated its influence. By 1620, it was the largest trading organization in Europe.

In the early phase of its expansion in Asia, the VOC took over several Portuguese ports in India and the Malay Archipelago, including Malacca (in mainland Malaya) in 1641 and Colombo (in modern-day Sri Lanka) in 1656. Further east, it established trading relations with the Chinese city of Canton

KEY DATES OF THE DUTCH EAST INDIA COMPANY

1595–97
The Dutch explorer Cornelis de Houtman's first voyage to Banten in Java, opening a new sea route from Europe to Indonesia

1600
The Dutch in Indonesia cooperate with the local Hituese in an anti-Portuguese alliance, in return for which they are given the sole right to purchase spices from Hitu

1600
The British East India Company is founded

1602
The States-General of the United Provinces (the Netherlands) grants a 21-year monopoly to the VOC to carry out colonial activities in Asia

1610
The post of governor-general is established in order to enable firmer control of the VOC's affairs in Asia

RIGHT: *A hand-colored engraved map of the East Indies from the 17th century, showing what is now Indonesia, Malaysia, Thailand, Cambodia, Vietnam, the Philippines, and New Guinea.*

(Guangzhou) and the southern Japanese port city of Nagasaki. Fueling this explosion of growth was an ever-growing demand for spices (such as cloves and nutmeg), a resource in which the region was rich. At the start of the 17th century the Portuguese controlled this trade, but the success of the VOC was such that the Dutch now became the dominant suppliers of spices to Europe.

POWER STRUGGLES

By 1669, the VOC employed over 10,000 soldiers, 40 warships, and 150 merchant ships. After this date, however, its fortunes began to decline. Internal power struggles led to increased corruption, and the company's hold on its foreign possessions grew unstable. The VOC also had to compete with the increasing power of England and France, whose colonies were expanding dramatically. In addition, resistance in China and Japan to what those countries saw as foreign bullying made the climate ever more unfriendly for the VOC's trade links in the Far East. The constant drain on the company's finances from the annual dividend was also a burden. These and other factors ensured that by the end of the 18th century the VOC was no longer a huge influence, and in 1800 it ceased to exist when its charter expired. However, it continued to exert a profound legacy into the 20th and 21st centuries as a model of how a multinational company might operate.

BELOW LEFT: *A 17th-century Dutch engraving of the headquarters of the British East India Company in London.*
BELOW: *The headquarters of the VOC at Batavia, now Jakarta, capital of Indonesia. Andriees Beeckman's painting from ca 1656–58 shows the castle from West Kali Besar.*

BRITISH EAST INDIA COMPANY

The Dutch were not the only nation to explore and colonize Asia in the 17th century. The British East India Company was set up in 1600 to trade with the East Indies, but later became heavily involved in India and China. The company mainly traded in tea, opium, dyes, silks, and cotton. Like the VOC, it dominated large areas of territory, using military power to further its commercial interests. The British East India Company effectively ruled most of India from the mid-18th century until 1858, when the British government assumed direct administration of the country.

1640
The VOC obtains the port of Galle in Sri Lanka, expelling the Portuguese

1652
Jan van Riebeeck establishes a settlement on the Cape of Good Hope, southern Africa

1669
The VOC is now the richest private company in the world and at the height of its influence

1672–74
The Third Anglo-Dutch War interrupts trade and causes pepper prices to increase dramatically, leading the British East India Company to begin competing with the VOC

1800
The VOC is dissolved after power struggles

THE THIRTY YEARS' WAR ⁓ 1618–48

The Thirty Years' War developed from an internal German religious conflict into an international struggle between the Catholic Austrian Habsburg dynasty and the Protestant states of northern Europe, as well as Catholic France. The impact of the war on the states of central Europe was immense, with the German population estimated to have declined between 15 and 30 percent through a combination of war, famine, disease, and internal displacement.

THE SACK OF MAGDEBURG

In May 1631, the army of the Catholic League under Tilly and Pappenheim captured and sacked the city of Magdeburg in Saxony in what was to become a byword for the excesses of the Thirty Years' War. Following the successful siege of the city, the imperial soldiers went out of control, setting fire to much of the city and massacring some 24,000 men, women, and children. The sack of the city caused an instant sensation and led to an escalation in the number of atrocities committed by both sides, with Protestant soldiers inflicting "Magdeburg justice" upon captured imperial soldiers.

ABOVE: *An engraving of the capture and sack of Magdeburg, Germany, on May 10, 1631, by the troops of Walloon general Jean T'Serclaes de Tilly.*

ORIGINS

The war sprang out of the uneasy peace that had existed between Protestants and Catholics since the signing of the Peace of Augsburg in 1555. The more immediate cause was the Bohemian Revolt of 1618, when disputes broke out between Ferdinand of Styria (the future Emperor Ferdinand II)—who was the newly elected ruler of Bohemia, part of the modern-day Czech Republic—and his Protestant subjects. These differences developed into a revolt after the Defenestration of Prague in May 1618, when Ferdinand's representatives were thrown from a window 65 feet above the ground in the Royal Palace of Prague. The Bohemian nobles then chose Frederick V, the Elector Palatinate, as king of Bohemia in his place. Ferdinand's election as Holy Roman emperor in 1619, however, transformed the revolt into a German-wide phenomenon.

Bolstered by support from the Spanish branch of the Habsburg family, as well as from the Duchy of Bavaria and the forces of the Catholic League, Ferdinand was able to crush the Bohemian Revolt at the Battle of White Mountain on November 8, 1620. The revolt had already spread throughout Austria and Hungary and into Frederick's lands in the Palatinate (southwest Germany), but the years leading up to 1624 saw a series of defeats for the Protestant cause at the hands of Spanish and Catholic League forces, which drove Frederick V into exile. There was no fighting in 1624, and the scene was set for a definitive Catholic victory.

However, in 1625 Denmark, supported financially by England, the Dutch, and the French, entered the war under the command of Christian IV. The Danish army was defeated by a Catholic army under Count Tilly at Lutter am Barenberge (in northwest Germany) on August 27, 1626, and the Danes were driven back to Holstein (part of the German region bordering Denmark). Christian IV retreated to the Baltic islands, before finally withdrawing to Denmark in September 1628 and quitting the war in 1629.

THE TURNING POINT

The same year saw Ferdinand II announce the Edict of Restitution, calling for Catholic property to be returned to its original owners, and this sparked new life into the Protestant cause—provoking Sweden to intervene in the war in 1630. Led by their renowned king and general,

KEY DATES OF THE THIRTY YEARS' WAR

1618
Defenestration of Prague instigates the Bohemian Revolt

1620
Battle of White Mountain ends the Bohemian Revolt

1629
Edict of Restitution provokes Sweden's entry into the war

1631
Sack of Magdeburg; first Battle of Breitenfeld

1632
Battles of Rain, Alte Veste, and Lützen, the last of which sees the death of Gustavus Adolphus on November 16

RIGHT: *King Gustavus II Adolphus of Sweden before the Battle of Lützen (near Leipzig, in modern-day Germany) in November 1632. Oil painting by Ludwig Braun, 1891.*
BELOW: *Oil painting of Austrian general Albrecht von Wallenstein (1583–1634).*
BELOW RIGHT: *King Gustavus II Adolphus of Sweden, an inspired military commander.*

Gustavus Adolphus, the Swedes won a major victory over the Catholic forces under Tilly at Breitenfeld (near Leipzig, eastern Germany) on September 17, 1631, before pressing south into Mainz and then into Bavaria in 1632, capturing Munich. However, the emperor recalled Albert of Wallenstein to command the imperial armies, and the new commander blocked the Swedes at Nuremberg in Bavaria before the two sides met at the Battle of Lützen near Leipzig on November 16, 1632, an encounter which resulted in a Swedish victory but also the death of Gustavus Adolphus.

The following year saw Wallenstein ousted and killed, and the leadership of imperial forces shifted to the future Emperor Ferdinand III. On September 6, 1634, his army met the Swedes at the Battle of Nördlingen, Bavaria, which ended in a crushing victory for the imperial army and led to the Peace of Prague in 1635 that saw most of the German rulers reach a settlement with the emperor. The stage was set for the final chapter of the war: the direct involvement of French forces against both Habsburg Spain and imperial forces in Germany from 1635 to 1648.

The French victory at Rocroi, France, on May 19, 1643 led to negotiations finally settled five years later with the Peace of Westphalia—signed on October 24, 1648—bringing the Thirty Years' War to a close.

GUSTAVUS ADOLPHUS (1594–1632)

The most famous commander of the Thirty Years' War, and one of the "great captains" of early modern warfare, was Gustavus Adolphus, King of Sweden and "lion of the north." Inheriting the throne of Sweden from his father in 1611 at the age of 17, he established his military credentials in a series of campaigns against Denmark, Russia, and Poland from 1611 through to 1629, in which he developed the use of combined-arms formations and his innovative deployment of mobile artillery. However, it was his victories at Breitenfeld and Rain in the Thirty Years' War that were his highest military achievements. He was killed at the Battle of Lützen in November 1632 at the age of 37.

1634
Battle of Nördlingen: Swedish forces comprehensively beaten by Spanish and imperial forces

1642
Second Battle of Breitenfeld, near Leipzig in Saxony

1643
Battle of Rocroi leads to negotiations between the major powers seeking an end to the war

MAY 1648
French win crushing victory over imperial army at Zusmarshausen in southern Germany

OCTOBER 1648
Peace of Westphalia ends the Thirty Years' War after five years of peace negotiations

THE ENLIGHTENMENT ~ CA 1620–1789

The Age of Enlightenment, which stretched from the mid-17th to the late 18th century, saw philosophical ideals of reason and rationalism take hold across the Western world, impacting on every aspect of life. With the growing general availability of knowledge, books, and technology came an explosion of scientific enquiry and a new reliance on reason and empirical evidence, rather than religious revelation, as a basis for legitimacy. This was a fundamental change of attitude that was equally evident in culture and socio-political thought.

Before this period, both popular and intellectual thought had been dominated for many centuries by beliefs derived from Ancient Greek Aristotelian philosophy and traditional Christianity. The Enlightenment, in contrast, was characterized by a decline in religious authority and the replacement of the medieval focus on the next world by a greater emphasis on mankind's place in this world. This shift would pave the way for new approaches such as humanism and liberalism.

THE POWER OF WORDS

Many of the Enlightenment's great thinkers interwove philosophy with science or politics, for instance by drawing conclusions about the nature of existence from what could be empirically perceived. Among these were the English empiricist and political philosopher John Locke (1632–1704), who wrote about personal liberty and property, and the Scottish empiricist philospher David Hume (1711–1776). Principles of reason were applied to political philosophy by the Englishman Thomas Hobbes (1588–1679) and the Swiss Jean-Jacques Rousseau (1712–88), who discussed morality and the ideal society. France contributed to the dissemination of Enlightenment ideas through the words of those such as the writer Voltaire (François-Marie Arouet, 1694–1778) and Denis Diderot (1713–84), the philosopher and founder of the great *Encyclopédie*. Through such men, the Enlightenment shaped the human rights ideals of Thomas Jefferson and Benjamin Franklin—expressed in the American Declaration of Independence—as well as Simón Bolívar in South America. Reason was taken to unreasonable extremes in the French Revolution, ending the era, but its values underlie modern political philosophy from democracy and capitalism to communism.

LEFT: *A portrait of the Swiss philosopher Jean-Jacques Rousseau, best known for his work* Du contrat social (The Social Contract).

RIGHT: *Microscopes from 1673 and 1685 belonging to the Dutch naturalist van Leeuwenhoek.*

THE ROYAL SOCIETY

Scientific societies, where leading minds would gather to discuss their theories, flourished during this period. Foremost among them was the Royal Society, officially the Royal Society of London for the Improvement of Natural Knowledge. Founded on July 15, 1662 by royal charter, it was set up as a place to discuss scientific theories and to enable peer review. Inspired by the foment of ideas at the time, other nations also established academies, including Germany in 1652 and France's Académie des Sciences in 1666. These all provided vital spaces for the new ideas of the Enlightenment to blossom.

KEY DATES OF THE ENLIGHTENMENT

1651 Thomas Hobbes publishes *Leviathan*, analyzing the structure of society and government

1661 Robert Boyle publishes *The Sceptical Chemist*, which puts forward his theories in the field of chemistry

1665 Robert Hooke's *Micrographia* is published, in which he coins the term "cell"

1751 First volume of Diderot's *Encyclopédie*, an encyclopedia of sciences, arts, and crafts

1674–82 Van Leeuwenhoek uses his microscope to see bacteria in the human mouth, muscle fibers, and spermatozoa

See pages from Carl Linnaeus' journal in Envelope II

ISAAC NEWTON

(1643–1727)

No account of the Enlightenment would be complete without mentioning the advances in physics made by the Englishman Isaac Newton. He developed the theory of gravity and laid the foundations of classical mechanics, expounding his theories in *Philosophiae Naturalis Principia Mathematica* in 1687. Newton's three laws of motion became the baseline of research in physics for three hundred years until the development of general and special relativity and quantum mechanics in the 20th century. He is also remembered for being a deeply religious man who sought to reconcile his Christian faith with the scientific discoveries of his day, leading to the emergence of the image of the scientist working to reveal the mysteries of God rather than to discredit them.

ABOVE: *An engraving of the influential English scientist Sir Isaac Newton.*
BELOW RIGHT: *A depiction of the Swedish botanist Carl Linnaeus classifying plants in a garden.*

ENLIGHTENMENT SCIENCE

The Enlightenment changed science, too. The first modern chemist was probably the Englishman Robert Boyle (1627–1691). Alchemy had been popular for centuries, its practitioners seeking to transform materials, primarily lead into gold, but it was discredited as a result of the new understanding provided by chemistry.

In biology, Antoni van Leeuwenhoek (1632–1723), a Dutchman considered to be the first microbiologist, used handmade microscopes (of which he made over 400) to observe single-celled organisms. He studied the flow of blood and the structure of muscle fibers, and in 1677 he discovered the existence of spermatozoa, causing concern in the Dutch religious community. In Sweden, Carl Linnaeus (1707–78) developed modern biological classification, while in England Robert Hooke (1635–1703) coined the term "cell" to describe the individual components of living things, and made many drawings of the world he saw through his microscope, capturing public admiration.

Public discussion of such discoveries was made ever more possible by the coffeehouses, salons, and societies where people could gather to discuss the affairs of the day. An increase in the number of books published, and their greater affordability, helped to disseminate information and provoke thought. This flow of information had profound consequences for the advance of knowledge and education, which was no longer the preserve of elite scholars in cloistered universities but part of the tapestry of public life.

1683
The Ashmolean Museum in Oxford is opened as the first public museum in England

1687
Newton publishes *Principia Mathematica*, establishing classical mechanical theory

1703
Newton is elected president of the Royal Society

1740
David Hume publishes *A Treatise on Human Nature*, a discussion of reason, morality, and free will

1789
The start of the French Revolution, generally seen as marking the end of the Age of Enlightenment

KANGXI & HIS EMPIRE ⁓ 1654–1722

Emperor Kangxi (or K'ang Hsi) was the third emperor of the Qing dynasty, and ruled when Chinese imperial power was at its height. He reigned from 1661 to 1722, ascending the throne when he was just six years old. Kangxi ruled for longer than any other Chinese emperor, and presided over a period that has become known as China's golden age. China's territorial domination reached its fullest extent during this time, stretching from Outer Mongolia and Manchuria in the north to the islands of Hainan and Taiwan in the south.

RIGHT: *The Hall of Prayer for Good Harvests in the Temple of Heaven, Beijing, where Ming and Qing emperors made regular prayers for good harvests.*

CULTURAL DIVERSITY

China's territory had never been greater, and controlling such a vast empire required considerable knowledge and skill. Consequently, the young Kangxi went about studying the various cultures and ethnicities that were subject to him, which included not only the majority Han Chinese but also Mongolians, Manchus, and Tibetans. This was also a time of variety in religious devotion, with the dominant spiritual tradition of Confucianism competing with Buddhism, Taoism, Catholicism, and Islam. Under Kangxi, these disparate cultural groups were tolerated as long as they did not threaten imperial power, an attitude that opened China up to greater cultural enrichment and social cohesion. Christian Jesuits were prominent visitors to Kangxi's court, and they were respected for their insights into foreign languages and military innovation. Kangxi was also the first Chinese emperor to have played the piano.

Kangxi's keen and inquiring mind led him to make six tours of southern China in order to know and understand his empire better. True to the inheritance of his nomadic Manchu ancestors, he favored an active lifestyle, in contrast to what he saw as the overly bookish tradition of the preceding Ming dynasty. His tours of the empire projected imperial presence and splendor far from the power center of Beijing,

LEFT: *An engraving of Kangxi by Perre Duflos, from* Recueil des Estampes, représentant les grades, les rangs et les signités, suivant le costume de toutes les nations existantes, *a survey of national costumes of the world and how they indicate rank, published in 1780 in Paris.*

KANGXI DICTIONARY

Though Emperor Kangxi commissioned many scholarly projects during his lifetime, perhaps the most famous is the *Kangxi Dictionary*. He ordered its compilation in 1710, and it was published six years later. Along with a preface written by the emperor himself, it contains more than 47,000 characters (including many obscure and rare ones), and became the standard Chinese dictionary of the 18th and 19th centuries. The commissioning of projects like these did much to ingratiate Kangxi with China's elites, and so helped cement his power as emperor.

KEY DATES OF KANGXI & HIS EMPIRE

MAY 4, 1654
Kangxi born to Shunzhi Emperor and Empress Xiao Kang Zhang

FEBRUARY 18, 1661
Kangxi inherits the throne, but is too young to rule by himself. The empire is governed by four senior advisers

1669
Kangxi has his adviser Oboi imprisoned, and begins to rule directly over his empire

1684
Taiwan is conquered and annexed into the empire

1685–86
Chinese troops clash with Russians in Manchuria, and drive them away from China's borders

ABOVE: *A 1699 pen, watercolor, and gouache on silk entitled* The Emperor Kangxi on Tour in the Southern Provinces. *Such tours increased the empire's sense of cohesion and mutual understanding between emperor and subjects.*
BELOW: *A porcelain pot for storing calligraphy brushes, decorated in* famille verte *enamels. This piece dates from the Kangxi period when, with the emperor's encouragement, Chinese arts reached new heights of skill and refinement.*

helping to consolidate the sense of a single Chinese identity among the people. They also increased his familiarity with the various climates, landscapes, and peoples of his territory.

PUBLICATIONS

The emperor's passion for learning was lifelong, and he became a great patron of scholarly projects. He sponsored the encyclopedic *Complete Collection of Illustrations and Writings of Ancient and Modern Times*, which was originally a private project but which was adopted by the state. It was published shortly before Kangxi's death, and ran to over 5,000 volumes. The *Quantangshi* was an anthology of poetry containing nearly 50,000 poems, commissioned by the emperor himself, and was published in 1707. The emperor was also a passionate calligrapher, and many examples of his writings survive today.

Initially, there were many amongst the Chinese elites who saw Kangxi, a Manchu, as a usurper of traditional Chinese culture and traditions. But, by the end of his reign, the emperor's generous patronage of the arts and scholarship, together with his open and generous attitude to different groups, had won over those who were sceptical of the Qing emperors. Under Kangxi, a new Chinese identity was being forged and the bloody history of warring dynasties drew to a close. Henceforth, China's enemies would come from beyond its borders.

CHRISTIAN MISSIONARIES

Kangxi's tolerance for various cultures and religions was most visibly marked by the number of foreign missionaries who arrived in China during his reign. In 1692, the emperor issued the Edict of Toleration, which officially recognized Catholicism and allowed the practice of Christianity within China. For many years this state of affairs continued. Yet many Christians were uncomfortable with tolerating what they saw as ungodly religious worship, and after the Pope declared Chinese Confucian practices heathenish in March 1715 through the *Ex illa die*, Emperor Kangxi responded by banning missionaries from operating in China.

1705
Kangxi issues an "Edict of Toleration," allowing Jesuits to operate legitimately within China

1707
The *Quantangshi* is published, containing nearly 50,000 poems

1715
Christian missionaries are banned from preaching in China

1716
The *Kangxi Dictionary* is published, containing more than 47,000 characters

DECEMBER 20, 1722
Kangxi dies, aged 68. A succession dispute ensues

CATHERINE THE GREAT ≈ 1729–96

The woman who became known as Catherine the Great was born Sophie Auguste Friedericke von Anhalt-Zerbst on May 2, 1729 in Stettin, which then belonged to Prussia. In 1744, she was betrothed to Peter II of Russia, the grandson of Peter the Great, and converted to the Russian Orthodox Church. It was at this time that she changed her name to Catherine. She gave birth to a son, Paul, on October 1, 1754. After the death of her mother-in-law, the Empress Elizabeth, on January 5, 1762, Peter took the throne, and he and Catherine moved to St. Petersburg.

A REFORMIST

Peter's rule was not to last, for on July 9 he was deposed in a bloodless coup while staying in Oranienbaum, away from his wife who had returned to St. Petersburg, and Catherine became the new Russian empress. Peter was then killed on July 17, just eight days after being deposed. It is not known whether Catherine herself had any part in this assassination, but the possibility has been the subject of much debate.

Under Catherine's rule, Russia enjoyed a period of great success. She expanded her adopted country's borders westwards and southwards, annexing the territories of the Crimea, Belarus, and Lithuania. She also negotiated with Prussia and Austria to divide Poland between them, with three partitions occurring in 1772, 1793, and 1795. Russia's influence and territory now stretched far into Europe, and it had established itself as one of the continent's "Great Powers."

Catherine's modernization of Russia forms an important part of her legacy. In 1766, she established a "Legislative Commission" of 564 deputies of various social and national backgrounds, where she put forward her ideas for a more enlightened and modern Russia. Though this convened for over 200 sittings, it achieved few practical reforms, partly because the ideas Catherine put forward were often too radical for the establishment to accept. Despite this, various reforms were implemented, including the Code of Commercial Navigation and the Salt Trade Code of 1781, the Police Ordinance of 1782, and the Charter to the Nobility in 1785. By the end of her reign, Russia had more than double the number of government officials as at its start, and they were spending six times as much on local government.

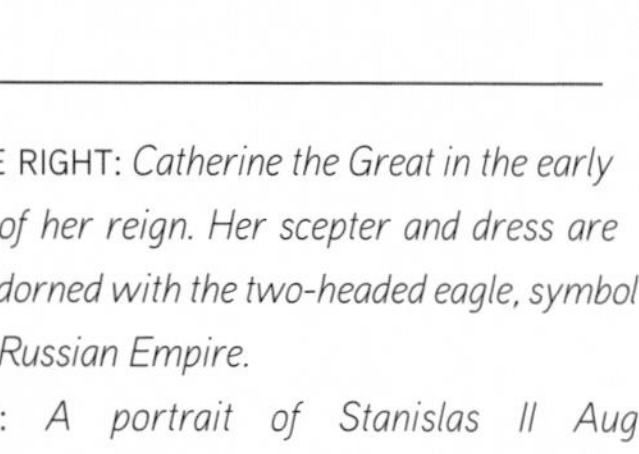

ABOVE RIGHT: *Catherine the Great in the early years of her reign. Her scepter and dress are both adorned with the two-headed eagle, symbol of the Russian Empire.*

RIGHT: *A portrait of Stanislas II Auguste Poniatowski (1732–98), one of Catherine's lovers, painted by Elisabeth Vigée-Lebrun (1755–1842).*

CATHERINE'S LOVERS

Catherine is as well known for her many romantic affairs as she is for her political achievements. Unhappy with her husband Peter, she had relations with many men over the years (often with several at the same time), both during their marriage and after Peter died. The most famous of these were Stanislas Poniatowski, who became king of Poland; Count Gregory Orlov, who was influential in helping Catherine ascend the throne after the death of her husband; and Gregory Potemkin, whom Catherine was rumored to have married in secret.

KEY DATES IN THE LIFE OF CATHERINE THE GREAT

MAY 2, 1729
The future Catherine the Great, Sophie, is born in Stettin, Prussia, daughter of a German nobleman

1745
Catherine marries Peter II of Russia, grandson of Peter the Great

OCTOBER 1, 1754
Catherine gives birth to her son Paul, who later becomes Russian ruler after his mother's death

JULY 1762
Catherine ascends the Russian throne, becoming Empress Catherine II

1764
Catherine's private art collection is gathered at the Hermitage in St. Petersburg

WARS WITH THE OTTOMAN EMPIRE

During Catherine's reign, Russia fought two wars against the Ottoman Empire to the south. Previous campaigns by Peter the Great had established Russian dominance on the edge of the Black Sea, and Catherine continued the conquest of new territory. During the first Russo-Turkish War (1768–74) the Ottomans were heavily defeated at the Battles of Chesma (July 5–7, 1770) and Kagul (July 21, 1770). This allowed Russia to expand across Ukraine, where the city of Yekaterinoslav was founded in Catherine's honor. Russia also gained access to the Black Sea, a move of great strategic importance.

PATRON OF THE ARTS

Catherine was a keen patron of the arts and education, and Russian culture flourished during her reign. The Hermitage Museum, which was founded in 1764, originally housed Catherine's private collection of paintings. It grew over the years, and today contains over three million items. She corresponded regularly with leading thinkers of the era, including Voltaire and Diderot. Her patronage opened up Russia to many classical and Western European influences, which in part inspired the Russian Enlightenment.

Catherine died on November 17, 1796, as the result of a stroke, and was succeeded by her son Paul. She was buried in the Peter and Paul Cathedral in St. Petersburg.

ABOVE LEFT: *The White Hall in the Winter Palace, St. Petersburg. The palace houses part of the stunning, extensive art collection of the Hermitage Museum.*
ABOVE: *French writer and philosopher Voltaire (1694–1778) greatly stimulated Catherine's intellectual development.*

1766
Catherine gathers the Legislative Commission in Moscow to discuss affairs of state

1774–75
The Pugachev Rebellion is violently put down by Russian military forces

1785
Catherine establishes the Charter to the Nobility, introducing several governmental reforms

1795
The third partition of Poland is signed between Russia, Austria, and Germany, expanding Russian territory into the heart of Europe

NOVEMBER 17, 1796
Catherine dies due to a stroke at the age of 67, having reigned for 24 influential years

JAMES COOK ≈ 1728–79

Captain James Cook was born on October 27, 1728 in the town of Marton in Yorkshire, England. He would go on to be one of Britain's foremost explorers, undertaking three voyages of discovery and circumnavigating the world twice, the first man to do so while remaining in just one ship. Cook began his service in the merchant navy when he was 18, joining the Royal Navy in 1755 at the age of 26.

THE TRANSIT OF VENUS

In 1768, he was appointed to lead a scientific expedition to Tahiti, to observe the transit of the planet Venus across the sun. Cook, at that time a lieutenant, set sail on August 26, in HMB *Endeavour*, arriving at his destination on April 13 the next year. The expedition was a success, for on June 3 the observatory successfully measured the time it took for Venus to traverse the sun.

ABOVE RIGHT: *A painting of Captain James Cook created in 1770 by Nathaniel Dance (1735–1811).*

BELOW: *A map of Otaheite (Tahiti in French Polynesia), drawn ca 1769, from Cook's first South Pacific voyage.*

This scientific accomplishment was significant in its own right, but Cook is best remembered for his voyages of discovery. In October 1769, he became the first European to set foot on the islands of New Zealand. Years previously, in 1642, they had been sighted by a Dutch ship, but never physically explored. Nevertheless, the country retained its Dutch name of New Zealand (from the province of Zeeland in Holland). Cook's most famous discovery was the east coast of Australia, which he sighted on April 19, 1770 and claimed three days later as British territory.

On his second voyage, Cook circled the then-undiscovered continent of Antarctica in HMS *Resolution*, but he could not find a way through the ice that surrounded it and he did not sight land. It was not until 1840 that this icy continent's existence was proved. Cook returned to Great Britain in 1775, where he was promoted to the rank of captain and elected as a fellow of the Royal Society, the country's foremost scientific institution.

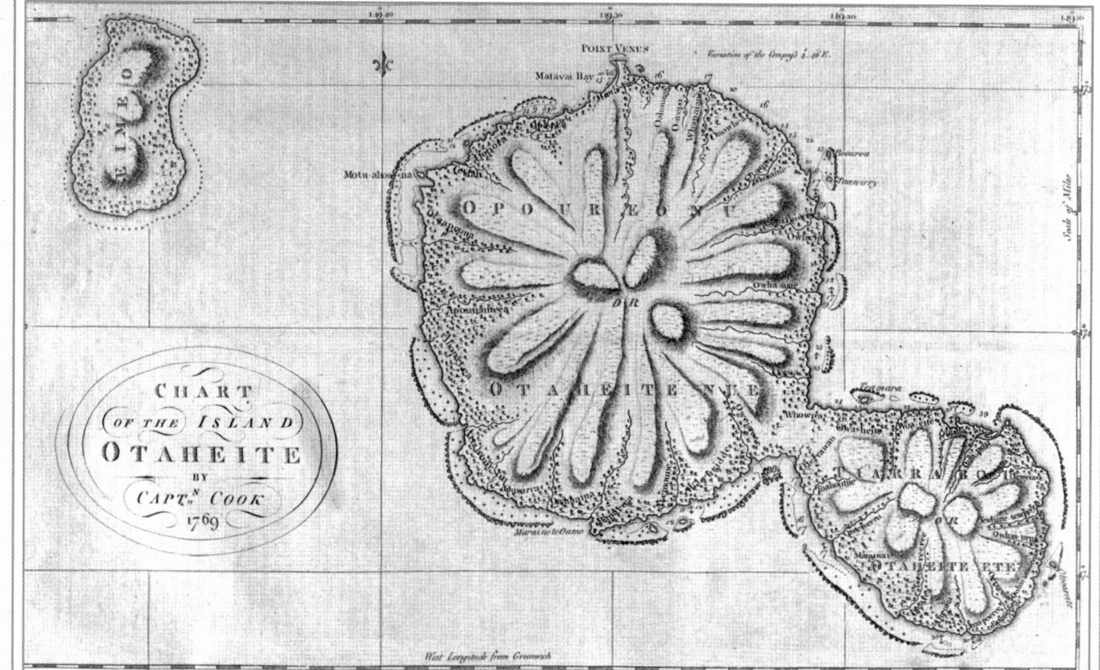

TERRA AUSTRALIS

The rumor that there existed a great mass of land to the south of the known world, known in Latin as Terra Australis Incognita (Unknown Southern Land), had been prevalent among European geographers since at least the 15th century. The idea was first put forward by Aristotle, and was later expanded in the first century A.D. by Ptolemy, who argued that the Indian Ocean was bordered to the south by land. He thought that the landmasses in the northern hemisphere must be balanced out by a similar amount of land in the southern hemisphere. Cook's voyages dispelled this idea, but the myth of Terra Australis did inspire the name of the new continent.

KEY DATES IN THE LIFE OF JAMES COOK

OCTOBER 27, 1728
James Cook is born in the town of Marton in Yorkshire, England

JUNE 1757
Cook passes his master's examination at Trinity House, Deptford, which qualifies him to navigate and handle a Royal Navy ship

1768
Cook is commissioned to lead a scientific expedition to Tahiti, and promoted to lieutenant

OCTOBER 1769
Cook becomes the first European to set foot on the islands of New Zealand

APRIL 19, 1770
Cook's expedition discovers the east coast of Australia

See an extract of one of the first convict lists in Envelope II

HMB *ENDEAVOUR*

HMB *Endeavour*, the ship that Cook commanded on his first voyage, is almost as famous as the man himself. It was a Royal Navy research vessel, purchased in 1768. While sailing along the coast of Australia, *Endeavour* ran aground on the Great Barrier Reef, and had to be beached for seven weeks in order for repairs to be carried out. The vessel returned home to England on July 12, 1771, having been at sea for nearly three years. *Endeavour* remained in service until 1778, when the ship was scuttled as part of a blockade of Narragansett Bay, Rhode Island, during the American Revolution.

HAWAII

Cook set out on his third voyage of discovery in July 1776, engaged in searching for the much-sought-after "Northwest Passage"—a sea route from Europe to Asia via North America and the Arctic. In January 1778, he became the first European to reach Hawaii, and from there he sailed along the western coast of North America, mapping it as he went, which was vitally important in allowing cartographers to map the extent of the Pacific Ocean. On reaching the Bering Strait, Cook found his way blocked by walls of ice. After a frustrating attempt to navigate the strait, he turned around and sailed back to Hawaii. On February 14, 1779, Cook was stabbed to death by Hawaiian natives as he investigated the theft of a boat. It was a tragic end for one of the age's most able naval explorers. After a further attempt to pass through the Bering Strait, HMS *Resolution* and HMS *Discovery* departed for home, now commanded by John Gore and Captain James King. The expedition arrived back in England in October 1780.

ABOVE: Triumph of the Navigators, *a 20th-century oil on canvas by Robin Brooks depicting* Endeavour *returning home through the Dover Strait from her first voyage in 1771.*
RIGHT: Death of Captain Cook, 1779, *oil on canvas painted in 1783 by George Carter.*

JANUARY 17, 1773
Cook's expedition becomes the first to cross the Antarctic Circle

1775
Cook is promoted to the rank of captain and becomes a fellow of the Royal Society

JUNE 3, 1768
Cook's expedition successfully takes astronomical observations of the eclipse of the sun by the planet Venus

JANUARY 1778
Cook becomes the first European to reach the Hawaiian islands

FEBRUARY 14, 1779
Cook is stabbed to death by Hawaiian natives as he attempts to recover a stolen boat

WOLFGANG AMADEUS MOZART 

The 18th century was a golden age for music. Many renowned composers were active during this period, among them one of the most famous of all, Wolfgang Amadeus Mozart. He was born on January 27, 1756 in Salzburg, Austria, and was surrounded by music from an early age, in large part due to his father's occupation as a composer, violinist, and concertmaster at the Salzburg court.

EARLY COMPOSITIONS

When he was only five years old, Mozart was already composing short but beautiful pieces of music, the first creations of a prolific career which eventually yielded more than 600 works.

Wolfgang's father saw an opportunity to showcase his son's talent to the world, and soon began to arrange public performances for the child prodigy. He devoted all his energies towards his son, recognizing that his own musical talent was insignificant in comparison. When he was just six, Wolfgang and his older sister traveled throughout the European courts, performing in cities such as Paris and London, where they played the violin and piano, impressing large numbers of people who came to enjoy their wonderful talents.

By the age of nine, Mozart had published his first composition and begun writing symphonies (which are performed by a full orchestra). He did not tour again until 1770, hoping to concentrate on improving his musical skills, but from 1770 to 1773 he visited Italy three times, during which period he wrote the operas *Mitridate*, *Ascanio in Alba*, and *Lucio Silla*. His ability to compose in the Italian style only heightened the admiration of his fans.

LEFT: Portrait of Wolfgang Amadeus Mozart, Aged Eight, Holding a Bird's Nest, *painted by the English-based German artist Johann Zoffany (1733–1810) in about 1764.*
BELOW: *A portrait of the Baroque composer Johann Sebastian Bach, who suffered from bad eyesight.*

VIENNA

Mozart realized that he would never be able to make the most of his prospects if he stayed in the regional town of Salzburg, and so he moved to Vienna in 1781, after brief stays in Munich and Paris. There he gave public performances, began teaching music, and published many of his compositions. He gained particular renown as a pianist, especially after performing before the Emperor Joseph on December 24, 1781. He also consolidated his reputation as a composer when he published the opera *Die Entführung aus dem Serail* (*The Abducton from the Seraglio*). This premiered on July 16, 1782, and became extremely popular. Mozart's meteoric rise to fame was now

J. S. BACH
(1685–1750)

Mozart was by no means the only talented composer active in the 18th century. He was born six years after the death of another giant, Johann Sebastian Bach. A German composer of the Baroque style, Bach enriched its form by introducing elements from French and Italian music. He played the organ and the violin, though it was as an organist that he was most respected by his contemporaries. It was only in the early 19th century, some years after his death, that Bach's abilities as a composer were fully celebrated. He had a strong influence on many talented composers who came after him, including Mozart.

KEY DATES IN THE LIFE OF WOLFGANG AMADEUS MOZART

MARCH 31, 1685
Johann Sebastian Bach is born in Eisenach, Germany

JANUARY 27, 1756
Wolfgang Amadeus Mozart is born in Salzburg, Austria

1759
At the age of three, Mozart begins to play the harpsichord

1761
Mozart begins to compose music, at the age of five: the start of a prolific career

DECEMBER 16, 1770
Ludwig van Beethoven is born in Bonn, Germany, son of a Kapellmeister

See pages from an original score by Mozart in Envelope II

complete. On August 4, 1782, he married Constanze Weber, with whom he was to have six children.

Mozart lived a comfortable life, but never gained complete financial security and often had to borrow from friends in order to make ends meet. He remained based in Vienna, but frequently traveled around Europe to perform on tour in operas and concerts. He died on December 5, 1791 at the early age of 35. It has been suggested that he may have been poisoned, but it is more likely that his death was due to illness. He left behind a rich catalog of compositions, including operas, sonatas, concertos, and symphonies.

LEFT: *The title page, in French, of the published score for Mozart's "Six Sonatas for the Clavichord or Piano, accompanied by the Violin."*

BELOW: *An early-19th-century watercolor of a view of the city of Salzburg, Austria, as seen from the Kapuzinerberg. The town has a lasting reputation as a musical center, and today is home to an annual music and drama festival.*

LUDWIG VAN BEETHOVEN

(1770–1827)

Ludwig van Beethoven was a German composer, born on December 16, 1770 in the town of Bonn in Germany. He moved to Vienna as a young man and soon gained a strong reputation as a virtuoso pianist. In the late 1790s, he began to lose his sense of hearing, a disaster for a man who relied upon music for his livelihood, not to mention his creative happiness. He eventually became completely deaf, but continued to compose music and even to perform publicly. Today, he is renowned as the key figure standing between the Classical and Romantic periods of classical music.

1770–73
Mozart tours Italy three times, and writes the operas *Mitridate, Ascanio in Alba,* and *Lucio Silla*

JULY 16, 1782
Mozart's opera *Die Entführung aus dem Serail* (*The Abduction from the Seraglio*) premieres

AUGUST 4, 1782
Mozart marries Constanze Weber, with whom he goes on to have six children

1785–86
Mozart composes the opera *Le Nozze di Figaro* (*The Marriage of Figaro*) in Vienna

DECEMBER 5, 1791
Mozart dies at the young age of 35, leaving over 600 compositions

THE AMERICAN REVOLUTION ≈ 1775–83

The American Revolution, which broke out in 1775, pitted "patriot," or pro-independence Americans in the Thirteen Colonies the British had established along the seaboard of the modern United States, against "loyalist" or pro-colonial Americans. A global war that ultimately drew in the French, Dutch, and Spanish, it ended with the establishment of the United States of America.

DEEP-SEATED TENSIONS

The causes of the war can be traced back to tensions that arose following the French and Indian War of 1755–62. British victories, including Wolfe's capture of Quebec in 1759, were confirmed by the Treaty of Paris, which marked the end of the conflict and granted most French territory in North America to the British. Britain faced financial difficulties following years of campaigning, and these were exacerbated by the costs associated with garrisoning and defending the newly gained territories. The British Parliament determined that the colonies themselves should meet some of the expenditure associated with their defense and introduced a series of taxes that many in the American colonies perceived as harsh and unfair. Meanwhile,

RIGHT: *Portrait of George Washington painted in 1796 by Jose Perovani.*

BELOW: *The death of the American general Joseph Warren during the Battle of Bunker Hill on June 17, 1775. It was a Pyrrhic victory for the British as they suffered huge losses.*

GEORGE WASHINGTON

(1732–99)

Born into a Virginia planter family, throughout his life George Washington pursued two linked interests: westward expansion and military affairs. Commissioned as a lieutenant colonel in 1754, his first military action was during the French and Indian War. In 1775, he was elected commander-in-chief of the Continental Army, and on July 3 of that year led his troops into six grueling years of war. With the end of the American Revolution, Washington felt compelled by patriotic duty to serve his country. The vote that made him President was unanimous, and he served two terms in the office before retiring to his home at Mount Vernon in 1797, where he died almost three years later.

KEY DATES OF THE AMERICAN REVOLUTION

1755–62
French and Indian War (the North American phase of the Seven Years' War)

1763
Treaty of Paris grants most French territory in North America to the British

DECEMBER 16, 1773
Boston Tea Party, the culmination of years of resentment at unfair taxation

APRIL 1775
Lexington Green—opening shots of the American Revolution

MID-1775
George Washington appointed commander-in-chief of colonial military forces

THE BOSTON TEA PARTY

On December 16, 1773, a band of American patriots boarded three British ships in Boston Harbor and destroyed the 342 crates of tea that they carried. This represented the culmination of years of American resentment at unfair taxation by the British parliament, which had authorized the East India Company to export the tea without paying duties in order to undercut and monopolize the local market. Following the unfavorable taxation already enshrined in law through the recent Sugar Act, Stamp Act, and Townshend Acts, this was a step too far and American resentment boiled over. The Boston Tea Party was symptomatic of the deteriorating relations between Britain and its American colonies, and represented a significant step on the road to war.

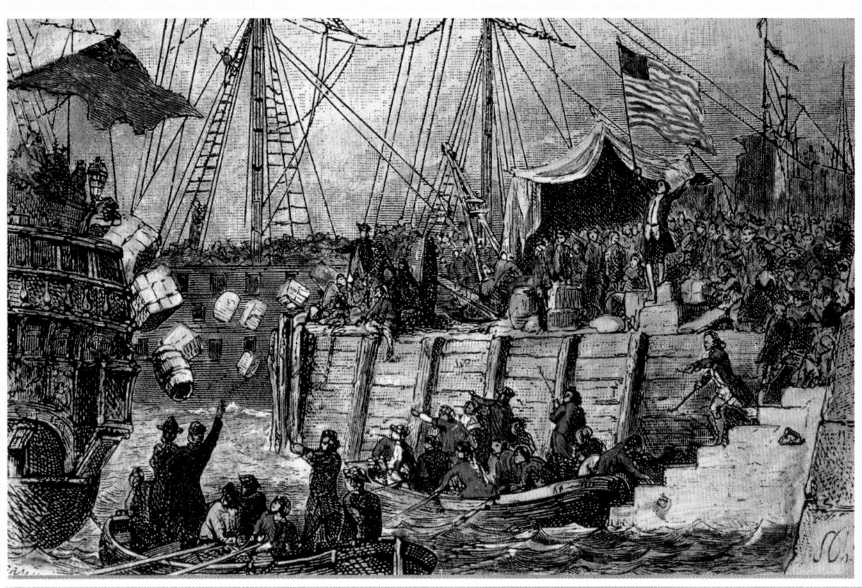

unrest simmered within the colonial militias themselves, as patriot American officers found themselves outranked by high-handed "royal" officers sent out from Britain.

Tensions escalated until, in April 1775, the British Lieutenant General Gage sent a force to seize patriot

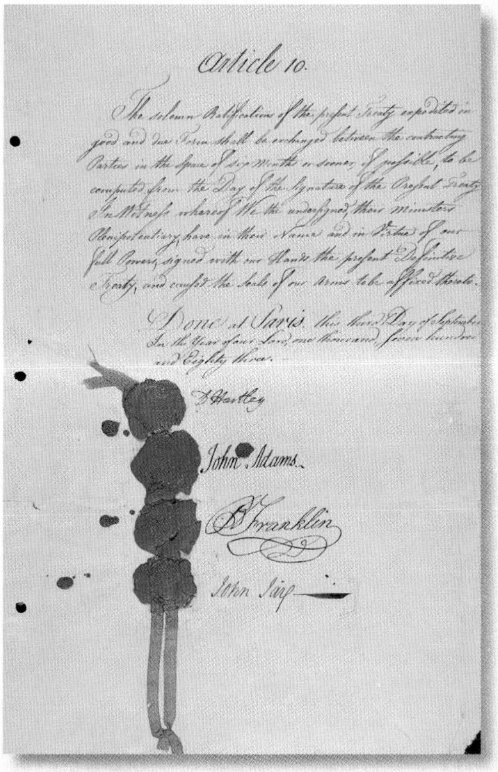

Article 10.

The solemn Ratification of the present Treaty expedited in good and due Form shall be exchanged between the contracting Parties in the Space of Six Months or sooner, if possible, to be computed from the Day of the Signature of the present Treaty. In Witness whereof We the undersigned their Ministers Plenipotentiary have in their Name and in Virtue of our full Powers, signed with our Hands the present Definitive Treaty, and caused the Seals of our Arms to be affixed thereto.

Done at Paris, this third Day of September In the Year of our Lord, one thousand, seven hundred and Eighty three.

D Hartley

John Adams.

B Franklin

John Jay

militia arms at Concord. His men became involved in a fire-fight at Lexington Green. The first shot fired there has been described as "the shot heard around the world." A bigger clash at Concord followed, and the British were forced to retreat to Boston, where they were blockaded in by colonial militias. Despite a victory for Gage's successor, William Howe, at Bunker Hill on June 17, they were unable to break free.

WASHINGTON'S COMMAND

Meanwhile, George Washington was appointed commander-in-chief of the patriot military units and set about recruiting the Continental Army, a force designed to replace the colonial militias, which he viewed as unreliable. Early success, as Washington forced the British to evacuate Boston by sea, was followed by dismal failure in an abortive attempt to invade Canada, and the loss of New York to the British under Howe in 1776.

The patriots' morale was bolstered by a small-scale victory at Trenton on Boxing Day that year, while in 1777 success for the British under Howe in Philadelphia was followed by a disastrous attempted invasion from Canada, which ended in September with the surrender of Lieutenant General Burgoyne and his entire army at Saratoga. Encouraged by news of this British defeat, the French, Spanish, and Dutch aligned themselves with the American patriots and entered the conflict; a French fleet arrived at the Delaware River in July 1778. Meanwhile, Howe had been replaced as British commander by Major General Clinton, who had ordered a retreat from Philadelphia, making New York his new headquarters.

The greatest British victory of the war came in the spring of 1780, when Clinton took Charleston by sea, and the British scored resounding victories at Camden (August 1780) and Guilford Courthouse (March 1781), before establishing a base at Yorktown. By August 1781, Cornwallis had begun to fortify his position there, but faced threats from both land and sea: George Washington was marching south with a combined patriot and French army, while a French fleet gathered off the York River. Cornwallis, insufficiently provisioned to withstand a siege and not strong enough to fight off an attack, was forced to surrender on October 19 before Clinton could arrive with much-needed support.

Although the war did not formally end until the signing of the Treaty of Paris in 1783, Cornwallis's surrender effectively represented the death of the British cause. American independence had been won.

ABOVE: *A late-18th-century print of the Boston Tea Party, which captures much of the drama and vigor of the action.*
LEFT: *The Treaty of Paris formally handed over the government of the American colonies to its inhabitants. It was signed by, among others, John Adams, Benjamin Franklin, and John Jay, who represented the United States.*

1776
New York captured by General Howe; victory for the patriots at Trenton, New Jersey in December

OCTOBER 1777
Lieutenant General Burgoyne surrenders at Saratoga, New York

MAY 1780
Victory for the British at Charleston, South Carolina

OCTOBER 19, 1781
Cornwallis surrenders at Yorktown, Virginia

APRIL 30, 1789
George Washington becomes President of the United States

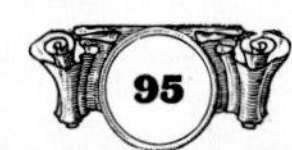

THE FRENCH REVOLUTION ≈ 1789–99

The French Revolution was the product of socio-economic change. France's emerging merchant class or "bourgeoisie" resented their exclusion from positions of influence; the peasant class increasingly chafed at their repression by the upper classes, and widespread crop failures led to food deprivation amongst the poor, polarizing the population between those with access to resources and those without. On top of this, France's involvement in the American Revolution (1775–83) had brought the government close to bankruptcy.

ATTACKING THE BASTILLE

The aristocracy's refusal to accept increased taxation to meet their country's budget deficits in 1789 led to a decision to summon the Estates General—a long-defunct legislative body consisting of the Clergy, the Nobility, and the "Third Estate" of commoners. This body was called to vote on proposed reforms to address the country's economic difficulties, but disputes over the electoral procedure spawned rumors of an "aristocratic conspiracy." A "great fear" soon gripped the nation, leading to the storming of the Bastille fortress in Paris on July 14, 1789, and peasant uprisings across the nation. In August, in an attempt to restore order, the newly formed National Constituent Assembly abolished the feudal system and introduced the "Declaration of the Rights of Man and of the Citizen."

RIGHT: Marie Antoinette and Her Children, *painted by Elisabeth Louise Vigée-Lebrun in 1787.*
BELOW: The Taking of the Bastille, July 14, 1789; *a key episode captured in a painting of the French School.*

MARIE ANTOINETTE

(CA 1755–93)

The daughter of the Holy Roman Emperor Francis I and Marie Theresa, Marie Antoinette married the future Louis XVI, grandson to Louis XV, in 1770. Initially a popular figure thanks to her glamorous looks and an outgoing personality that contrasted with her husband's withdrawn manners, she fell from favor as the French became suspicious of her extravagance. Following the storming of the Bastille on July 14, 1789, she was accused of insensitivity towards the near-starving peasantry. Imprisoned in 1792, Louis XVI and Marie Antoinette were executed the following year, in January and October respectively.

KEY DATES OF THE FRENCH REVOLUTION

1774
Louis XVI ascends the throne of France, aged 19

JULY 14, 1789
Storming of the Bastille, commemorated today as modern France's national day

AUGUST 26, 1789
Declaration of the Rights of Man and of the Citizen, a key influence on human rights worldwide

APRIL 20, 1792
France declares war on Austria in the first of the revolutionary wars

APRIL 25, 1792
First use of the guillotine, intended to make execution more humane

See Marie Antoinette's last letter in Envelope II

These measures were embraced by the populace, who marched on the royal palace at Versailles to bring the royal family back to Paris. The National Constituent Assembly went on to nationalize lands held by the Roman Catholic Church to pay off the country's debt, redistributing property across the nation and establishing the system of *départements.*

As the revolution gained momentum, members of the nobility and the clergy fled. The royal family attempted to escape confinement, but were arrested at Varennes in June 1791. The following year, France declared war on Austria. The revolutionaries desired to spread their principles further afield, while the king hoped that foreign intervention might lead to his release. However, early defeats led to suspicions of treachery by the French aristocracy, and a revolutionary mob stormed the royal family's home at the Tuileries and imprisoned the king and queen. On September 21, 1792, the newly formed National Convention proclaimed the abolition of the monarchy and the establishment of the Republic.

POLITICAL FIGHTING

The National Convention was divided between the Girondins, who favored a bourgeois republic, and Robespierre's more extreme Montagnards, who sought greater power for the lower classes. Despite Girondin objections, Louis XVI and Marie Antoinette were tried and executed for treason in 1793. The Montagnards' power grew, as they won the support of the Parisian working class or "*sans-culottes,*" adopting radical policies including the nationalization of prices, assistance for the poor or disabled, free education, and increased taxation on the rich. Those who resisted became victims of Robespierre's 11-month "Reign of Terror," during which 300,000 people were arrested and over 17,000 executed. This dark period only ended with the execution of Robespierre himself in July 1794.

On the demise of Robespierre, royalists attempted to seize power in Paris, only to be crushed by the young Napoleon Bonaparte in 1795. The National Convention dispersed days later. The government of France now rested with a Directory of five members and the Corps Legislatif (composed of the Council of Ancients and the Council of the Five Hundred). Disputes between these bodies were rife, until on November 9, 1799, Bonaparte intervened to abolish the Directory and appoint himself France's "first consul." In 1804, he named himself emperor, marking the end of the French Revolution.

RIGHT: *A late-18th-century portrait of the revolutionary leader Maximilien de Robespierre (1758–94) at his desk, painted by L. L. Boilly.*

BELOW LEFT: An Execution by Guillotine in Paris during the French Revolution, *a popular spectacle immortalized by Pierre Antoine De Machy (ca 1722–1807).*

THE GUILLOTINE

The guillotine, icon of the French Revolution, was the brainchild of the reformer Dr. Joseph Ignace Guillotin. Ironically, Guillotin was committed to overthrowing the death penalty completely. His invention was intended as an interim measure to replace the barbaric practice of quartering, the fate of poor criminals who could not afford to buy a less painful death by hanging or beheading. Guillotin envisaged that his invention would offer a dignified and painless death for all convicts. The first use of the guillotine came on April 25, 1792, and thousands of individuals were publicly guillotined during the course of the revolution. It was last used on September 10, 1977.

AUGUST 10, 1792
Storming of the Tuileries: imprisonment of the king and queen

SEPTEMBER 1792
Establishment of the First French Republic, abolishing the monarchy

1793
King Louis XVI and Queen Marie Antoinette executed (in January and October)

SEPTEMBER 5, 1973–JULY 27, 1974
Reign of Terror: thousands of people targeted, for many and various reasons

NOVEMBER 9, 1799
Napoleon Bonaparte becomes "first consul" of France

THE CORPS OF DISCOVERY ⸻ 1804–06

Lewis and Clark's great voyage of discovery in the early 19th century opened up new territories for the westward expansion of the infant United States, pioneering routes along which thousands of homesteaders would follow in their steps over the coming years. Commissioned by President Thomas Jefferson, their task was to discover a water route from the eastern seaboard to the Pacific.

SETTING OUT

With a party of nearly 50, they set out from St. Louis in May 1804, heading up the Missouri, where Clark charted the river's course while Lewis studied geology, flora, and fauna.

Jefferson's instructions were that the group should establish cordial relations with the powerful Sioux nation. While the expedition's early encounter with the Yankton Sioux went well, first contact with the warlike Teton Sioux proved less cordial, almost deteriorating into conflict when the Native Americans demanded one of their boats in return for safe passage.

The expedition wintered in Mandan territory, building a fort by the Missouri when the river froze. From December to April 1805, they survived temperatures of 0°F, subsisting on buffalo and other game while Lewis and Clark wrote up their experiences. Here they recruited the translator Toussaint Charbonneau, whose Shoshone wife, Sacagawea, proved invaluable when the party came to trade with the Shoshone the following summer.

The expedition departed from Fort Mandan in April, and on June 13, Lewis became the first white man to see the Great Falls of the Missouri River when he led a scouting party ahead of the main group. Following a month-long portage around the 12 miles of falls, they met the horse-rich Shoshone, from whom they obtained mounts on which to cross the Rockies. Despite trading more horses and food from Flathead and Nez Perce tribes, the party was

LEWIS AND CLARK

(1774–1809 & 1774–1838)

Meriwether Lewis and William Clark were young men when they set out on their historic expedition: born in 1774 and 1770 respectively, they were just 29 and 33. Both had proven leadership skills, following stints in the United States Infantry, and it was while serving with the army—Lewis as a captain in the 1st Infantry and Clark in the 4th—that their friendship grew. On the basis of this old comradeship, Lewis called upon Clark to be his co-commander in the "Corps of Discovery" expedition of 1804–06. Upon their return, both men went on to serve as governors, Lewis in Louisiana Territory and Clark in Missouri Territory as well as holding an appointment as Superintendent of Indian Affairs in St. Louis.

THE CORPS OF DISCOVERY 1803–1806

Lewis and Clark, 1803–1806
Clark, July–August 1806 (where different from the original route)
Lewis, July–August 1806 (where different from the original route)

ABOVE: *A portrait of William Clark.*

LEFT: *A map of Lewis and Clark's journey of 1803–06, including stretches where one of them deviated from the original route on the return journey.*

KEY DATES FOR THE CORPS OF DISCOVERY

AUGUST 1, 1770
The soldier and explorer William Clark born

AUGUST 18, 1774
The soldier and explorer Meriwether Lewis born

MAY 20, 1804
Lewis and Clark's expedition or "Corps of Discovery" begins its journey

AUGUST 2, 1804
First Indian encounter, with Sioux along the Missouri River

JUNE 13, 1805
Lewis becomes first white man to see the Great Falls of the Missouri

close to starvation by the time the snowy mountains were behind them.

At the Clearwater River, they hollowed out dugout canoes and, setting off on October 7, reached the Columbia within days. They rode that river's currents to the Pacific, achieving its shores in mid-November, when they resigned themselves to a winter on the coast. It was not until March that conditions were clement enough to set out again. Retracing their steps, the men battled strong currents and the hostile attentions of the Chinookan Native Americans all the way back up the Columbia.

BELOW: *William Clark's detailed log and diary that he kept while on the expedition.*

ABOVE: *Lewis and Clark and the Corps of Discovery on the Lower Columbia River in Washington State.*

RIGHT: *Sacagawea with Meriwether Lewis as they discuss which route to take.*

SPLITTING UP

After a month among the Nez Perce, the party's first attempt to cross the range was thwarted by snow, but with the aid of Indian guides, they at last made it to Traveler's Rest. Here the expedition split, with Lewis heading for the Marias River while Clark and the others set out for the Yellowstone.

Lewis's group became involved in a skirmish with local Blackfeet, fleeing 120 miles in 24 hours after an incident in which two Indians died. Clark, meanwhile, lost half of his horses to a Crow raiding expedition. The two parties were reunited by chance, and the group set off as a single unit again, passing through Mandan lands to re-enter Teton Sioux territory. There, they steered a course straight down the middle of the river, avoiding over 100 hostile warriors who lined the shores.

Now progressing homeward at a rate of up to 80 miles a day, the party reached St. Louis on September 23, 1806. It was almost two and a half years after their departure, and they had been all but given up for dead.

LEWIS AND CLARK AND THE SHOSHONE

Also known as the "Snake Nation," the Shoshone were a tribe of tepee-dwelling buffalo hunters living to the east and west of the Rockies. The arrival of Lewis and Clark's expedition in Shoshone territory in August 1805 represented the tribe's first ever encounter with white men. Without the horses that they obtained through trade with the Shoshone, the expedition would have been doomed. By a stroke of luck, it happened that Sacagawea—wife to Lewis and Clark's translator—was the sister of the Shoshone chief, Cameahwait. With Sacagawea as translator, the expedition was able to obtain the horses it needed as well as gaining vital intelligence about the territory that lay ahead.

NOVEMBER 1805
Expedition reaches the Pacific at the mouth of the Columbia River

MARCH 23, 1806
The return journey begins, retracing the route back up the Columbia River

JUNE 30, 1806
Lewis and Clark part company, taking different routes homeward

AUGUST 11, 1806
Lewis allegedly shot by a member of Clark's party; expeditions reunited

SEPTEMBER 23, 1806
Lewis and Clark welcomed home to St. Louis

NAPOLEON BONAPARTE ≈ 1769–1821

Out of the bloody aftermath of the French Revolution of 1789 arose one of the world's greatest military commanders. Napoleon Bonaparte, who declared himself emperor of France in 1804, deployed his unmatched military strategy to conquer much of Europe. His reputation as a tyrant and dictator is balanced by his status as a French national hero and military genius.

LEFT: *Jean Auguste Dominique Ingres's famous portrait of Napoleon Bonaparte in his emperor's robes, from ca 1804.*
RIGHT: *This portrait of Napoleon's first wife, Josephine Beauharnais, hangs in the Château Malmaison, her home near Paris, France.*

A MILITARY CAREER

Napoleon was born on August 15, 1769 on the Mediterranean island of Corsica, which had come under French rule the previous year. He was educated at military school, where he excelled, and when he graduated in September 1785 he was given a commission as second lieutenant in the artillery. He rose rapidly through the ranks, and by 1796 he was commander of the French Army of Italy, where he began to put many of his military ideas into effect, achieving enormous success. The campaign resulted in Napoleon's forces capturing 150,000 prisoners, 540 cannon, and 170 standards by the time it ended in April 1797.

Success on the field of battle also increased Napoleon's political influence in France. He published three newspapers, which were circulated among his troops but also found their way into the hands of private citizens in France. His popularity rose meteorically, and he took advantage of this by staging a coup d'état against the Directory in November 1799, becoming first consul, the most powerful person in France. In 1802 he was given the position for life.

EMPEROR

In January 1804, Napoleon discovered an assassination plot against him, and used this as an excuse to reinstitute a hereditary monarchy. He was crowned emperor on December 2, 1804, at Notre Dame Cathedral in Paris. Napoleon was now supremely powerful, and was poised to become one of the most influential figures in European history.

NAPOLEONIC CODE

The Napoleonic Code entered into force on March 21, 1804. It codified certain aspects of law, and established freedom of religion, meritocratic promotion in government, and the abolition of hereditary privileges. It is an important example of the rise of the rule of law in Western Europe during this time, and established a more centralized and coherent civic society, protected by a legally binding document. No longer could the whims of rulers affect every aspect of civil life. The code was imposed in countries conquered by Napoleon, and elements of it were adopted by others, providing a key element in the legal systems of many European nations.

KEY DATES IN THE LIFE OF NAPOLEON BONAPARTE

AUGUST 15, 1769
Napoleon Bonaparte is born on the island of Corsica, the son of Carlo Bonaparte and Letizia Ramolino

SEPTEMBER 1785
Napoleon graduates from military school and is given a commission as a second lieutenant

NOVEMBER 1799
Napoleon stages a coup d'état against the Directory, becoming first consul

MARCH 21, 1804
Napoleonic Code is established, doing much to establish the rule of law in France

OCTOBER 21, 1805
Battle of Trafalgar, where French naval forces are defeated by the British Royal Navy

See a love letter from Napoleon to Joséphine in Envelope III

RIGHT: *Now in the Musée de Versailles, this depiction of the Battle of Austerlitz shows Napoleon on the right in the heat of the action.*

Over the following years, he embarked upon a series of military campaigns against shifting coalitions of allies—including Britain, Russia, Prussia, and Austria. His plans to invade England were scuppered after the defeat of his naval forces at the Battle of Trafalgar off the coast of Spain on October 21, 1805. After this he turned his attention eastward, defeating Austro-Russian forces resoundingly on December 2 at the Battle of Austerlitz (in the present-day Czech Republic). France's conquered territory now stretched all the way to Prussia. Countries that neighbored France soon became puppet states, led by men loyal to Napoleon. It was the peak of his military success.

On June 23, 1812, Napoleon invaded Russia, which resulted in a disastrous defeat. His army had set off for Moscow with over 400,000 troops, but the harsh winter and grueling battles reduced this to less than 40,000 men by the time they turned for home. The allies now took the offensive, and in 1814 they captured Paris. Napoleon was sent into exile on the Mediterranean island of Elba. He was not finished yet, however, and in March 1815 he escaped and returned to France. During this period, known as the Hundred Days, he quickly reimposed his authority over France's army. Napoleon's second reign was cut short by defeat at the Battle of Waterloo (in present-day Belgium) on June 18. The victorious allies exiled him again, this time to the remote Atlantic island of St. Helena, where he spent the rest of his days until his death on May 5, 1821.

BELOW: *A dramatic depiction by the German artist Johann Moritz Rugendas of Napoleon on the battlefield at Waterloo, where he suffered his final defeat.*

THE BATTLE OF WATERLOO

Napoleon's final engagement as a military commander was the Battle of Waterloo, a name that has become firmly entrenched in the popular imagination as a byword for defeat. Despite this, it was a very close result and could easily have had a completely different outcome. On Sunday, June 18, 1815, Napoleon faced the armies of the Seventh Coalition, made up of British and Prussian troops. After throwing itself against the British forces placed along the Mont St. Jean escarpment, Napoleon's army was attacked in the flank by the newly arrived Prussian force. The British, led by the Duke of Wellington, then counter-attacked and routed the French.

DECEMBER 2, 1805
Battle of Austerlitz, where Napoleon defeats a Russo-Austrian army, enabling him to consolidate his power in central Europe

JUNE 23, 1812
Napoleon begins his invasion of Russia, which ends in disaster and retreat

MARCH 1815
After being exiled, Napoleon returns to France and begins the Hundred Days campaign

18 JUNE 1815
Napoleon is defeated at the Battle of Waterloo by British and Prussian forces

MAY 5, 1821
Napoleon dies from stomach cancer on the island of St. Helena, while in British custody

SIMÓN BOLÍVAR ≈ 1783–1830

Simón Bolívar was born into a wealthy family in Caracas in Venezuela on July 24, 1783. After the death of his parents at an early age, he was raised by his uncle, Carlos Palacios, and educated by tutors. At the age of 16 he was sent to Spain to continue his education.

LEFT: *Engraving of Simón Bolívar by M. N. Bate, ca 1825, as he was reaching the apex of his power.*

At 19, Bolívar married a Spanish noblewoman before returning home to Caracas in 1802, but his new wife died from yellow fever within a year of their arrival in Venezuela. Depressed and broken-hearted, he vowed he would never marry again, and he never did. He returned to Europe and traveled throughout Italy and France, beginning to study the works of philosophers such as Rousseau, Locke, and Voltaire. He became fascinated with the personal accomplishments of Napoleon and, after visiting the United States, he returned to Venezuela in 1807, convinced that he could lead his country in a similar fight for independence from Spain.

VENEZUELA

In 1810, Venezuela declared its secession from Spain, and Bolívar, together with key figures Andrés Bello and Luis Lopez Mendez, was sent on a diplomatic mission to Europe to raise money for the struggle. Bolívar returned to Venezuela in 1811 and fought in the Battle of Valencia under the command of Francisco de Miranda, a veteran of the Venezuelan independence struggle. Miranda acted as the dictator of Venezuela until the Spanish royal forces recaptured the Venezuelan city of Valencia the following year and imprisoned him. Bolívar then travelled to Cartagena, capital of New Granada (which included modern Colombia, Ecuador, and Panama), where he wrote the *Cartagena Manifesto* in which he encouraged cooperation between Venezuela and New Granada in order to achieve victory over Spain.

With the support of New Granada, Bolívar led the attack on Venezuela, where he secured the cities of Merida and Caracas and was proclaimed El Libertador ("the Liberator"). Spanish military successes forced him to take refuge in Haiti in 1816 but, with the help of the newly independent Haitians,

THE LIBERTADORES

Libertadores ("liberators") was the name given to the leaders of the Latin American independence movement during the early 19th century. For the most part they were well-educated South American noblemen or men from prosperous families, who were inspired by European or American liberalism. While Simón Bolívar was the most prominent of them, their ranks also included the Argentinian patriot José de San Martín (1778–1850), the Uruguayan liberator José Gervasio Artigas (1764–1850), Bernardo O'Higgins (1778–1842), who was a Chilean of Irish descent, the Venezuelan Antonio José de Sucre (1795–1830), and the Ecuadorian poet José Joaquín de Olmedo (1780–1847).

KEY DATES IN THE LIFE OF SIMÓN BOLÍVAR

1808
Venezuela declares its independence from Spain. Bolívar travels to Europe to secure support for Venezuelan independence

1811
Bolívar returns to Venezuela to join the military struggle against Spain

1812
The *Cartagena Manifesto* encourages cooperation between Venezuela and New Granada

1816
Bolívar seeks temporary refuge in Haiti

1817
The struggle is renewed, as Bolívar returns to Venezuela with money, arms, and men

THE BRITISH LEGION

During his military career Simón Bolívar fought several battles, but probably his most influential victory was the Battle of Boyacá in August 1819. Fought in New Granada (now Colombia) in the foothills of the Andes, it freed the country from the Spanish, allowing it to declare its independence. It also secured the political survival of Venezuela, and established Bolívar as the leading figure in the Latin American independence movement. At Boyacá Bolívar commanded a force of around 3,000 Venezuelan and Colombian Republican "Patriots," supported by a British Legion of 400 volunteers, the majority of whom were experienced veterans of the Napoleonic Wars. After the battle, Bolívar declared that he owed his victory to the British who spearheaded his assault.

ABOVE: *A statue of Simón Bolívar, dating from ca 1956, stands in front of a monument to the Heroes of Independence in Caracas, capital of Venezuela.*

he returned to Venezuela in 1817, eager to renew the struggle. After his victory at Boyacá (1819), Bolivar was proclaimed president of Venezuela, and continued to safeguard the country's newly won independence through military and political efforts. A victory at Pichincha in May 1822 saw the liberation of northern South America, and in 1824 Bolívar convincingly defeated the Spanish army at the Battle of Junin in Peru, one of the last engagements in the struggle for the complete independence of South America.

LEFT: *Bernardo O'Higgins, Chilean soldier, statesman, and liberator; an English mezzotint of 1829.*

BELOW: *An engraving by an unknown artist of the Battle of Boyacá, 1819, which won Colombia independence from Spain.*

A HERO

Simón Bolívar was now the most powerful man in the continent and in August 1825 the Congress of Upper Peru created the Republic of Bolivia in his honor. Bolívar wrote the Bolivian Constitution in 1826, but it was never enacted, and his vision for a united South America went unfulfilled. By the time of his death from tuberculosis in December 1830, Bolívar had survived an assassination attempt and his popularity had dwindled. However, his reputation has since been restored, and Simón Bolívar is once again revered as South America's greatest hero.

1819
The Battle of Boyaca results in the independence of Colombia

1821
Venezuela and Colombia unified under Bolívar's presidency

1822
Battle of Pichincha —Bolívar achieves independence for Ecuador

1824
Battle of Junin—Bolívar secures the independence of Peru

1830
Bolívar ousted as president of Colombia, as Venezuela and Ecuador secede from the country. Bolívar dies in Colombia, while preparing for exile in Europe

ENDING THE SLAVE TRADE ~ CA 1807

For over two centuries, Great Britain was one of the world's leading slave-trading nations, and British slave ships transported millions of enslaved Africans from their homeland to the Americas. Then, in 1807, Britain became a pioneering champion of the abolition movement. This dramatic change of policy was the result of a lengthy political and moral campaign, championed by William Wilberforce, a member of Parliament.

REFORMER

Wilberforce won his seat in 1780, when he was just 21. By this time, he had embraced evangelical Christianity, and he became a member of the "Clapham Set" of evangelical reformers. He used his political influence to campaign for social change, and in 1789 he spoke in Parliament in opposition to the slave trade.

Wilberforce became a figurehead for the anti-slavery movement, which had been championed by the Society of Friends and the Society for the Mitigation and Gradual Abolition of the Slave Trade. Until Wilberforce joined them, most abolitionists had been Whigs, but as a Tory, Wilberforce helped the campaigners transcend party politics. His first anti-slavery bill was rejected in 1791, but the abolitionists redoubled their efforts. While the leading proponents of abolition, Thomas Clarkson and Granville Sharp, compiled evidence of the slave trade, Wilberforce concentrated on the political campaign, lobbying MPs and changing attitudes through debate, fueled by the fresh evidence supplied by his colleagues.

LEFT: *William Wilberforce (1759–1833), English philanthropist and member of Parliament from 1780.*
BELOW: *Engraving of a slave ship, 1858. While this may not be an exact map of the human cargo's distribution, it gives an accurate idea of the tightly packed conditions on board.*

THE TRIANGULAR TRADE

Slavery was an extremely lucrative business, and the "triangular trade" provided great financial rewards for shipowners. Slave ships would leave European ports carrying trade goods, which would be exchanged on the West African coast for a cargo of slaves. In most cases, the middle men in West Africa were Africans themselves. The slaves were then shipped to the Americas, a journey known as The "Middle Passage," On reaching their destination—usually the islands of the Caribbean—they were sold. The profit was used to purchase a cargo of rum, sugar, or other local commodity, which was then transported to Europe in the newly empty vessel.

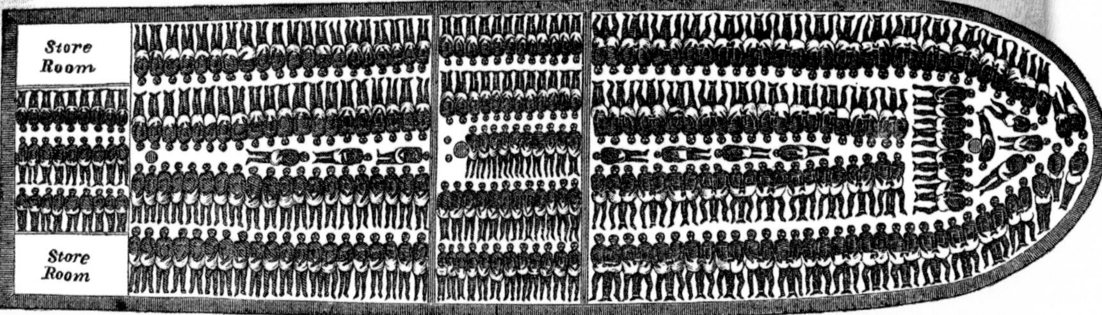

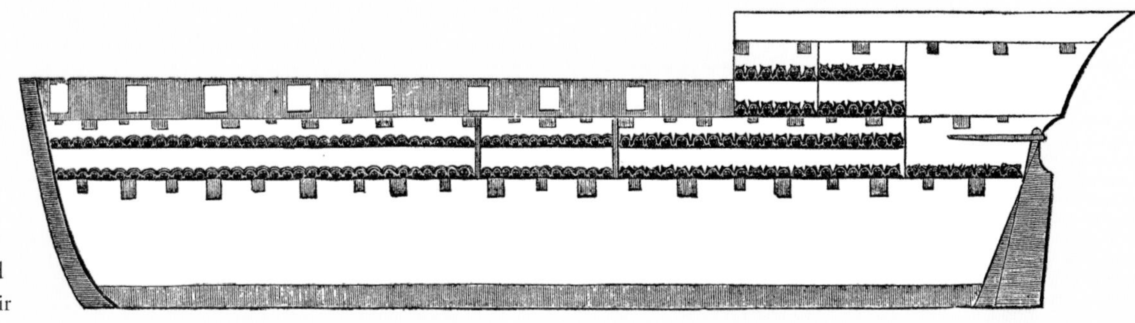

KEY DATES IN THE ENDING OF THE SLAVE TRADE

1772
The practice of slave ownership abolished in England (Scotland follows suit in 1799)

1777
Slavery abolished in Vermont, followed by Pennsylvania (1780), and Massachusetts (1783), U.S.A.

1787
Society for the Mitigation and Gradual Abolition of the Slave Trade founded in Great Britain

1794
Slavery abolished in France and its overseas colonies

1803
Slavery abolished in Lower Canada, a British colony

leading European statesmen abolished slavery in their respective countries, a decision based on "principles of humanity and universal morality." Slavery was banned in some American states before the United States won its independence in 1783, and the abolitionist movement gained ground during the decades that followed. After the American Civil War (1861–65), the slave trade was abolished, the legislation being enshrined in the Thirteenth Amendment to the Constitution (1865). Illegal slavery still continues today in some parts of the world, but for the past century all Western countries have abhorred the practice.

LEFT: *Lord Grenville, who championed the abolition of slavery in the British Parliament and served briefly as prime minister.*

BELOW: *A painting by the French artist François Auguste Biard (1799–1882), from 1849, showing the proclamation of the emancipation of slaves in the French colonies in 1848.*

THE SCALE OF THE BUSINESS

As early as 1500, there are records of African slaves being shipped to the Spanish settlements of the New World. The Portuguese had a virtual monopoly of the trans-Atlantic slave trade until the mid-17th century, when English and French slave traders claimed the business for themselves. By the 18th century, English and American colonial ships dominated the slave trade, although Portuguese slavers still served the needs of their colony in Brazil. It has been estimated that between 1502 and 1807, over 11 million enslaved Africans were transported to the Americas, and one in eight of these unfortunate captives died during the passage.

THE SLAVE TRADE BILL

In 1805 the House of Commons passed a bill making it illegal for a British subject to capture or transport slaves, but the bill was blocked by the House of Lords, whose ranks contained several prominent slave traders. In early 1806, a new Whig government was formed under the leadership of Lord Grenville, an opponent of the slave trade. In a fresh round of campaigning, Wilberforce extended his support within the Commons, while Grenville harangued the Lords. As a result, the Abolition of the Slave Trade Bill was finally passed in February 1807, and it became law on March 25, 1807.

Illegal slave trading in British ships continued, despite the efforts of the Royal Navy, and, rather than face heavy fines, slaver captains often threw their human cargo overboard if they were stopped. It was not until 1833 that the Slavery Abolition Act finally made slavery illegal in British-controlled territories, closing the last loopholes that had allowed the trade to survive. Other countries followed Britain's example, although France had already abolished slavery in 1794, as part of its French Revolutionary legislation, and Portugal had instituted a partial abolition in 1761. In 1815, at the Congress of Vienna, the

1807
Abolition of the Slave Trade Act is passed in Great Britain after two decades of campaigning

1811
Spain abolishes slavery and the slave trade in most of its colonies

1815
The Congress of Vienna passes the Abolition of the Slave Trade

1833
The Slavery Abolition Act passed in Great Britain

1865
Thirteenth Amendment passed, abolishing slavery in the United States

THE RISE OF INDUSTRY — 1780s–1850s

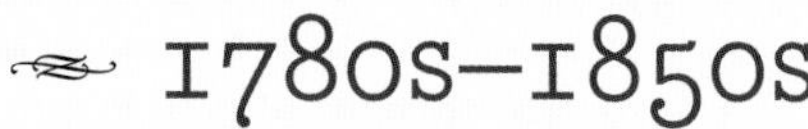

LEFT: *Printing calico in an 1830s cotton mill. The textile industry was a key part of the Industrial Revolution, both taking advantage of the possibilities of mechanization and triggering further new inventions.*
BELOW: *Luddite rioters in 1811. After violent clashes, some Luddites were arrested and were even transported to penal colonies or executed.*

THE LUDDITES

The huge changes brought about by the Industrial Revolution did not please everybody, and many people were appalled by the destruction of their old ways of life. One group who took this attitude to an extreme were the Luddites, a band of textile workers who were active in Britain in 1811–15. They fought against the loss of their traditional ways of life by destroying the new machinery that threatened to replace them. They also protested against the poor working conditions in the new textile mills, and hoped by their actions to delay or defeat the Industrial Revolution by force.

The Industrial Revolution stands out as a period of radical change in almost every aspect of people's lives. Marked by an unprecedented growth in industrial output and technology, it was characterized by a complete restructuring of society in the countries affected by such "revolutionary" change. Beginning in the late 18th century, parts of Britain's economy began the transition towards mechanization, most notably in the textile industry.

THE STEAM ENGINE

This, along with better communications brought about by steam trains and canal networks, led to an explosion in productive capacity. Soon, the cottage industries that had produced much of Britain's manufactured goods were rendered obsolete, replaced with factories and mills using standardized parts and advanced new technology.

The key piece of equipment behind this shift was the steam engine. It was invented by Isaac Newton, but the first practical version of the machine was built by James Watt in 1763–75. It soon became the workhorse of manufacturing centers throughout Britain, replacing the waterwheels and windmills that had been the main means of powering machinery. Coal had to be mined in much greater quantities to fuel these engines, spurring on the development of a large coal-mining industry predominantly in the north of England.

KEY DATES OF THE INDUSTRIAL REVOLUTION

1763–75
Watt's steam engine is developed, paving the way for the Industrial Revolution

1777
The Grand Trunk Canal links the Rivers Mersey and Trent, connecting the industrial Midlands to the ports of Bristol, Liverpool, and Hull

1801
London's population is 959,300, just under a million

1811–15
Luddite riots: workers attack factories and break up the machines, fearing the loss of their livelihoods

1830
The Liverpool and Manchester Railway begins first regular commercial rail service

ABOVE: *Mr. Cowell, a labor leader, addresses strking textile workers in Preston, Lancashire, in the northwest of England, in 1853. This well-attended meeting was held in the open air, in an orchard. A wood engraving from a contemporary English newspaper.*

THE STEAM ENGINE

The key invention behind the Industrial Revolution was the steam engine, and the period is sometimes known as the "age of steam." The key principle behind the engine was that coal could be burnt to heat water, which in turn became steam that could be pressurized and used to drive both machinery and vehicles. Its applications were extensive, and additionally, it enabled manufacturing machinery to be powered anywhere a source of coal or wood was available. Industry was no longer tied to natural features such as rivers, and it could be concentrated on a much larger scale.

MIGRATION

The ability to manufacture so much in such a relatively confined space led to great shifts in the labor force. Britain in the 19th century experienced the mass movement of people into burgeoning urban centers, especially northern industrial cities such as Liverpool and Manchester. This large-scale movement of labor created an entirely new set of living conditions, with urban workers living in high-density housing close to their places of work. In turn, this led to overcrowding and unsanitary conditions, especially as many cities lacked the modern sewer systems needed to cope with such a high population density. By the end of the 19th century, most of Europe and especially Britain was completely altered from a century earlier. Throughout the country, cities were no longer merely centers of commerce but great manufacturing centers, and they contained many more people. London had a population of 959,300 in 1801; by 1891 this had rocketed to a total of 5,572,012.

Conditions in the workplace were also extremely harsh, with long working hours and scant wages common, together with the many dangers caused by the presence of so much moving machinery. It was not long before this created an impetus to improve life for the new "working class," with organized groups springing up demanding a better way of life. Workers were no longer separated from one another by large physical distances, and this, along with a greater prevalence of print literature, made it relatively easy to organize large groups of people. The first trade unions were formed around the middle of the 19th century, and proved to be a potent political force. The Industrial Revolution also created the conditions necessary for socialism to emerge as a political philosophy, and as European countries completed the transition to fully industrialized economies, the political landscape ended up being reshaped as much as the social one had been.

ABOVE: *The first rotary steam engine designed by James Watt (1736–1819), the beginning of industrial and social changes that were truly revolutionary. A 19th-century wood engraving.*

1837
Morse develops the telegraph and Morse code, out of frustration that there was no way to communicate quickly when his wife was dying

1858
The first trans-Atlantic cable is laid, allowing telegraph communication between the U.S.A. and Britain. It is met with an outburst of enthusiasm

1867
Alfred Nobel produces dynamite, the first explosive that can be safely handled

1879
Thomas Edison invents the incandescent lamp, using heat to emit light

1891
London's population has grown to a staggering 5,572,012

CHARLES DARWIN ≈ 1809–82

Charles Darwin, the naturalist credited with developing the theory of evolution, was born on February 12, 1809, to a wealthy and prestigious family in Shropshire, England. Charles was the grandson of Erasmus Darwin, a popular poet and leading 18th-century intellectual.

EARLY INTERESTS

Originally destined for a career in medicine, in 1825 Charles headed to Edinburgh University to embark upon his medical studies. It was in Edinburgh that his interest in the natural world developed, as he studied marine invertebrates and found himself fascinated by all forms of natural history. Darwin soon realized that a medical career was not for him, and swapped his course at Edinburgh for divinity at Christ's College, Cambridge. It was his hope that life as a country parson would afford him the free time to continue his investigations of the natural world. While studying at Cambridge, he became acquainted with the botanist John Steven Henslow, who changed the course of history by recommending Darwin as the naturalist

BELOW: *1878 photograph of Charles Darwin, by this point established as the patriarch of natural history. His theories would stimulate debate and thought for centuries to come.*

RIGHT: *Title page of Darwin's* On The Origin of Species by Means of Natural Selection, *published in London in 1859.*

ON

THE ORIGIN OF SPECIES

BY MEANS OF NATURAL SELECTION,

OR THE

PRESERVATION OF FAVOURED RACES IN THE STRUGGLE FOR LIFE.

BY CHARLES DARWIN, M.A.,

FELLOW OF THE ROYAL, GEOLOGICAL, LINNÆAN, ETC., SOCIETIES; AUTHOR OF 'JOURNAL OF RESEARCHES DURING H. M. S. BEAGLE'S VOYAGE ROUND THE WORLD.'

LONDON:
JOHN MURRAY, ALBEMARLE STREET.
1859.

The right of Translation is reserved.

673.24 DARWIN: ORIGIN OF THE SPECIES, 1859.
Credit: The Granger Collection, New York

ON THE ORIGIN OF SPECIES

Darwin's most famous and most controversial work, *On The Origin of Species*, was first published in 1859. In it, Darwin set out his theory that organisms and species are not fixed in their nature. Taking familiar domestic plants and animals as his examples, he pointed out the ways in which these had changed over the course of man's relationship with them. He went on to show how species evolve and change in response to prevailing conditions, including predation and environmental factors such as food, climate, and space. His theory of natural selection showed that the strongest or best-adapted organisms survived to reproduce, passing on their defining genetic characteristics to their descendants, so securing the future of their species.

KEY DATES IN THE LIFE OF CHARLES DARWIN

FEBRUARY 12, 1809
Charles Darwin born in Shropshire, in the west of England

1825
Darwin begins his medical studies at Edinburgh University in Scotland

1828
Darwin graduates from Cambridge University

1831
Charles Darwin sets out for South America on HMS *Beagle* as the ship's naturalist

1836
Darwin returns to England, with much data to discuss with naturalists and others

ABOVE: *A red marine iguana on Fernandina Island in the Galapagos. Darwin was inspired to new understanding by the creatures he encountered in the Galapagos.*

to accompany Captain Robert Fitzroy on a five-year survey journey aboard HMS *Beagle*, which set sail from Devonport on December 27, 1831. During his travels, Darwin read extensively. Lyell's *Principles of Geology*, with its suggestion that fossils found in rocks were evidence of ancient organisms, influenced him profoundly, as did the writings of John Herschel and Alexander von Humboldt. Drawing upon his own observations and these seminal writings, Darwin made a close study of the geology of South America, as well as surveying and collecting the animal and plant life that he encountered on his journey. His collection of samples formed the basis of his five-volume work *The Zoology of the Voyage of the HMS Beagle*, published upon his return.

BREAKTHROUGH

In the Galapagos Islands, Darwin made his major breakthrough as he recognized that each island supported its own population of finches, and that these birds differed in significant particulars. Returning to England, he consulted with animal breeders to understand how they worked to develop distinct breeds and types. His discoveries reaffirmed the growing belief that species evolve in response to prevailing circumstances, and that the similarities between different kinds of organisms could be explained by a theory of common ancestry. After reading Malthus's *Essay on the Principle of Evolution* (1798), Darwin developed this theory further. Malthus's assertion that the human population would balloon to outstrip the world's resources led Darwin to note that a vast proportion of organisms die before they can reproduce. This became the germ of his theory of sexual selection and the survival of the fittest.

Although fellow naturalist Alfred Russel Wallace formulated very similar theories and there was initially intense rivalry as to who made the discovery first, they later became friends. Darwin came across the other man's essay "On the Tendency of Varieties to Depart Indefinitely from the Original Type" and was struck by the similarities between their theories. Their theories were presented jointly to London's Linnean Society in July 1858 and formed the basis of Darwin's most famous publication, *On The Origin of Species by Means of Natural Selection*, the following year.

While the evolution of *Homo sapiens* was by no means the primary focus of Darwin's book, his suggestion that human beings may be simply another product of evolution and one among many species of animal made the work highly controversial. The church, in particular, was threatened by this theory, and Darwin was attacked and ridiculed. Ultimately, however, his ideas gained widespread acceptance and today provide the basis for our understanding of how evolution occurs.

BELOW: *The exploratory voyage of HMS* Beagle, *on which Charles Darwin sailed as ship's naturalist from 1831 to 1836.*

DARWIN AND THE HMS *BEAGLE*

Charles Darwin's famous voyage on board HMS *Beagle* was in fact the ship's second survey voyage. Tasked with charting parts of South America and running a chain of chronometric readings, the ship's captain, Robert FitzRoy, foresaw that the new voyage would provide an excellent opportunity for the study of natural history and the collection of samples. The captain proposed the idea to Captain Francis Beaufort, hydrographer of the navy, who in turn consulted with Cambridge professors he knew and came up with the name of Charles Darwin—describing him as "a young man of promising ability, extremely fond of geology, and indeed of all branches of natural history."

1839
Darwin marries his cousin, Emma Wedgwood, a happy, close marriage

1842
Darwin publishes his first essay expounding the theory of natural selection

1858
Darwin and Alfred Russel Wallace announce their theories to the scientific world

1859
On The Origin of Species, Darwin's most famous work, published

APRIL 19, 1882
Darwin dies, having transformed scientific thought

THE OPIUM WARS ≈ 1839–60

No event in modern Chinese history is as bitterly remembered as the Opium Wars, which resulted in a humiliating defeat for China and capitulation to a foreign power, Britain. The conflict started as a dispute over China's high custom duties on imported goods, and attempts by the Chinese government to prevent the importation of opium, a highly addictive drug whose trade had proven extremely lucrative for British merchants.

ABOVE: *An engraving of the East India Company's steamer* Nemesis *and other boats destroying Chinese war junks in Anson's Bay during the First Opium War, January 7, 1841.*

ABOVE: *An opium poppy,* Papaver somniferum, *from the King's College Collection at the Royal Botanical Gardens, Kew, on the outskirts of London, England.*

THE FIRST OPIUM WAR

Although it had been officially banned in 1796, the drug was extremely popular in China, with large numbers of habitual users. This had created an enormous and profitable market, and Western traders were angered that this was being denied to them. The ruling Qing dynasty, on the other hand, saw the trade as an insidious attempt to poison China's population and dominate them through the drug.

By the 1830s, China's balance of trade was negative, and it is likely that it was the large-scale opium imports that were largely to blame for the imbalance. In the late 1830s, more than 30,000 chests of opium were being imported annually. The First Opium War was sparked off when Chinese officials in Canton (Guangzhou) in southern China confiscated and destroyed 20,000 chests of opium in early June 1839. In

OPIUM

Opium had been used in China since the 15th century, but it was relatively rare and very expensive. Its use first became widespread in the 17th century, mixed with tobacco. Its danger as a potent addictive drug was recognized early, and it was officially banned in 1796, yet it continued to grow in popularity. The success of the British after the Opium Wars led to an even greater increase in recreational use, as supplies poured into the country. By 1905, a quarter of the male Chinese population were regular users.

KEY DATES OF THE OPIUM WARS

15TH CENTURY
Opium first used in China as a recreational drug

17TH CENTURY
Opium use is widespread and popular in China and other countries

1796
Opium is banned in China, but usage continues regardless

LATE 1830S
Over 30,000 chests of opium are being imported into China annually, mostly from British traders

JUNE 1839
First Opium War breaks out after large stocks of opium are confiscated by port authorities in Canton (Guangzhou)

LEFT: *The signing of the Treaty of Tianjin (or Tientsin), which ended the Second Opium War in July 1858. Its signatories were China, Britain, France, Russia, and the U.S.A..*

BELOW: *The Treat of Nanking (or Nanjing), signed between Britain and China on August 29, 1842. As well as ending the First Opium War, it established marked commercial advantages for Britain.*

response, British troops surrounded the city. From their point of view, China was unfairly restricting trade and must be brought to heel. On August 26, 1839, British forces seized Hong Kong to use as a base from which to launch further military action.

FURTHER CONFLICT

The Chinese could not match the technological and tactical superiority of the British, and by 1842 they had been thoroughly defeated. British troops occupied the mouth of the Yangtze River and the city of Shanghai, which meant that they now controlled China's major trade routes. The conflict ended in August 1842 with the signing of the Treaty of Nanking, whose terms included the cession of Hong Kong to Britain, the opening to British trade of five Chinese ports (including Canton), and the payment by China of a huge indemnity, including financial compensation for the opium that had been burned in 1839. The treaty left the Chinese sharply humiliated before a Western power, and created a bitterness that would help galvanize Chinese nationalist sentiment in the next century. Even today, it remains strong in the collective cultural memory of the Chinese. For them, the war was not simply a matter of trade policy, but a struggle for self-identity, national sovereignty, and cultural freedom.

The Second Opium War broke out in 1856 over the search by Chinese officials of a British ship, the *Arrow*. This prompted the outraged British to resume their siege of Canton in late 1856. The French were also active belligerents in the second war, and there were several joint attacks by British and French forces upon Chinese targets, notably against the Taku forts on the approach to Beijing in May 1858. With the capital under threat, the Chinese agreed to sign the Treaty of Tianjin in July 1858, which incorporated the "most favored nation" clause that gave all major foreign powers the same benefits as the British had previously enjoyed. Nevertheless, fighting continued, and British and French troops burned the Summer Palace and Old Summer Palace in Beijing to the ground. Peace was finally achieved in 1860, when the Treaty of Tianjin was ratified at the Convention of Beijing.

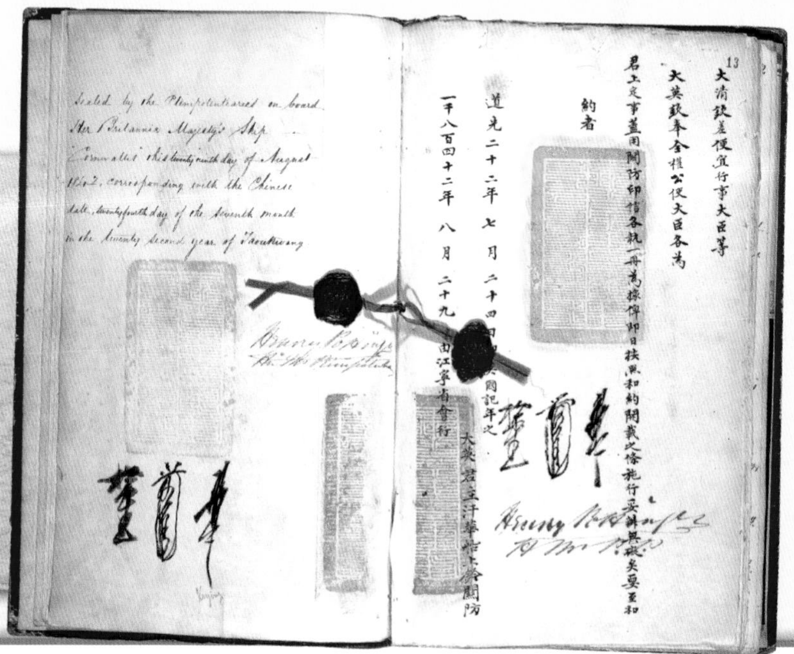

13

大清欽差便宜行事大臣等

大英欽奉全權公使大臣各為

道光二十二年七月二十四日

一千八百四十二年八月二十九

Sealed by the Plenipotentiaries on board Her Britannic Majesty's Ship "Cornwallis" this twenty ninth day of August 1842, corresponding with the Chinese date, twenty fourth day of the seventh month in the twenty second year of Taoukwang

TREATY OF NANKING

This is widely regarded as one of the world's first "unequal treaties," where one signatory is significantly favored over the other. In this case, Britain gained much from the treaty, while China lost a great deal. The treaty abolished the Canton System, which had regulated trade in China since 1760, and opened up five ports for trade with Britain. The Qing government had to pay large reparations payments to Britain for the opium they had confiscated, and for the cost of the war. They also released all British prisoners of war, and made the island of Hong Kong a crown colony, ceding it to Britain "in perpetuity."

AUGUST 26, 1839
British forces seize Hong Kong, using it as a base from which to launch further military action

AUGUST 29, 1842
The Treaty of Nanking is signed, granting Britain trade rights and possession of Hong Kong

1856
The Second Opium War breaks out after the British ship *Arrow* is seized and searched by Chinese officials

1858
The Treaty of Tianjin is signed, incorporating a "most favored nation" clause for all the major foreign powers

1860
The Treaty of Tianjin is ratified at the Convention of Beijing

KARL MARX — 1818–83

Karl Marx is one of the most well-known political thinkers of modern history. He formulated the ideas that gave rise to communism, an ideology which would dominate global political discourse during the 19th and 20th centuries. Marx was born on May 5, 1818 in Trier, which was then part of Prussia.

At his father's insistence, he studied law at the Universities of Bonn and Berlin, Germany, but his real interests lay in politics and philosophy. As he became older, Marx's political philosophy developed along increasingly radical lines. The Prussian government grew alarmed at the socialist views being propagated and attempted to suppress Marx by censoring his newspaper, the *Rheinische Zeitung*, which had campaigned for increased reforms and democracy. The paper was shut down on March 31, 1843, and Marx moved to France later that year. He stayed in Paris until ordered to leave on account of his views in 1845, when he moved to Belgium.

COMMUNISM

Marx put his political views forward most clearly in his *Communist Manifesto* (published in February 1848), a work which had been commissioned by the Communist League, an organization

Manifest

der

Kommunistischen Partei.

Veröffentlicht im Februar 1848.

Proletarier aller Länder vereinigt Euch!

London.

Gedruckt in der Office der „Bildungs-Gesellschaft für Arbeiter"
von J. E. Burghard.
46, Liverpool Street, Bishopsgate.

LEFT: *A photograph of Karl Marx taken in later life.*

RIGHT: *A first edition of the* Manifesto of the Communist Party, *published in German in London, England, in 1848.*

REACTIONS TO MARXISM

Marxism laid the foundation for a variety of other political philosophies, the most well-known of which is Marxist-Leninism, which took root in Russia in the early 20th century and eventually shaped the official Communist ideology of the Soviet Union. Lenin held that he had taken the core principles of Marxism and adapted them for the practical needs of revolution. The Chinese Communist leader Mao Zedong also used Marxism, but maintained that peasants, not just industrial workers, were key to any class struggle. The prevalence of Marx's views, and their adaptability to different cultures and times, makes him the single most important left-wing thinker in modern political thought.

KEY DATES IN THE LIFE OF KARL MARX

MAY 5, 1818
Karl Marx is born in Trier, a town in modern Germany that was then in Prussia

MARCH 31, 1843
The newspaper that Marx edits, the *Rheinische Zeitung*, is shut down

JUNE 19, 1843
Marx marries Jenny von Westphalen, the daughter of a Prussian baron, with whom he will have seven children

JANUARY 1845
Marx is ordered to leave Paris by the French authorities, and he moves to Belgium

1847
Marx writes *The Poverty Of Philosophy*, a critique of French socialist thought

FRIEDRICH ENGELS
(1820–95)

Friedrich Engels was Marx's close friend and political confidant, and together they developed Marx's system of political philosophy. In 1845, Engels published *The Condition of the Working Class in England*, a critical study of living and working conditions for the urban poor. Later, in 1847 and 1848, he helped Marx write the *Communist Manifesto*. When Marx was living in England, Engels ran a textile factory and supported his poverty-stricken friend as he devoted himself to his writing. After Marx died, Engels published the remaining volumes of *Das Kapital*, and became a life-long vocal advocate of Marxism.

of German workers based in Paris. In it he clearly outlined the positions of the League, and with them an examination of what it thought was wrong with the current capitalist system. He formulated the idea that all struggles in history actually represent an underlying struggle between the proletariat and the bourgeoisie. With this, Marx created not only an analysis of his own time's economic conditions, but also a school of historical thought.

In Europe, 1848 was a tumultuous year, with many protests and violent uprisings. As a radical figure, Marx came under suspicion from the Belgian authorities, and was soon expelled from the country. After initially returning to Paris, he moved to London, where he spent the remainder of his life and wrote *Das Kapital*, a work in which he fully laid out his political philosophy. *Das Kapital* spanned three volumes, but only the first was published during its author's lifetime. It did not sell, and Marx remained quite poor until his death on March 14, 1883.

LEGACY

Marx's legacy was a political philosophy that laid the foundations for socialism and communism, the dominant ideologies of the 20th century. Marxism, as his ideas became called, is a world view that sees history as fundamentally a struggle between social classes, and holds that economic conditions profoundly shape the social fabric of a society by dividing people according to material status. Marxism maintains that the working classes have great value as they produce labor, but that they are unfairly prevented from reaping the rewards of their work because the bourgeoisie controls the means of production. Marx advocated that the only way to transform these unjust conditions was through a revolution, after which the means for producing wealth would be owned collectively, and material inequality between classes would disappear.

LEFT: *Friedrich Engels, Marx's loyal colleague.*
BELOW: *The title page of* Das Kapital: A Critique of Political Economy (Volume 1: The Production Process of Capital), *published in Hamburg, Germany, in 1867.*

Das Kapital.

Kritik der politischen Oekonomie

Von

Karl Marx.

Erster Band.

Buch I. Der Produktionsprocess des Kapitals.

Das Recht der Uebersetzung wird vorbehalten.

Hamburg

Verlag von Otto Meissner.

1867.

New-York: L. W. Schmidt. 24 Barclay-Street.

FEBRUARY 21, 1848
The *Communist Manifesto* is published, the first step of a revolution in political philosophy

MAY 1849
Marx moves to London, where he remains for the rest of his life

1867
The first volume of *Das Kapital* is published, but does not sell well

DECEMBER 1881
Marx's wife dies, and he becomes plagued by ill health for the rest of his life

MARCH 14, 1883
Marx dies in London of bronchitis and pleurisy at the age of 64

THE AMERICAN CIVIL WAR ~ 1861–65

The American Civil War, fought between the northern states of the United States (the Union) and 13 southern states (the Confederacy) over the issue of slavery, was the world's first industrialized war and one of its bloodiest. It is estimated that over 620,000 soldiers died, with diseases including typhoid, dysentery, malaria, and smallpox killing far more soldiers than were wounded in battle. The shape of warfare was changed forever: the old-fashioned charges favored by Robert E. Lee, the Confederacy's leading general, were shown to be useless in the face of modern firearms at the Battle of Gettysburg in 1863.

On the Union side, General Sherman gave the world its first taste of total war, with his infamous March to the Sea, while naval warfare progressed apace as the CSS *Hunley* became the very first submarine to sink a ship.

SLAVERY

The years immediately preceding the outbreak of war had seen a rift widen between the increasingly industrialized north and the slave-based agricultural economies of the southern states. As westward expansion created new states, tensions rose over whether each one would be slave-holding or free. Finally, with the election of the anti-slavery Republican Abraham Lincoln as President in 1860, the southern states seceded from the Union to form the Confederate States of America, with Jefferson

LEFT: *The Battle of Gettysburg in July 1863 signaled the advent of modern firearms and changed the face of warfare. It was a major victory for the Union.*

THIRTEENTH AMENDMENT

The Thirteenth Amendment was passed by Congress on January 31, 1865, and ratified in December of that year. Whereas before the Civil War, campaigners had hoped for a gradual abolition of slavery, the Union victory meant a complete and instant end to the practice. The Thirteenth Amendment as we know it today provides that "neither slavery nor involuntary servitude, except as a punishment for crime whereof the party shall have been duly convicted, shall exist within the United States, or any place subject to their jurisdiction."

KEY DATES LEADING UP TO THE AMERICAN CIVIL WAR

1774 Rhode Island becomes the first state to abolish slavery

1804 New Jersey becomes the final northern state to enact gradual abolition of slavery

1820 The Missouri Compromise admits Maine to the Union as a free state, and Missouri as a slave state

1849 California Gold Rush populates northern California with migrants from northern U.S., making it likely to become a free state

1854 Passing of the Kansas–Nebraska Act states that these territories should decide for themselves on "all questions pertaining to slavery"

☛ See the Wanted poster for John Wilkes Booth in Envelope III

RIGHT: *The 107th U.S. Colored Infantry during the Civil War. With the future of slavery such a key aspect of the war, free African Americans took up arms to fight for their rights.*

Davis as their president. Months of tension between the two sides following the secession of the first state (South Carolina) from the Union was followed by the outbreak of war on April 12, 1861, when Confederate troops opened fire on Fort Sumter, South Carolina.

With more than double the population of the South, and the material advantages of an established manufacturing industry and transport infrastructure, the Union held an apparently unstoppable advantage. Nevertheless, the Confederacy emerged victorious from the First Battle of Bull Run in July 1861, forcing the Union forces to retreat to Washington and review their military training and recruitment practices.

THE COURSE OF THE WAR

The coming years brought an ebb and flow of supremacy, with Union victories in western Tennessee, at Shiloh, and at New Orleans followed by triumphs for Robert E. Lee's Confederate troops in the Seven Days' Battles. A Union success at Antietam in 1862 spurred Lincoln to issue his Emancipation Proclamation, yet, even so, the Confederacy went on to seize the upper hand at Fredericksburg and Chancellorsville, finally invading the North and challenging the Union forces at Gettysburg in July 1863. Here, Union victory came at a cost of 60,000 lives, but halted the last major Confederate thrust towards Washington, while victory at Vicksburg deprived the Confederacy of a valuable port, and broke it into two. As Grant wore down Lee's troops at Petersburg, Sherman captured Atlanta and embarked upon his March to the Sea of 1864, an attritional campaign which devastated those southern states it traversed. Richmond fell to Grant on April 3, 1865, and within six days Lee was forced to surrender to the Union general. On April 26, Joseph E. Johnston surrendered to Sherman in North Carolina, and the war was finally over.

ROBERT E. LEE

(1807–70)

Born in Stratford, Virginia, in 1807, Robert E. Lee graduated from the U.S. Military Academy at West Point in 1829. He served as superintendent at West Point and as a lieutenant colonel in the 2nd Cavalry in Texas. Lincoln offered him the post of Field Commander of the Union Army but, loyal to his home state, Lee resigned his commission, going on to lead the Confederate Army for much of the war. Following his surrender at Appomattox Court House, Lee was paroled, and took on the presidency of Washington College. He died from heart disease in 1870.

ABOVE: *A lithograph based on* Terrific Combat Between the Monitor 2 Guns & Merrimac 10 Guns *by F. E. Palmer. This was the first fight between ironclad ships of war, 1862; the smaller vessel won.*

LEFT: *A 19th-century steel engraving of Confederate general Robert E. Lee.*

1855–56
Violence erupts in "Bleeding Kansas" and is seen as a presage to the Civil War

1857
"Panic of 1857"—short-lived economic depression in major cities

1859
John Brown attempts to ignite slave rebellion with the attack on Harper's Ferry

1860
Abraham Lincoln wins the election; process of secession begins with South Carolina

1861
Jefferson Davis elected President of the Confederacy; ten more states secede; war erupts

HEADING WEST ~ 1800–1900

During the 19th century, the United States of America tripled in size. Prior to the Louisiana Purchase of 1803, the country's land area stood at some 800,000 square miles. Just one hundred years later, it had reached three million square miles.

As the frontier pushed westward, the population followed. The western territories, inhabited by less than 10 percent of the population at the start of the century, were home to some 60 percent of Americans by the dawn of the 20th century.

FRENCH SALE

At the time of the Louisiana Purchase in 1803, President Thomas Jefferson was already harboring dreams of westward expansion. He had tasked Meriwether Lewis with an expedition through what was still French territory to establish a trade route to the Pacific. Before the expedition departed, Jefferson was astonished when Napoleon voluntarily sold him the 827,000 square miles of Louisiana Territory for $15,000,000. The United States now extended from the Mississippi to the Rockies, and from the Gulf of Mexico to the border of Canada.

Further territorial acquisitions swiftly followed. West Florida and East Florida were absorbed in

LEFT: *A drawing by William Henry Jackson of a wagon train following the Oregon Trail in Wyoming along the Sweetwater River by Devil's Gate.*
BELOW: The Awful Slaughter at Wounded Knee Creek, South Dakota, December 29. *Sioux Indians are massacred by the U.S. 7th Cavalry in 1890, in this engraving from a contemporary newspaper.*

THE FATE OF THE NATIVE AMERICANS

For America's native peoples, the westward expansion of the United States was a catastrophe. As white settlers, hungry for land, gold, and adventure, flooded into the plains, mountains, and prairies, the tribes who had inhabited those lands for centuries were robbed of their homelands, their heritage, their rights, and their way of life. The first white men to come to America had brought the Native Americans new breeds of horse, sheep, and firearms, but as demand for land mounted, settlers and the United States government were increasingly unwilling to share territory and natural resources with the Indian tribes. The relationships between white men and Native Americans were sullied by misunderstandings and betrayals, leading to such atrocities as the 1890 Massacre at Wounded Knee.

KEY DATES OF WESTWARD EXPANSION IN THE UNITED STATES

JULY 1803
The Louisiana Purchase sees the United States double in size

1845
The United States annexes Texas as the 28th state

1846
Compromise with Britain leaves half of Oregon in U.S. hands

JANUARY 1848
James Marshall finds gold at Coloma near Sacramento, California

1848
End of the war with Mexico, as a result of which Mexico cedes over 500,000 square miles of land to the U.S.

1810 and 1819, while in the five years from 1845 to 1850, the United States' area grew by one-third. The 390,000 square miles of the Texas Republic was annexed in 1845, and the next year negotiations with Britain left half of Oregon—285,000 square miles—in American hands. The war with Mexico ended in 1848, leaving 529,000 square miles of territories including California, Nevada, Utah, parts of Arizona, Colorado, New Mexico, and Wyoming under American control, and the Gadsden Purchase of 1853 added a further 30,000 square miles of land to the United States.

THE FRONTIER

Occupation soon followed acquisition. Pioneers returned from the West with tales of open country, fertile soil, abundant game, and the promise of wealth: the concept of the Frontier was born. Under the terms of the Homestead Act of 1862, any individual was entitled to 160 acres of land in the West, in return for no more than a small filing fee and an undertaking to improve the land. Thousands of families gathered their belongings and joined the wagon trains heading out to the prairies in search of a new life.

Technological advances throughout the 19th century added momentum to the United States' westward expansion, as the railway network grew. The first transcontinental railway was completed in 1869, rendering the West ever more accessible, not only to settlers but also to a burgeoning tourist industry that catered for eastern entrepreneurs eager for a sanitized sighting of the legendary Wild West.

The West represented a promise of riches for the people of East Coast America. For those further afield, it offered a steady job, and thousands of migrant workers traveled from China and other distant lands to work, often on the railways.

The westward expansion of America was an important time in the development of the United States as a geographical entity, but its impact on the American psyche was no less significant. The expansion of the Frontier became synonymous with independence, with a liberating sense of possibility and, in the widest possible sense, with the image of the great American Dream.

RIGHT: *Chinese workers constructing the Southern Pacific Railroad's Secrettown Trestle, Sierra Nevada, USA, 1877.*

BELOW: *Main Street in the Gold Rush town of Dawson, Yukon Territory, in Canada's remote northwest, during the Gold Rush years, ca 1898.*

THE CALIFORNIA GOLD RUSH

January 1848: James Marshall, head of a work crew tasked with building a sawmill on the American River near Sacramento in northern California, made a momentous discovery. In amongst the river's pebbles, he spotted a few tiny nuggets of gold—and with his find triggered one of the greatest human migrations in history. Marshall's find was publicized in the March 15 issue of *The Californian*, and it was not long before gold had been found in the Feather and Trinity Rivers. A Gold Rush was soon underway. By 1850, the year in which California became a state, gold mining had begun in the quartz deposits of Grass Valley; the following year brought the discovery of gold in Kern County. Within four years of Marshall's discovery, California's annual gold production had reached a staggering $81 million.

1853
The Gadsden Purchase by the United States of a further 29,670 square miles of territory from Mexico

1862
The Homestead Act grants the head of every family title to 160 acres of Western land

1864
California Gold Rush is over as the surface and river-bed levels are exhausted

1869
The first Transcontinental Railroad is complete, with the final stretch finished between Sacramento and Oakland, California

1890
The Massacre at Wounded Knee, South Dakota

THE FIRST POWERED FLIGHT ~ 1903

The dream of powered flight became a reality in December 1903, when Orville Wright took to the air in the 1903 *Wright Flyer*, a machine which he had designed together with his brother Wilbur. Key to the brothers' success was their step-by-step scientific approach to solving the challenges of flight. In 1899, Wilbur requested information from the Smithsonian Institution on the experiments in flight that had been conducted to that time, and they studied the work of George Cayley, Samuel Pierpont Langley, and Otto Lilienthal.

TOP RIGHT: *The brothers Orville (left) and Wilbur Wright, photographed together in May 1909.*
ABOVE: *Wilbur Wright (right) and Dan Tate fly an unmanned kite-like biplane glider at Kitty Hawk.*

GLIDERS

The brothers' first flying machine was their 1899 biplane glider, flown unmanned as a kite, with which they tested their concept of "wing warping"—a means of arching the wing-tips in order to control an aircraft's balance. Their study of birds had led them to note the way in which birds' wings alter their shape as the creatures maneuver in the air. The brothers recognized that in-flight control would be the greatest problem facing any flying machine that they designed, and became convinced that they should be able to apply the birds' technique to their creations.

In 1900, the brothers successfully flew a 50-pound, 17-foot-wingspan glider at Kitty Hawk, North Carolina, choosing this as their test site on account of its remote location, wind, and hills. The machine was flown unmanned as a kite, before becoming the world's first piloted glider. Their attempts to up-scale their creation the following year proved less successful, when their larger contraption with its 22-foot wingspan lacked lift and tended to spin out of control.

Bouncing back from initial disappointment, the brothers reviewed their design and came up with the idea of a wind tunnel in which they could test a range of wing shapes. On the basis of their wind tunnel experiments, they developed an unprecedented understanding of how wings work, which informed the design for their 1902 glider—bigger than ever before, with a 32-foot wingspan and stabilizing tail. Further testing led them to develop a moveable tail, and they incorporated this into the design of their glider while beginning work on plans for a powered aircraft.

THE WRIGHT FAMILY

Orville and Wilbur Wright, sons of Milton and Susan Wright, had two older brothers, Lorin and Reuchlin, and a younger sister, Katharine. Milton was a bishop with the United Brethren Church, and he and his wife were committed to raising their children to be intellectually curious and self-confident. Both Wilbur and Orville excelled in math and science at school and, although neither received a formal university education, both were awarded numerous honorary degrees from institutions including Harvard and Yale. In 1892, the brothers founded the Wright Cycle Company, and the company's profits funded their early experiments in flight. Neither brother married, both living in the family home until their deaths.

KEY DATES IN THE STORY OF THE WRIGHT BROTHERS' FLIGHT

APRIL 16, 1867
Wilbur Wright born near Millville, Indiana, third son of Milton and Susan Wright

AUGUST 19, 1871
Orville Wright born in Dayton, Ohio, fourth son of Milton and Susan

1892
Foundation of the Wright Cycle Company, a bicycle shop, in Dayton, Ohio

OCTOBER 22, 1900
The Wright brothers make their first glider flight

MARCH 23, 1903
The Wright brothers apply for patents on their improved glider and flying machine

 See a letter from Wilbur Wright about the first flight in Envelope III

ABOVE: *The first heavier-than-air flight, by the Wright brothers, at Kitty Hawk, North Carolina, on December 17, 1903. The asymmetry of the wings is clearly visible.*
BELOW: *The front page of the* Virginian-Pilot, *December 18, 1903. The story lacked accurate detail of the first flight, but gave an evocative impression of the historic event.*

1903 WRIGHT FLYER

On December 17, 1903, the *Wright Flyer* became the first heavier-than-air, powered aircraft to complete a sustained, controlled, piloted flight. The contraption took to the air four times at Kitty Hawk, North Carolina that day, its best flight covering 852 feet in just under a minute. Its design was based on that of the Wrights' 1899 kite, and the key to its success lay in a three-axis control system. The right wing of the flyer was four inches longer than the left, compensating for the weight of the engine which was located to the right of the pilot, while a slight droop to the wings' rigging was designed to combat the effects of crosswinds.

12 Pages
Virginian-Pilot.
NORFOLK, VA., FRIDAY, DECEMBER 18, 1903. TWELVE PAGES.
FLYING MACHINE SOARS 3 MILES IN TEETH OF HIGH WIND OVER SAND HILLS AND WAVES AT KITTY HAWK ON CAROLINA COAST
TALLY SHEETS WILL DECIDE CONTEST
U. S. LANDING PARTY FINDS STRONG CAMP OF COLOMBIAN TROOPS
TO DEEPEN THE HARBOR AT NORFOLK
"WANTS CANAL BUILT WITHOUT SUSPICION OF NATIONAL DISHONOR"
NO BALLOON ATTACHED TO AID IT

POWERED FLIGHT

The following year, the 600-pound aircraft *Wright Flyer* emerged from the brothers' workshops. After two failed attempts and one minor crash, the machine made its first successful flight, with Orville at the controls, on December 17, 1903. Manned aviation had truly taken off, and more "firsts" quickly followed: the very next year, Wilbur made the first flight of over five minutes' duration in the *Flyer II*, extending this just a month later to a 39-minute flight. In 1909, the U.S. government bought its first aeroplane, sold to them by the Wright brothers for $25,000 plus a $5,000 bonus for exceeding a speed of 40 miles per hour, and 1911 brought the first aerial crossing of the United States, again by a Wright-built machine, the *Vin Fiz*. By 1907, military aviation had come of age, with the establishment of an Aeronautical Division of the Signal Corps, equipped with Wright brothers airplanes.

DECEMBER 17, 1903
The *Wright Flyer* makes its first manned flight, on the windy sand at Kitty Hawk

MAY 14, 1908
Wright brothers pilot the first passenger flight. The passenger was their mechanic, Charles Furnas

SEPTEMBER 17, 1908
First fatal air crash: Thomas E. Selfridge was in a plane piloted by Orville Wright at Fort Myer, Virginia

MAY 25, 1910
Orville and Wilbur Wright make their only flight together

1911
The Wrights' *Vin Fiz* becomes the first aircraft to cross the U.S.

THE RUSSO-JAPANESE WAR ≈ 1904–05

The conflict between Tsarist Russia and Japan, which began in 1904, highlighted the rise of Far Eastern powers at the dawn of the 20th century. By its end Japan had become the first such nation to defeat a Western power in the modern era. The seeds of the war lay in the rivalry between Russia and Japan over territory in Manchuria and Korea. In 1895, Russia had intervened on China's behalf against Japan at the end of the Sino-Japanese War, and was granted the right to extend the Trans-Siberian Railway across Manchuria.

GEOPOLITICAL IMPLICATIONS

Observers around the world were stunned at Japan's string of victories against Russia, the world's largest nation and a "Great Power." After the war, the Treaty of Portsmouth, which was mediated by United States President Theodore Roosevelt, granted Japan control of the Liaotung Peninsula, including Port Arthur and the railway that led from it. They were also granted the southern half of Sakhalin Island, and their control of Korea was recognized. Japan was now well placed to become the dominant power in the region. As for Russia, where the war was unpopular and remote, it had hardly ended before Tsar Nicholas II was forced to issue the October Manifesto granting certain civil liberties to appease a revolt against his rule.

ABOVE: *Russian soldiers at a hillside battery with a six-inch naval gun, Port Arthur, Manchuria.*
RIGHT: *Left to right, Russians Sergei Witte and Roman Rosen, U.S. President Theodore Roosevelt, and Japanese Jutaro Komura and Kogoro Takahira at the signing of the treaty.*

This allowed it to complete a vital communications link with Vladivostok, greatly increasing the strategic value of that Pacific seaport. In addition, in 1898, China granted Russia a lease on the port of Port Arthur, in southern Manchuria. The Russians valued this warm-water harbor, as Vladivostok was only operational during the summer months. Japan, in contrast, regarded these Russian moves as severe threats to its regional hegemony.

ATTACK

Aware that their forces were still superior to Russia's in the region, the Japanese decided to attack before the Russians could significantly strengthen their position in the Far East. When Russia refused to discuss a withdrawal of its troops from Manchuria in 1903, Japan used this as its *casus belli*. On February 8, 1904, the Japanese fleet attacked Russian ships in Port Arthur, quickly followed by a land invasion of Korea in March. By May 26, the Liaotung Peninsula had been cut off by another Japanese force, and the Russians in Port Arthur were isolated. Knowing that they held the initiative, the Japanese drove the Russian army north to Mukden (now Shenyang). By October that year, the Russians had managed to stage a few

KEY DATES LEADING UP TO AND INCLUDING THE RUSSO–JAPANESE WAR

1895
Russia joins in an alliance with China against Japan, and is granted the right to extend the Trans-Siberian Railway across Manchuria

1898
China grants Russia a lease on the port of Port Arthur

FEBRUARY 8, 1904
The Japanese naval fleet attacks Russian ships in Port Arthur

MAY 26, 1904
The Japanese cut off the Liaotung Peninsula, isolating the Russians in Port Arthur

AUGUST 10, 1904
Battle of the Yellow Sea—the Russian fleet attempts to break out of Port Arthur, but is driven back by Japanese ships

counter-attacks, but these were largely ineffective in pushing the Japanese back.

SIEGE

Throughout this time, Port Arthur had been under siege, and on January 2, 1905 the commander of the city's garrison suddenly decided to surrender, even though he had many months' worth of supplies left. This greatly helped the Japanese, who launched an assault against the Russians at Mukden on February 20. After heavy fighting and appalling losses—over half the troops on each side became casualties—on March 10, the Russian forces withdrew, and the Japanese occupied the city.

Though the Russians had been defeated, it was not the decisive blow. That was struck through naval power, and it came at the Battle of Tsushima on May 27–28. In October 1904, the Russians had sent a fleet to the Far East in the hope of relieving Port Arthur. It encountered the Japanese in late May 1905. The huge guns of both sides' ships hammered away at each other, and the Japanese eventually prevailed. Peace between the two countries was agreed soon afterwards, as both were exhausted by the conflict. Russia had been soundly defeated and Japan was now a major power in the East.

ABOVE: *The Japanese miltary parade celebrating the nation's victory in the Russo–Japanese war, 1905.*

RIGHT: *Japanese marines on board the battleship* Mikasa, *Admiral Togo's flagship at the Battle of Tsushima.*

BATTLESHIPS

The Russo–Japanese War was the high point of battleship warfare, when these behemoths truly ruled the waves. They were huge, heavily armed with several large-caliber guns and protected by thick steel armor. Commanders envisaged that battleships would close with their enemy in a fleet action and blast them apart with superior firepower. At the Battle of Tsushima, however, the fighting was actually conducted at great range due to the size of the ships' guns. It was to be the only decisive battle in battleship history, as they later became vulnerable to torpedoes, mines, and air power.

OCTOBER 1904
The Russians send a fleet from the Baltic to relieve Port Arthur

JANUARY 2, 1905
The commander of Port Arthur's garrison surrenders the city to the Japanese

FEBRUARY 20, 1905
The Battle of Mukden results in heavy casualties on both sides. On March 10 the Russian forces withdraw, and the Japanese occupy the city

MAY 27–28, 1905
The naval Battle of Tsushima, fought between fleets of battleships, ends in a Russian defeat

SEPTEMBER 5, 1905
The Treaty of Portsmouth is signed, ending the war and granting large amounts of territory to Japan

THE RACE TO THE SOUTH POLE ~ 1911

On December 14, 1911, the Norwegian Roald Amundsen and his four companions became the first men to stand at the South Pole. Amundsen had originally hoped to conquer the North Pole; however, in September 1909 the news reached him that the American Robert Peary had already achieved that distinction, and a swift re-think saw him plotting a route south.

PLANS

Amundsen's plans were clandestine: the explorer had many debts, and he believed that sponsors would look more favorably upon an Arctic mission of scientific exploration than a headline-snatching attempt on the South Pole. Up until the eve of his departure, his brother and the *Fram*'s captain, Thorvald Nilsen, were the only two other men who knew of the plans to head south. It was not until the *Fram* docked at Madeira in September that Amundsen revealed his destination to the rest of the crew, at the same time cabling Robert Falcon Scott, the leader of a rival British expedition, who was then in Melbourne, Australia, with the message, "Beg leave inform you *Fram* proceeding Antarctic. Amundsen." He reached the Bay of Whales in January and set about creating a winter headquarters—which they called Framheim—and depots at 80, 81, and 82 degrees south.

They had to wait through a winter which lasted from April 21 until August 24. Following a false start on September 8, Amundsen's party began their journey to the pole on October 20, 1911. Throughout the long wait, the men had busied themselves studying the area and making final preparations. Now, the expedition split in two, with Amundsen and four companions taking four sledges and 52 dogs to the Pole itself, while two others went to explore King Edward VII Land.

Traveling around 20 miles in five hours each day, Amundsen made it to 82 degrees by November 4. The men would set out early, stop at lunch time, build a cairn, and rest for what remained of the day. The 340-mile final push began on November 17, when the team (with 42 dogs and enough supplies for 30 days) climbed mountains that Amundsen named Queen Maud's Range. All but 18 dogs were slaughtered on the way to the Pole, with six of the final 18 shot to provide meat for the others on the return journey back to Framheim.

LEFT: *Roald Amundsen, wearing a fur parka. May 1923.*
ABOVE RIGHT: *"The Fram in the Bay of Whales," a photo from* The South Pole: An Account of the Norwegian Antarctic Expedition in the "Fram" 1910–12.

THE *FRAM*

Designed and built with polar voyaging in mind, the round-bottomed Norwegian ship *Fram* was about one-third as wide as she was long. Her unusual proportions were calculated to safeguard against the danger of being crushed by pack ice, with a shape that enabled her to be pushed up above the ice by its squeezing pressure until she rested on top of it. Constructed in Larvik, Norway, in 1892, *Fram*'s first polar adventures were in the north under the captaincy of the explorer Nansen. In 1911, *Fram* was the ship that bore Roald Amundsen on his journey to conquer the Antarctic.

KEY DATES IN THE RACE TO THE SOUTH POLE

JANUARY 1773
Captain James Cook crosses the Antarctic Circle

1820
James Bransfield discovers the shore of the Antarctic Peninsula

1821
Captain John Davis becomes the first man to land on the Antarctic Peninsula

1902
Scott and Shackleton make their first attempt to reach the South Pole

1904
Carl Larsen builds the first whaling station at Grytviken, South Georgia

See an extract from Amundsen's diary in Envelope III

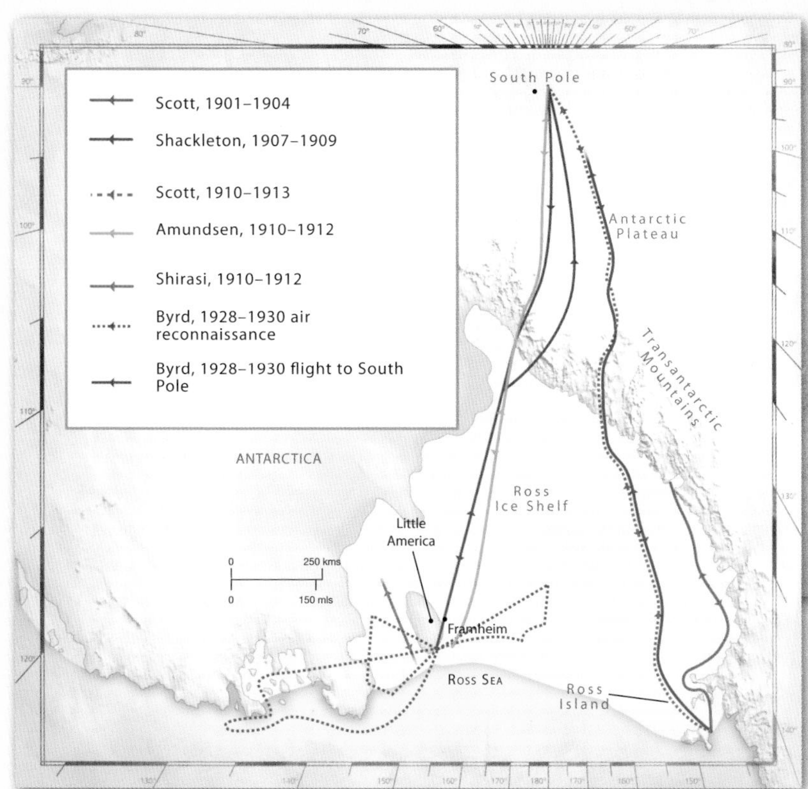

ABOVE: *A map showing the various routes taken across the Antarctic by Scott, Shackleton, Amundsen, Shirasi, and Byrd.*

ANTARCTICA TODAY

Today, Antarctica is one of the few regions of the world that has never been affected by war and where the environment and the requirements of scientific research take priority. The whole region is preserved for peaceful purposes under the terms of the Antarctic Treaty of 1961. Now signed by 46 countries (in effect representing around 80 percent of the global population), the treaty was designed to safeguard the area south of 60 degrees south from nuclear testing and the disposal of radioactive waste. It promotes international scientific cooperation in the Antarctic, setting aside disputes over territorial sovereignty.

SUCCESS

Exhausted, frostbitten, yet driven by the fear that Scott might already have beaten them, the team pushed on until, at 3.00 p.m. on December 14, 1911, they arrived. All four men grasped the Norwegian flag and planted it at the South Pole, naming the plain King Haakon VII's Plateau. Celebrations ensued, with expedition member Bjaaland surprising his colleagues with a box of cigars at dinner. The party stayed for four days at "Poleheim," making observations, before leaving messages for Scott and King Haakon and setting out back to Framheim.

Just under a month later, on January 17, 1912, the ill-fated Scott and his party were devastated to find Amundsen's tent in place when they reached the Pole. By this time, Amundsen was already on his way back to Framheim, where he arrived "hale and hearty"with his four companions on January 25. None of Scott's party would return from Antarctica alive.

BELOW: *Scott's ill-fated group at the South Pole on January 17, 1912. Left to right: Laurence Oates, H. R. Bowers, Robert F. Scott, Edward A. Wilson, and Edgar Evans.*

1908
Shackleton abandons a second attempt to reach the South Pole

JANUARY 1909
Edgeworth David, Douglas Mawson, and Alistair McKay reach the south magnetic pole

DECEMBER 14, 1911
Norwegian Roald Amundsen becomes the first person to reach the South Pole

JANUARY 17, 1912
Robert F. Scott's expedition reaches the South Pole

JUNE 23, 1961
The Antarctic Treaty comes into force after ratification by 12 of the original 44 countries

ALEXANDER GRAHAM BELL ~ 1847–1922

Few inventions have revolutionized human communication as much as the telephone, a device that allows people to talk to each other in real time while great distances apart. For those who first used the device, it must have seemed a miracle of modern technology.

SCOTTISH ROOTS

Alexander Graham Bell, the man behind the new invention, was born on March 3, 1847 to Alexander Melville Bell and Eliza Grace Bell. He grew up in Edinburgh, Scotland, where he studied at the Royal High School until he was 15, after which he moved to London, England to stay with his grandfather. After a spell as a teacher at Weston House Academy, he attended courses at the University of Edinburgh.

Bell's father was a well-known elocutionist, and Bell himself became highly knowledgeable in the field. He had a particular fascination with how deaf people communicated, and could recognize many different types of sign language. It was this interest that led him to experiment with sound and how it was produced. In 1863, Bell and his older brother Melville laboriously built a human head that could utter a few words by manipulating an artificial windpipe. After reading Hermann von Helmholtz's book *On The Sensations Of Tone*, he was convinced that he could simulate consonant sounds using electricity.

RIGHT: *Alexander Graham Bell, photographed with sketches for some of his early inventions.*

BELOW: *A wood engraving of Bell demonstrating his telephone at Salem, Massachusetts, over a line to Boston, on March 15, 1877, from a contemporary American newspaper.*

BELL'S OTHER INVENTIONS

Although the telephone is Bell's most well-known invention, and the one that propelled him to international fame, his inquisitive mind was responsible for many others. He successfully claimed 18 patents, and another 14 that he shared with other people. Bell created a rudimentary metal detector in 1881, with which he attempted to find the bullet lodged in the body of President Garfield after he was shot on July 2. Bell also created a hydrofoil seaplane, which went through many prototypes. On September 9, 1919, his model HD-4 set a world marine speed record of 70.86 miles per hour.

KEY DATES IN THE LIFE OF ALEXANDER GRAHAM BELL

MARCH 3, 1847
Alexander Graham Bell is born to Alexander Melville Bell and Eliza Grace Bell

1863
Bell and his older brother Melville build a human head that can speak a few distinguishable words

FEBRUARY 14, 1876
Bell's lawyer files a patent for the first "acoustic telegraph" at the U.S. Patent Office

MARCH 10, 1876
Bell makes the first telephone call in his Boston laboratory

JULY 9, 1877
Bell Telephone Company is founded by Bell and Gardiner Green Hubbard

BELL TELEPHONE COMPANY

Bell founded his telephone company on July 9, 1877. On February 17, 1879, the Bell Telephone Company merged with its sister company, the New England Telephone and Telegraph Company, and they became the National Bell Telephone Company. In the same year, the company acquired Thomas Edison's carbon microphone, which allowed a much clearer quality of sound over long distances. On December 30, 1899, the Bell Telephone Company was bought by American Telephone & Telegraph, which had been its own subsidiary. AT&T continues to operate today, continuing Bell's legacy.

BELOW: *The drawing for Bell's patent for "improvements to telegraphy," which is in fact considered to be the patent for the telephone. The patent was granted on March 7, 1876.*

2 Sheets—Sheet 2.
A. G. BELL.
TELEGRAPHY.
No. 174,465. Patented March 7, 1876.

Fig 6.

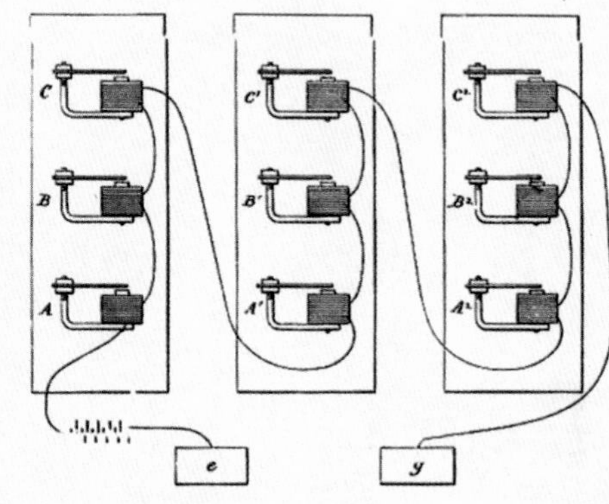

Fig. 7

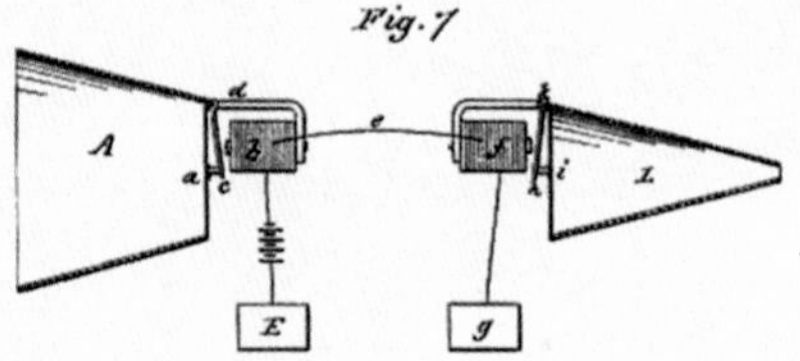

Witnesses

Inventor:
A. Graham Bell

PATENT

On February 14, 1876, Bell's lawyer filed a patent for the first "acoustic telegraph" at the U.S. Patent Office (Bell was now living in the United States). Another man, Elisha Gray, also submitted a patent on the very day, and there remains some controversy over who had come up with the idea first. Bell's patent was for "the method of, and apparatus for, transmitting vocal or other sounds telegraphically ... by causing electrical undulations, similar in form to the vibrations of the air accompanying the said vocal or other sound." On March 10, Bell successfully spoke to his assistant Thomas Watson using a telephone apparatus at his Boston laboratory, speaking the first ever words communicating on a telephone, "Mr. Watson, come here, I want to see you," an instruction which his assistant in the next room could hear clearly. The invention was a success. Over the following months, Bell exhibited his new device to many famous people, including the Emperor of Brazil and Queen Victoria of England.

The huge level of interest in the telephone helped launch it onto the world stage and achieve its future success. Over the years to follow, the telephone developed from a sensational novelty to a viable commercial enterprise. In 1877, the Bell Telephone Company was established, and in 1878 Bell set up the first telephone exchange, in New Haven, Connecticut. By 1884, telephone cables were operational between Boston and New York City, and in 1886 over 150,000 Americans owned telephones. The design for the telephone was much improved over the years, and long-distance calls became practical. On January 25, 1915, Bell made a call from New York City to San Francisco, over a distance of just under 3,000 miles and across three time zones.

BELOW: *Bell's first telephone transmitter and receiver, constructed from the invention patented in March 1876 and used for the first phone call.*

1878
The first telephone exchange in the world is set up in New Haven, Connecticut

1886
Over 150,000 people in the U.S. own telephones, most of which use Edison/Berliner carbon transmitters

1888
Bell becomes one of the founding members of the National Geographic Society

DECEMBER 30, 1899
The Bell Telephone Company is bought by American Telephone & Telegraph

AUGUST 2, 1922
The inventor Alexander Graham Bell dies at the age of 75

THE SINKING OF THE *TITANIC* ≈ 1912

The largest ocean liner of her time, the *Titanic* made history when she sank just four days into her maiden voyage from Southampton, England, to New York under the captaincy of Edward J. Smith. The tragedy of the *Titanic*—which had a capacity of 3,511 passengers—lay largely in the inadequacy of her lifeboat provision. Contemporary regulations demanded that a ship of her size should provide lifeboats for 962. The *Titanic*'s owners, White Star Line, had in fact furnished an extra four collapsible lifeboats, taking their total potential capacity up to 1,178, yet only 706 of the 2,223 people on board the *Titanic* survived her sinking in the flat, calm waters of the early hours of April 15, 1912.

CONSTRUCTION

Built by the Irish shipyard Harland and Wolff of Belfast, the *Titanic* was not designed for speed or maneuverability: her one superlative lay in her great size; at 882 feet, she was the longest ship at sea. The shipbuilder's claim that she was "practically unsinkable" would haunt both Harland and Wolff and the White Star Line in the years that followed the ship's ill-fated maiden voyage.

At the time of the Titanic's construction, White Star's competitor, Cunard, held all of the records for speedy Atlantic crossings. The Cunard vessels, *Mauretania* and *Lusitania*, both launched in 1906, held the coveted Blue Riband for record speed across the Atlantic thanks to their engine technologies, borrowed from warship construction. These sister ships boasted steam turbines driving quadruple screws, each with its own rudder, which rendered them speedier and easier to turn than their White Star Line counterparts. The *Titanic*, meanwhile, was an enlarged version of the smaller ships that had preceded her. With an economic triple-screw propulsion system that combined two expansion engines with a low-pressure turbine, she had a cruising speed of just 21 knots and could not come close to the 26 knots regularly recorded by Cunard. Her design owed more to the sailing ships of the preceding century than to the latest technological advances, and her single long,

ABOVE: *Undeterred by cumbersome clothing, passengers make use of the gymnasium aboard the* Titanic.

BELOW: *The immense four-funneled bulk of the* Titanic *sails out of Southampton, England, in 1912.*

KEY MOMENTS IN THE SINKING OF THE *TITANIC*

MARCH 31, 1912
Outfitting of the *Titanic* is completed in Belfast, Northern Ireland

APRIL 10, 1912, 7:00 A.M.
Captain Smith boards the *Titanic* to take command

APRIL 10, 1912, 12:00 P.M.
Titanic sets sail from Southampton, England for Cherbourg, France

APRIL 14, 1912, 1:45 P.M.
Amerika warns of ice ahead —the message is not relayed to the *Titanic*'s bridge

APRIL 14, 1912, 11:00 P.M.
Wireless operator of the nearby *Californian* warns *Titanic* of ice ahead

See a blueprint of the *Titanic* in Envelope III

AN EYEWITNESS ACCOUNT

Governess Elizabeth Shutes was on board the *Titanic* when it sank. As she recalled, "a queer quivering ran under me, apparently the whole length of the ship. Startled by the very strangeness of the shivering motion, I sprang to the floor... An officer's cap passed the door. I asked: 'Is there an accident or danger of any kind?' 'None, so far as I know,' was his courteous answer... This same officer then entered a cabin a little distance down the companionway... I listened intently, and distinctly heard, 'We can keep the water out for a while.' Then, and not until then, did I realize the horror of an accident at sea."

ABOVE RIGHT: *The stanchion of the ship's wheel stands out clearly amid the underwater ruins of the* Titanic's *bridge, photographed in 1995.*

BELOW RIGHT: *Captain Edward Smith on* Titanic *in April 1912 en route to Cherbourg, France and then Queenstown, Ireland, on the first leg of the fateful trip. This photograph was taken by Rev. F.M. Browne, who disembarked at Queenstown.*

elegant rudder would prove her undoing, as it failed to provide the crew with the responsive maneuverability that they needed to steer clear of the iceberg that destroyed the ship.

THE VOYAGE

The *Titanic* set sail from Southampton at midday on April 10, 1912, amidst a great fanfare of excitement. The water that the ship displaced caused the nearby *New York* to break from her moorings and swing towards the *Titanic*, an event retrospectively viewed by those who witnessed it as an ill omen. Myths surrounding the sinking of the *Titanic* suggest that the ship was striving to set a new record for trans-Atlantic passage. Yet not only her engine capacity, but also her route—the longer southerly Atlantic passage, generally considered safer from the dangers of ice—suggest otherwise. The true reasons for *Titanic*'s fateful collision with an iceberg late at night on April 14 will never be known. Both Captain Smith and Joseph Ismay, Managing Director of White Star Line and one of the survivors of the wreck, have been cast by history as the heroes or the villains of the piece, variously blamed and commended by eyewitnesses and the press for their actions on that tragic night. Regardless of what reprisals or commendations were deserved, within two hours and 40 minutes of her impact with the iceberg, the ship had vanished without trace, taking with her the captain and over 1,500 passengers and crew.

CAPTAIN SMITH

(1850–1912)

Sixty-two years old at the time of taking command of the brand-new *Titanic*, Captain Edward John Smith had served with the White Star Line since 1880. Nicknamed the "millionaires' captain," he had a well-earned reputation as a "safe pair of hands," having received the transport medal for his service in the Boer War in 1903 and becoming commodore of the White Star Line the following year. From that time onward, it became routine for him to command the line's new ships on their maiden voyages, and the *Titanic* was his fourth such command. Captain Smith died when the *Titanic* sank in the early morning of April 15, although the circumstances of his death remain unknown. His body was never recovered.

APRIL 14, 1912, 11:40 P.M.
The *Titanic* strikes an iceberg, having been traveling at 22½ knots

APRIL 15, 1912, 0:40 A.M.
First lifeboat of 20 (four of which were collapsible) is lowered

APRIL 15, 1912, 2:20 A.M.
Two hours and 40 minutes after hitting the iceberg, the *Titanic* sinks

APRIL 15, 1912, 4:10–8:30 A.M.
RMS *Carpathia*, commanded by Captain Rostron, picks up the survivors

APRIL 18, 1912
RMS *Carpathia* docks in New York after three days of stormy weather

HENRY FORD ≈ 1863–1947

LEFT: *Henry Ford, photographed in front of a Model T in approximately 1920. From 1918, about half of all cars in the U.S. were Model Ts.*
BELOW: *A Model T dating from 1915, when the design was coming into its prime.*

THE MODEL T

Developed throughout 1907 and 1908 at the Ford Piquette Avenue plant in Detroit, the Model T Ford was launched to the world on September 27, 1908, with only 11 cars being built in the first month of production. By the time production of the Model T ceased in 1927, over 15,007,034 had been built, first at the Piquette plant and then at the Highland Park plant. The Model T was priced to make it affordable to the middle classes, while its simplicity of construction enabled Ford to introduce mass production techniques that would revolutionize the industry.

Henry Ford was neither the inventor of the motorcar nor the first industrialist to use assembly-line methods to speed up its production. However, his application of these techniques revolutionized the automobile industry, developing the techniques of mass production that would define 20th-century industry, while at the same time creating an affordable car that would do much to popularize driving, first in the United States and then throughout the world.

THE EARLY YEARS

Henry Ford was born on July 30, 1863 into a farming family near what became Dearborn, Michigan. Although he was expected to follow in his father's footsteps and become a farmer, the young Henry was fascinated by all things mechanical, leaving home aged 16 to become an apprentice machinist in Detroit. Although he returned to the family farm after three years, he resumed his vocation in 1891 as an engineer with the Edison Illuminating Company. Here, Henry started to develop his first automobiles. Leaving the

KEY DATES OF THE FORD MOTOR COMPANY

JULY 30, 1863
Birth of Henry Ford in Greenfield Township, Michigan

1891
Henry Ford becomes an engineer with the Edison Illuminating Company

JUNE 16, 1903
The Ford Motor Company founded, with investment from 12 backers

SEPTEMBER 27, 1908
First Model T Ford comes off the production line in Detroit, Michigan

1913
First moving assembly line used in automobile production

LEFT: *A poster for Ford dating from about 1920 clearly links the car with the good life and with the excitment and modernity of big cities.*
BELOW RIGHT: *United Auto Workers union members picket the Ford plant in St. Louis, Missouri, in December 1937, at the height of the conflict.*

Edison company in 1899, he established the Detroit Automobile Company the same year, and the Henry Ford Company in 1901 (later renamed the Cadillac Automobile Company), before finally founding the Ford Motor Company in 1903. Ford introduced a range of models branded A through S (though excluding D and E), but it was the introduction of the Model T Ford, the "Tin Lizzie," in 1908 that was to transform the company and the industry through its pioneering design and construction techniques.

THE ASSEMBLY LINE

Those techniques took a while to introduce, and the first Model Ts were built in a traditional handmade fashion at the Ford Piquette Avenue plant in Detroit. After this, production was moved to a purpose-built factory at Highland Park. It was at this facility that the first moving automobile assembly line was introduced in 1913, with workers only focusing on one stage of the process before the vehicle moved down the production line to the next stage. This new way of operating led to the construction time of a Model T Ford dropping from 12 hours and 30 minutes before the line was introduced to just 93 minutes by 1914.

That same year saw Ford introduce changes to his labor practices that would also help revolutionize the industry: he reduced the working day to eight hours and doubled his workers' pay to $5 a day—both reducing the high levels of staff turnover at his factory and transforming his workforce into potential customers for his cars. Although Henry was generous towards his employees, he had major issues with the labor unions, refusing to recognize the United Automobile Workers (UAW) when it formed in the 1930s. This antagonism culminated in the "Battle of the Overpass" in 1937 between Ford employees and union representatives. Ford was finally compelled to recognize the UAW in 1941 following a long strike.

By this point the Ford Motor Company had moved to the River Rouge complex, where the raw materials were processed, parts manufactured, and cars assembled, all on the same site. Although production of the Model T ceased in 1927, the redesigned Model A proved to be a major seller, as did the later V-8s. Ford also provided huge amounts of war materiel for the United States during the Second World War, building over 8,600 B-24 Liberator bombers.

THE *DEARBORN INDEPENDENT*

From 1919 to 1927, Henry Ford ran a newspaper that would do much to taint his reputation for later generations. This paper, the *Dearborn Independent*, was founded in 1901 but had been running at a loss when acquired by Ford in 1919. Under his ownership, circulation increased to 900,000 in 1925, but not without controversy, as the paper ran a series of anti-Semitic articles, including an English-language translation of the notorious "Protocols of the Elders of Zion." Ford shut down the paper once he became involved in a court case to do with the material, and later apologized to the Jewish community, though he also accepted the Grand Cross of the German Eagle from the Nazis in 1938.

DECEMBER 2, 1927
First sale of the Model A Ford, which was available in four colors, but not black

1928
Completion of the River Rouge complex: a single site for all stages of manufacture

MAY 26, 1937
Battle of the Overpass between union organizers and Ford security staff

1941
Ford compelled to recognize the UAW, following a long strike

APRIL 7, 1947
Death of the engineer and industrialist Henry Ford, aged 83

PABLO PICASSO ~ 1881–1973

Artist and sculptor Pablo Ruiz y Picasso was a pioneer of artistic style and form, as well as one of history's most prolific artists, creating over 20,000 artistic works during his lifetime. Picasso was just 27 when he first met fellow artist Georges Braque in Paris. Together, they founded one of the most influential artistic movements of the 20th century.

The human figure, together with letters, musical instruments, bottles and pitchers, and still-life studies, remained some of the most popular subjects for Cubist painting—as this style was known—as it evolved. Cubism rejected traditional techniques of perspective, refuting the notion of art as a reflection of nature in favor of presenting a new vision of reality. The traditionally imitative use of color in art was abandoned in favor of monochromatic tans, mauves, grays, greens, and browns, focusing the viewer's attention on the artists' primary preoccupation: the deconstruction of form.

Some critics described Cubist canvases as "a field of broken glass." Picasso and Braque reinvented the concept of space and perspective, representing objects not as they are perceived by the retina, but as they might exist within the mind's eye. The objects of their art were recreated in a series of angular shapes, concave and convex, representing several facets of a given object in order to create a new artistic "whole."

TOWARDS CUBISM

Picasso's "protocubist" period began in the summer of 1906, influenced by Greek, Iberian, and African art. His key work of the period, *Les Demoiselles d'Avignon*, was hailed by some as the first example of 20th-century art. For many critics at the time, however, the work's reduction of the female form to a series of harsh, angular shapes was much too radical for them fully to appreciate.

ABOVE: *Picasso preparing for a summer exhibition of his work in Vallauris, France, photographed on March 25, 1953.*
RIGHT: *The French artist Georges Braque.*

THE INFLUENCE OF CEZANNE

Georges Braque's 1908 painting *Houses at L'Estaque* was the first work to which the term "cubist" was applied, and Picasso and Braque's earliest Cubist work was deeply inspired by Paul Cézanne's landscapes, in which color was used to render perspective. The earliest phase of Cubist art, from 1908 to 1910, is referred to as Analytical Cubism. The artists were preoccupied with the analysis of form, and significant works of this period include Picasso's *Girl with a Mandolin* and *Portrait of Ambroise Vollard*.

GEORGES BRAQUE
(1882–1963)

Co-founder of the Cubist movement, Georges Braque studied art at the Paris Académie Humbert and École des Beaux-Arts under Leon Bonnat, executing his early works (1903–05) in an Impressionist style. Influenced by Matisse and Derain, he went through a Fauve period before discovering Cézanne in 1907. He met Picasso at the same time, and the two artists worked together over the years that followed to invent Analytical Cubism. The term Cubism itself was first used by art critic Louis Vauxcelles in a derisive description of one of Braque's works, which he said was "full of little cubes." Braque's best-known works include *Woman with a Guitar* and *Violin and Candlestick.*

KEY DATES IN THE LIFE OF PABLO PICASSO

OCTOBER 25, 1881
Pablo Ruiz y Picasso is born in Malaga, Spain to Don José Ruiz y Blasco and his wife, Maria Picasso y Lopez

MAY 13, 1882
Georges Braque is born in Argenteuil, France, the son of a painter and decorator

1906
Picasso executes works in the "protocubist" style, notably *Portrait of Gertude Stein*

1908
Georges Braque paints *Houses at L'Estaque*, the first work to be described as "cubist"

1908–11
Analytical Cubism is the first stage in the Cubist period and focuses on analysing the form of the motifs

The influence of Cubism on 20th-century art, sculpture, and architecture was profound, informing the work of artists such as Juan Gris and Marcel Duchamp, as well as Alexander Archipenko, Raymond Duchamp-Villon, and the architect Le Corbusier. In 1971, Picasso became just the second living artist (the first being Georges Braque) to have his work shown at the Paris Louvre, in an exhibition honoring his 90th birthday.

LEFT: *Picasso's seminal work* Guernica, *emblem of the Spanish Civil War in all its brutality.*

BELOW: Les Demoiselles d'Avignon *(1907), an example of Picasso's protocubist painting.*

GUERNICA

Perhaps Picasso's most famous work, the painting *Guernica* now hangs in Madrid's Reina Sofia Museum. Depicting the bombing of the town of Guernica in the Basque Country on April 26, 1937, the vast 11 foot 6 inch x 25 foot 6 inch painting in blue, black, and white is regarded today as an anti-war symbol and emblem of peace. When asked about the symbolism within his work, however, the artist insisted, "this bull is a bull and this horse is a horse ... If you give a meaning to certain things in my paintings it may be very true, but it is not my idea to give this meaning."

From around 1912, the artists' work evolved into Synthetic Cubism, with its focus on the synthesis of different forms and surfaces. Objects, including unpainted newspapers and tobacco wrappers, were pasted onto partially painted canvases, posing questions as to what is real and what is illusion in art. Picasso's first collage to be created in this style was *Still Life with Chair Caning*. He continued to practice Cubist painting throughout his career, often simultaneously alongside experimentation in other styles, including Realism, Surrealism, and his "Ingresesque" style influenced by the French neoclassical artist.

1912
The development of Synthetic Cubism in which the artist combines traditional painting techniques with different textures

1915
Picasso paints the Synthetic Cubist work *Harlequin*

JUNE 1937
Picasso completes perhaps his most famous work, *Guernica*

1971
Picasso's work exhibited at the Louvre, Paris, in honor of the artist's 90th birthday

APRIL 8, 1973
Death of the artist and sculptor Pablo Ruiz y Picasso in the South of France

THE FIRST WORLD WAR ≈ 1914–18

The First World War was the first truly global war. It is also known as "The Great War," a testament to its vast scale—involving most of the world's great powers—and its huge cost, and a recognition that it was the largest armed conflict the world had seen at that time. The assassination on June 28, 1914 of Archduke Ferdinand, the heir to the Austro-Hungarian throne, in the Bosnian town of Sarajevo, is seen as the trigger that started the war.

ALLIANCES

The European powers had built a complex web of alliances and pacts over the previous decades in preparation for conflict, and the assassination precipitated a series of military mobilizations, as countries aligned in support of Austro-Hungary and Serbia. The Allied Powers (France, Britain, and Russia) supported Serbia, and the Central Powers, including Germany, declared support for Austro-Hungary.

The Germans hoped to knock France out of the war early, but their offensive faltered at the Battle of the Marne in France in September, and for the remainder of the war the opposing armies

ABOVE: *A pilot being strapped into a German Fokker triplane DR1 before take-off, winter 1917–18.*

ABOVE RIGHT: *Lord Horatio Herbert Kitchener on a British recruiting poster of 1914. This was to inspire the well-known "I Want You for the U.S. Army" poster of 1918.*

RIGHT: *A British Mark IV tank on the Amiens Road in northern France on August 10, 1918.*

THE TANK

One new invention designed to break through the trench systems that dominated the Western Front was the tank, a "landship" that could resist the machine-gun fire, which was so deadly to exposed infantry, and cross no man's land intact. Introduced at the Battle of the Somme in 1916, these new weapons proved their worth at the Battle of Cambrai in 1917. They saw widespread use in the battles of the summer and autumn of 1918, though they remained mechanically unreliable and both difficult and dangerous to operate throughout the war.

KEY DATES OF WORLD WAR I

JUNE 28, 1914
Archduke Franz Ferdinand is assassinated in Sarajevo, Bosnia, an event generally seen as setting in motion the build-up to the war

AUGUST 3, 1914
Germany declares war on France, which mobilized two days earlier

AUGUST 4, 1914
Germany invades Belgium, and Britain declares war on Germany in response

APRIL 2, 1915
Second Battle of Ypres, where German forces use poison gas on a large scale for the first time

APRIL–AUGUST 1915
British troops attack Gallipoli. The campaign ends in failure

LEFT: *French soldiers wait in the grim conditions of the trenches on the Western Front, ca 1916.*

BOTTOM: *An oil painting by John Singer Sargent (1856–1925) of soldiers blinded by gas in World War I.*

on the Western Front faced each other from fortified trench lines. A vast increase in fire-power—including the introduction of the machine-gun—meant armies could not rely on maneuver to defeat an enemy. Huge offensives such as the Battles of the Somme and Verdun in 1916 cost hundreds of thousands of lives, but gained at most a few square miles of land for the attackers.

TANKS & PLANES

To try and break the stalemate, new technology was developed, such as the tank. Flight technology was still in its infancy, so airplanes were used mostly for reconnaissance, though some small-scale bombing and strafing was attempted.

As the Western Front settled into a stalemate in 1915–16, the Germans concentrated much of their offensive effort against Russia in the east. The British tried to relieve the Russians by attacking the Ottoman Empire (one of Germany's allies) through the Gallipoli Peninsula. The campaign deployed soldiers from Australia and New Zealand, but failed to achieve its initial objectives and ended in an evacuation.

German unrestricted submarine warfare—which involved attacking merchant and civilian vessels of countries that were not actually engaged in the war—provoked the United States to enter the conflict on the Allied side in 1917. The Germans decided to launch a major attack to bring the war to a close in early 1918. This "Spring Offensive" made large territorial gains, but it overstretched the German army and a massive Allied counter-offensive followed, which forced Germany to seek an armistice in November 1918.

The cost of the First World War was appallingly high, with nearly ten million dead. Furthermore, the League of Nations and the Treaty of Versailles (1919) that ended the First World War contained the seeds of a new conflict.

GENERAL DOUGLAS HAIG (1861–1928)

General Haig was the senior commander of British forces from 1915. He was (and remains) a controversial figure. Many junior officers accused him of throwing away soldiers' lives unnecessarily in costly attacks, and they claimed that he failed to understand the true nature of trench warfare. These accusations stuck, leading to Haig being nicknamed "The Butcher of the Somme." Today, historians are divided, with some defending him as effectively using a strategy of attrition to wear down the German army to the point of surrender.

JULY 1–NOVEMBER 18, 1916
Battle of the Somme, France, one of the most controversial battles of the war, which resulted in over 350,000 British casualties

APRIL 6, 1917
U.S. declares war on Germany, ending a long period of isolationism in international affairs

DECEMBER 1917
Treaty of Brest-Litovsk is signed, marking Russia's exit from the war

NOVEMBER 9, 1918
German Kaiser abdicates and flees to the Netherlands

NOVEMBER 11, 1918
Armistice with Germany is signed. A ceasefire comes into effect at 11 a.m. on November 11, 1918, "the eleventh hour of the eleventh day of the eleventh month"

THE RUSSIAN REVOLUTION ~ 1917

The roots of Russia's 1917 revolution lie in the reign of Tsar Nicholas II (1894–1917), who had become increasingly unpopular as the years went on. One particular event stands out: the January 22, 1905 massacre of unarmed protesters in the then capital, St. Petersburg.

BELOW LEFT: The Storming of the Winter Palace in Petrograd (St. Petersburg), *October 1917 (by the Russian calendar), a painting by Gemälde von Surikow.*
BELOW: *Tsar Nicholas II at Tsarskoye Selo with his family. Left to right: an army officer (partly visible); the tsar; his daughters Grand Duchesses Tatiana, Olga, Marie, and Anastasia; his sons Tsarevitch Alexei and Prince Vasily. Behind are his nephews, Nikita, Rostislav, and Dimitry.*

TSAR NICHOLAS II
(1868–1918)

Tsar Nicholas II was the last of the Russian tsars, and a member of the House of Holstein-Gottorp-Romanov. He ruled from May 26, 1894 to March 15, 1917, when he was deposed in the "February Revolution." He is best remembered today for his acts of brutal repression against his people and the disastrous state of Russia after it entered World War I. After he abdicated in 1917, he was taken, along with his family and servants, to Ipatiev House in Yekaterinburg, where they were all executed by Bolsheviks on July 16, 1918.

This event became known as "Bloody Sunday," and triggered a wave of discontent, including widespread strikes and violence, across Russia and its empire. The protesters had been marching to present a petition of grievances to the tsar, and their brutal treatment at the hands of the Imperial Guard turned much of the population against Nicholas's rule, fatally undermining his authority.

ECONOMIC PROBLEMS

By 1917, Russia was losing its part of World War I against Germany, due to inadequate communication networks and a lack of industrial resources. The war also led to soaring unemployment and inflation, and dwindling supplies of food. In Petrograd (formerly St. Petersburg) the situation was particularly dire, and things came to a head when 200,000 workers went on strike and demanded a redistribution of land. The military garrison refused to quell the uprising, and on February 28 Tsar Nicholas II abdicated, ending the line of tsars that had ruled Russia for centuries. His replacement was the Provisional Government, composed of a mixture of liberals and moderate socialists. In opposition to this, several soviets (or workers' councils) were formed, acting as rival centers of power, particularly in Petrograd.

Despite the change in government, Russia continued to suffer; it carried on losing the war

KEY DATES OF THE RUSSIAN REVOLUTION AND SURROUNDING ERA

JANUARY 22, 1905
"Bloody Sunday"—tsarist troops open fire on a peaceful demonstration of workers in St. Petersburg

1914
Russia enters into World War I. It achieves little military success before it makes peace with Germany in 1918

MARCH 15, 1917
Tsar Nicholas II abdicates his position as head of state, and is replaced by the Provisional Government

JULY 21, 1917
Alexander Kerensky becomes head of the Provisional Government

NOVEMBER 7, 1917
Bolsheviks storm the Winter Palace in Petrograd and arrest some members of the Provisional Government

against Germany and food remained scarce. Several newly released political prisoners incited yet greater unrest, and the Provisional Government was widely seen as ineffective. In response, it tried to crackdown on troublemakers, further alienating the workers.

VLADIMIR LENIN

A key figure who emerged during this time was Vladimir Lenin, leader of the Bolshevik faction among the Communists. He garnered great popular support for ending the war and redistributing wealth. Alexander Kerensky, who had become head of the Provisional Government on July 21, 1917, was acting in an increasingly dictatorial manner. The Bolsheviks opposed him and, on November 7 (October 24 according to the unreformed Julian calendar then in use in Russia), their supporters stormed the Winter Palace in Petrograd, where the Provisional Government was based, and arrested several ministers. The next day, at the Second Congress of Soviets, Lenin orchestrated proceedings to award his Bolsheviks a majority of seats in the government. The "bloodless coup" of October 1917 was directly organized by Lenin, and was a carefully planned operation.

Dissent soon burgeoned against the new regime, and in response the Bolsheviks banned non-Bolsheviks from joining soviets and dissolved the Constituent Assembly. This was followed by the Russian Civil War, a struggle between the Bolshevik Red Army and a loose coalition of their opponents, known as the "Whites." This latter group had backing from France, Great Britain, Japan, and the United States, who were keen to suppress the socialist state emerging in Russia. The war ended in 1923 with victory for the Reds, while the previous year had seen the establishment of the Union of Soviet Socialist Republics (U.S.S.R.).

RIGHT: *A 1917 poster calling all women workers and peasants to vote with the men and annihilate the bourgeoisie.*

BELOW RIGHT: *Lenin addresses a May Day gathering in Mocow's Red Square, 1918. May 1, International Workers' Day, became an occasion for vast Soviet military parades.*

VLADIMIR LENIN
(1870–1924)

Vladimir Ilyich Lenin is the man most responsible for the October Revolution and the eventual establishment of the U.S.S.R. His ideas about Marxist socialism (known as Marxism-Leninism) became the basis for Russian Communism, and he was revered as a hero by the Communist cause. A powerful orator, Lenin successfully encouraged people to revolt against the Provincial Government through his fiery speeches and by appealing to people's needs. He was responsible for the consolidation of Bolshevik power during the Russian Civil War and for instigating the creation of a socialist economic system. Joseph Stalin succeeded him as General Secretary of the Communist Party of the Soviet Union in 1922.

NOVEMBER 10, 1917
All ranks and titles are abolished; many Russian nobles then flee to Europe

JULY 16, 1918
Tsar Nicholas II, his family, and servants are executed at Yekaterinburg in the Ural Mountains

DECEMBER 30, 1922
The Treaty on the Creation of the U.S.S.R. is ratified, formally establishing the U.S.S.R. as a new nation

1923
The Reds win the Russian Civil War, consolidating Bolshevik power throughout the U.S.S.R.

JANUARY 21, 1924
Lenin, the man most responsible for the October Revolution, dies

WOMEN'S SUFFRAGE ⁓ 1848–1984

The word suffrage simply means "the right to vote," a right that women were denied, even in the 19th century as suffrage was extended to men of modest economic means. The campaign to secure that right for women in the United States began, in a modest way, in 1829 with a book entitled *Course of Popular Lectures* by Fanny Wright. The book was extremely controversial and largely dismissed, as Wright also advocated the end of slavery.

PROVOCATION

In 1840, Lucretia Mott and Elizabeth Cady Stanton traveled to London, England to attend the World Anti-Slavery Convention, only to find that females were prohibited from speaking at the meeting. Outraged, Mott and Stanton returned home to America and organized a women's rights convention at Seneca Falls, New York in 1848, which passed a resolution stating that "the duty of the women of this country is to secure to themselves the sacred right of the elective franchise." The movement made little progress until Susan B. Anthony joined forces with Stanton in 1869 to form the National Woman Suffrage Association. The N.W.S.A. had its first victory the same year when the territory of Wyoming gave women the vote.

In 1890 the N.W.S.A. merged with a rival group, the American Women Suffrage Association, to form the National American Women Suffrage Association. Their efforts began to succeed and by 1914, 11 states had allowed women the right to vote. President Woodrow Wilson argued that granting women the right to vote was needed as a "war measure" but two efforts in 1918–19 to pass legislation in Congress both failed. Eventually, when Tennessee became the 33rd state to succumb to the suffrage movement, the measure gained enough support to pass both houses of Congress. On August 26, 1920, the Nineteenth Amendment to the U.S. Constitution became law and all American women were granted the right to vote.

SUSAN B. ANTHONY (1820–1906)

Susan B. Anthony was born on February 15, 1820 near Adams, Massachusetts. She was raised as a Quaker and taught at a Quaker school, eventually becoming its headmistress. In her late twenties, Anthony became involved in abolitionism (the effort to end slavery), which led to a meeting with Elizabeth Cady Stanton. The two women were lifelong proponents of the women's suffrage movement. Anthony is the only woman ever to be depicted on the currency of the United States: the Susan B. Anthony dollar coin was first minted in Philadelphia and Denver in 1979. Anthony died on March 13, 1906, 14 years before the ratification of the Nineteenth Amendment that saw American women win the right to vote.

SUFFRAGETTES

In Britain, the philosopher John Stuart Mill introduced a petition in Parliament seeking the right to vote for women in the Reform Act of 1867, and the same year, Lydia Becker established the first Women's Suffrage Committee in Manchester, England. In 1903, Emmeline Pankhurst, along with her daughters Christabel and Sylvia, founded the Women's Social and Political Union. This was a more militant group, whose members were frequently arrested and who were the first to be called "suffragettes." In 1918, their campaign finally proved successful when women over the age of 30 were granted the right to vote. In 1928 women over 21 were enfranchised, giving them the same voting rights as men.

Many European countries also began to allow women the vote, with Finland granting female suffrage in 1906, Norway in 1913, and Denmark in 1915. The U.S.S.R. followed in 1917. Austria and Poland passed suffrage reform laws in 1918, followed by Sweden, Germany, Luxembourg and the Netherlands the next year. Spain gave women the vote in 1931. France extended the ballot to women in 1944, with Italy, Romania, and Yugoslavia waiting until 1946, and Belgium following suit two years later. Switzerland did not fully enfranchise its women until 1971, and Lichtenstein in 1984.

ABOVE: *A 19th-century engraving of Frances (Fanny) Wright (1795–1852), Scottish-born U.S. feminist and social reformer.*
BELOW: *A 1979 U.S. dollar coin features activist for women's rights Susan B. Anthony.*

KEY DATES IN THE WOMEN'S SUFFRAGE MOVEMENT

1829 Fanny Wright's *Course of Popular Lectures* published in the U.S.

1840 Foundation of women's rights convention in U.S. by Mott and Stanton

1867 John Stuart Mill raises issue of women's suffrage in British Parliament. Women's Suffrage Committee formed in Britain

1869 National Woman Suffrage Association founded in U.S.

1890 Wyoming becomes the first U.S. state to allow women the vote

See a poster used by Suffragettes in Envelope IV

EMMELINE PANKHURST

(1858–1928)

Emmeline ("Emily") Pankhurst was born on July 15, 1858 in Manchester, England. In 1889, Pankhurst formed the Women's Franchise League, which sought to allow married women the right to vote in local elections. Like many suffragettes, Pankhurst was arrested frequently over the years and often went on hunger strikes to bring publicity to the suffrage cause. This provoked the government to pass the "Cat and Mouse Act" of 1913 which allowed the release of prisoners on hunger strike until they had regained their strength, at which time they would be arrested again. Emmeline Pankhurst died on June 14, 1928, shortly after equal voting rights for men and women were established in Britain.

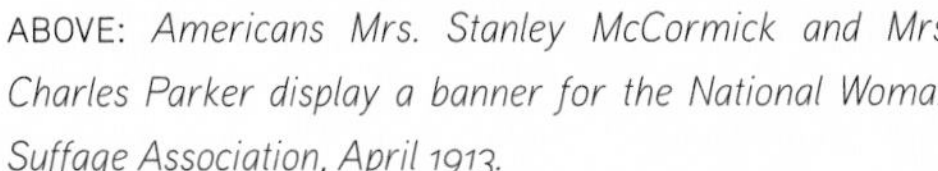

ABOVE: *Americans Mrs. Stanley McCormick and Mrs. Charles Parker display a banner for the National Woman Suffage Association, April 1913.*

ABOVE RIGHT: *British suffragette Emmeline Pankhurst is arrested and bodily removed from a demonstration in June 1914.*

1897
National Union of Women's Suffrage Societies formed in Britain

1913
"Cat and Mouse Act" passed in Britain, allowing the release and rearrest of prisoners who go on hunger strike

1918
Representation of the People Act grants full suffrage in Britain to women over 30

1920
The Nineteenth Amendment guarantees women's suffrage in the United States

1928
Voting age for women in Britain lowered to 21, in line with the voting age for men

HOLLYWOOD SPEAKS ~ 1923

If the introduction of the first motion pictures during the last years of the 19th century transformed the world of popular entertainment, the integration of sound and motion pictures in the 1920s revolutionized the film industry, helping to make Hollywood the entertainment capital of the world.

NEW TECHNOLOGY

The silent film, with no synchronized recorded sound to accompany it, relied on exaggerated facial expressions, gestures, and title cards to help tell the story. These limitations failed to reduce the explosion of interest in motion pictures during the first decades of the 20th century, and by the early 1920s the Hollywood-based film industry had become a dominant cultural force. Some silent films, such as *The Birth of a Nation* (1915), *Ben Hur* (1925), or Charlie Chaplin's *The Gold Rush* (1925), remain amongst the most successful and highly acclaimed films of all time. However, technicians had been working on the problems facing the use of synchronized sound, and by 1920 it was clear that the era of the silent film would soon be over.

The first experiments with sound film were carried out in the 1890s—William Dickson's *Experimental Sound Film* (1894) suggested the way forward, harnessing the Kinetoscope projection system developed by Dickson and Thomas Edison. The problem lay in finding a way to synchronize the sound recording with the film, as Dickson's little 17-second film relied on a separate wax-cylinder sound recording which lasted six times as long. There was no attempt to combine sound and moving image onto one integrated film, and the quality of both was also too poor to allow them to be commercially viable.

SOUND ON DISC

By the First World War, developments in sound-on-disc technology permitted the integration of gramophone recordings with silent films, but these remained separate entities, even though they were designed to be played together. The secret of synchronization clearly lay in developing a reliable sound-on-film system. In 1926, Warner Brothers screened *Don Juan*, the first film to use synchronized sound, which relied on a sound-on-disc system. At that time the sound-on-disc quality was better than sound on film, but technical and timing problems meant that the latter system was preferable. By late 1927, improvements in sound-on-film recording and amplification rendered sound on disc obsolete.

LEFT: *Charlie Chaplin in a still from the classic silent movie* The Gold Rush *(1925), which he not only starred in but also wrote and directed.*

DEVELOPMENTS

In 1902, Léon Gaumont patented the Chronophone, which showed promise but still lacked both the quality and reliability needed to make the device a commercial success. Four years later, another Frenchman, Eugène Lauste, patented a sound-on-film system based on celluloid film, but technical problems halted any further development. In the end, two rival

KEY DATES IN THE HISTORY OF FILM SOUND DEVELOPMENT

1894
William Dickson produces the first film to include a sound accompaniment

1895
American inventor Thomas Edison pioneers his Kinetoscope projection system

1902
French inventor Léon Gaumont introduces the Chronophone, an early sound-on-disc system

1907
French inventor Eugène Lauste develops one of the first sound-on-film systems

1919
Lee De Forest develops a workable sound-on-film system

systems emerged. In 1919, the American inventor Lee De Forest produced a reliable method of combining pictures and sound onto one film strip, and, together with Theodore Case, he then worked on improving the reliability of his system. Simultaneously, the Polish immigrant Joseph Tykociński-Tykociner developed a similar system, but he lacked the financial backing of De Forest, and so it was the latter's system that made sound on film a reality. In April 1923, he demonstrated his new system in New York's Rivoli Theater.

Over the next few years, the De Forest system was adopted by the Hollywood film studios, which collectively recognized its incredible potential. In February 1927, the leading Hollywood film companies elected to fully back sound-on-film technology and abandoned silent or sound-on-disc film. While this change created a revolution in Hollywood, *The Jazz Singer*, released in October, demonstrated to cinema audiences the full potential of the new technology. The brief era of the silent movie had come to an end, and a new golden age of sound film-making had begun.

ABOVE LEFT: *Thomas Edison (1847–1931), the American scientist whose inventions paved the way for the possibilty of sound in film. A photograph taken ca 1922.*

BELOW: *Edison's Kinetoscope, pioneered in 1895.*

THE JAZZ SINGER (1927)

This musical film starring Al Jolson was the first feature-length motion picture to use synchronized dialog and moving film, using the proven Vitaphone sound-on-disc system. The 90-minute film was essentially a musical medley—Jolson sang six songs, including "Toot Toot Tootsie." There was also dialog, the first spoken words being Jolson's catch phrase "You ain't heard nothin' yet." The story centered around a young Jewish musician who defied tradition in order to follow a musical career, and the film proved an overnight box-office success, thereby demonstrating the huge commercial power of the motion picture.

RIGHT: *A poster for* The Jazz Singer, *the first movie to make the most of sound—for music as well as speech.*

1923
First screening of a commercial moving motion picture using synchronized sound

1926
Warner Brothers release *Don Juan*, the first commercial synchronized-sound film

1927
The major Hollywood studios agree to adopt sound motion-picture technology

1927
The Jazz Singer premiers, and becomes a major box-office success

2010
Avatar, directed by James Cameron, breaks all box-office records

THE GREAT DEPRESSION ~ 1929–40s

What became known as the Great Depression was a period of worldwide economic decline precipitated by the Wall Street Crash of 1929. This American stock market crash sent share prices spiraling downwards after a decade of economic strength during which stocks had become grossly overvalued. The collapse in the stocks' prices had severe consequences for economies across the globe, as American companies called in loans from abroad, prompting a collapse in international lending. This in turn led to a decade of high unemployment and poverty, as international trade, commodity prices, and industrial output all fell sharply, leaving many people out of work and with little hope of finding employment.

EFFECTS

The price of wheat, which had been artificially subsidized by the United States government, plummeted to 60 cents a bushel, causing enormous hardships to farmers and agricultural laborers.

ABOVE: *The tiny, somber but neat huts of a "Hooverville" shanty town on the edge of Seattle, photographed in July 1934.*
BELOW: *Traders crowd the sidewalks in panic outside the New York Stock Exchange after the financial crash in 1929.*

HOOVERVILLES

One of the most visible effects of the Great Depression in the United States was the rise of "Hoovervilles"—shanty towns on the outskirts of settlements, named after the unpopular President Hoover, whom many blamed for the Depression. They were mostly occupied by homeless people or displaced migrant workers. They were often set up close to potential sources of work, or around charitable services such as soup kitchens. Conditions in the makeshift camps were typically poor and unsanitary, and local authorities did not officially tolerate them. Often, however, they were accepted as a necessary consequence of the economic circumstances afflicting the nation, and as a way of containing "undesirable" elements of the population.

KEY DATES OF THE GREAT DEPRESSION

OCTOBER 24, 1929
Wall Street Crash begins, marking the end of over a decade of economic prosperity

1931
Food riots occur in various regions of the United States

1932
American GNP has fallen 31 percent, and over 13 million Americans have lost their jobs since 1929

JANUARY 30, 1933
Adolf Hitler, leader of the National Socialist German Workers' Party, becomes chancellor of Germany

MARCH 4, 1933
Franklin Delano Roosevelt becomes President of the United States, promising a "New Deal" for the American people

See the front page of Variety newspaper in Envelope IV

THE JARROW MARCH

The industrial northeast of England was particularly badly affected by the Great Depression, including the town of Jarrow in Yorkshire, where many worked in the shipyards and coal mines. In October 1936, unemployed workers organized a march to London to draw attention to their plight. They walked the entire distance of 300 miles, and were given food and even shelter along the way by people sympathetic to their situation. When they arrived in London, a month after setting out, little attention was paid to their complaints by the government, and they were sent home. Nevertheless, the march remains an iconic symbol of the Depression.

In Britain, the effects of the Depression were not spread equally: there were specific areas of the country particularly hard hit. In the coal-mining areas of south Wales and the northeast, where industries relied upon industrial demand, unemployment soared and many were left in desperate poverty. Elsewhere, however, particularly in the south and southeast, economic conditions were not so badly affected. In fact, the late 1930s were a time of relative prosperity there, as a house-building boom and new industries stimulated the economy. Mass production of consumer goods led to an increased standard of living for many.

Agricultural communities were also badly affected by the weakened economy, as reduced demand meant that their products fetched much lower prices on the open market. Although poverty was less visible and concentrated than it was in urban areas, many rural families were badly affected. In the United States, the problem was confounded by a series of dust storms that afflicted much of the center of the country. Farmland became useless, and hundreds of thousands of people became migrants in an attempt to find work. They were known as "Okies," as many of them came from the state of Oklahoma, and they became a symbol of the Depression era in the United States.

ABOVE: *Escorted by a policeman, protesters on the Jarrow March, or Jarrow Crusade, brave a rainy English October.*
BELOW: *A poor migrant family living in a trailer in Amarillo, Texas, in 1940. Simply parked in a field, they have no sanitation or running water.*

Europe was just as badly affected. In Germany, the Weimar Republic was reliant on American loans to sustain its economic development, and when they began to be recalled after the Wall Street Crash, the German economy spiraled into decline. In 1932, its unemployment rate approached 30 percent. The desperate economic conditions in Germany led to an increase in support for extremist political parties, as people became more desperate for solutions, and Hitler's National Socialist (Nazi) Party came to power in January 1933.

ACTION

As a means of resolving the economic crisis afflicting their countries, many national governments initiated a system of public-works programs to stimulate economic demand and alleviate unemployment along principles advocated by the British economist John Maynard Keynes. In the United States, the Roosevelt administration invested heavily in public infrastructure projects, and many of the country's most iconic landmarks—such as the Hoover Dam and Golden Gate Bridge—were constructed as part of these programs. Ultimately, while the measures did help millions, the global economy only began to recover robustly during the Second World War, as industrial production soared to meet the need for armaments and munitions.

1935
The U.S. government creates the Works Progress Administration (WPA), which employs millions of people as unskilled labor on public-works projects

OCTOBER 1936
The Jarrow March begins in Britain, as hundreds of unemployed men walk from Jarrow to London, drawing attention to poverty in the industrial north of England

MAY 27, 1937
The Golden Gate Bridge is opened across the Golden Gate Bay in California

1939
John Steinbeck's Pulitzer Prize-winning novel, *The Grapes of Wrath,* is published

SEPTEMBER 1939
World War II breaks out in Europe when Germany invades Poland

ALBERT EINSTEIN ⁓ 1879–1955

Albert Einstein was born in Ulm, Germany, on March 14, 1879. As a child, he displayed signs of a patient and inquiring mind, often building models and mechanical devices for amusement. At the age of five he was intrigued by the way a compass needle would always point north, a sign of an early fascination with physics and the way the world worked, and as a teenager, he displayed brilliance in both mathematics and physics. When the family business failed in 1894, the Einsteins decided to move to Milan in Italy.

BELOW LEFT: *Albert Einstein in later years. Perhaps more than any other academic, this quintessential genius emanates consideration and intelligence, along with a hint of the classically eccentric professor.*

BELOW: *A detail of Einstein's "Manuscript on the Special Theory of Relativity," written in Zurich and Prague in 1912.*

THE THEORIES OF RELATIVITY AND QUANTUM MECHANICS

Einstein's theories of relativity were contradicted by the theory of quantum mechanics. This examined the universe on the smallest of scales, that of sub-atomic particles, rather than the huge distances considered by the theories of relativity. Indeed, quantum mechanics directly opposes relativity by holding that objects do not exist in one place at one time, but can in fact exist in several places simultaneously. The leading proponent of this theory was Niels Bohr, and he and Einstein were to clash several times. Einstein famously rejected quantum mechanics by writing: "I, at any rate, am convinced that He [God] does not throw dice."

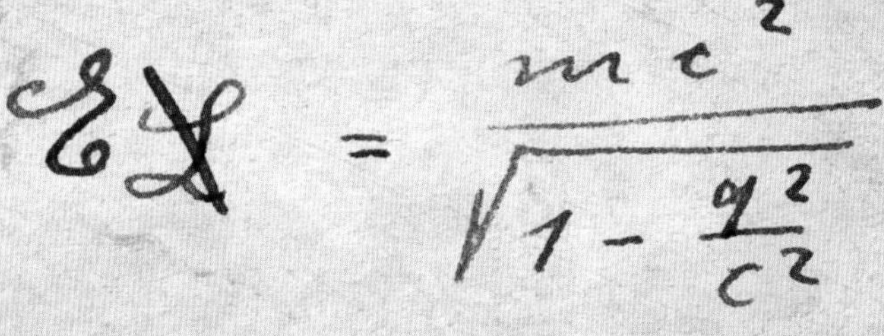

SWITZERLAND

Einstein soon transferred to Aarau in Switzerland to finish secondary school, where he renounced his German citizenship in order to avoid military service. He returned in 1896 to the Swiss Federal Institute of Technology, where he graduated in 1900 as a secondary-school teacher of mathematics and physics. Unfortunately, he found it difficult to find a job and eventually ended up working in the Swiss patent office in Bern. It was while he was employed there (from 1902 to 1909) that Einstein developed much of his scientific thinking, and he published a large amount on theoretical physics. Eventually, his efforts led to him obtaining a doctorate from the University of Zurich, and in 1909 he received an appointment there as associate professor of Physics.

THE THEORIES OF RELATIVITY

In the world of science, Einstein is best known for his ground-breaking theories of Special Relativity and of General Relativity. In 1905, he published a paper introducing the idea that the speed of light in a vacuum is constant. It was through his work on Special Relativity that Einstein deduced the equation

KEY DATES IN THE LIFE OF ALBERT EINSTEIN

MARCH 14, 1879
Albert Einstein is born in the German town of Ulm

1905
Einstein's Special Theory of Relativity is published

1912
The Einsteins move to Zurich, where Albert is given a position as professor of Theoretical Physics

1915
Einstein completes the General Theory of Relativity

1922
Einstein is awarded the Nobel Prize in Physics for 1921

$E=MC^2$. This equation suggested that minute amounts of mass could be converted into enormous amounts of energy, a discovery that would have profound consequences in later years when these principles formed the basis of the research into nuclear weapons.

The theory of General Relativity (1915) introduced the idea that space and time are inherently related, and that objects of sufficient mass exert influence upon this "spacetime," causing it to bend. Objects of an enormously massive nature can become "black holes"—regions of space where the "spacetime continuum" is distorted so strongly that nothing can escape, not even light.

In 1933, Einstein moved to the United States, partly to escape Nazi persecution for being Jewish. During his long life, he became extremely famous in his adopted country, having already been recognized internationally by the award of the 1921 Nobel Prize in Physics. He died on the morning of April 18, 1955, from internal bleeding caused by an aortic aneurism. In his lifetime, Einstein published over 300 scientific and 150 non-scientific works, and he is seen today as one of the most well-known and iconic figures of the 20th century. He is also regarded as one of the most intelligent men of recent times, so much so that the name "Einstein" has become a synonym for genius. In 1999, Albert Einstein was named "Person of the Century" by *Time* magazine.

ABOVE: *An illustration of Einstein's thought experiment on light and its relative speed from moving objects.*
RIGHT: *The house in Princeton, New Jersey, where Einstein lived after emigrating from Europe.*

POLITICAL VIEWS

Einstein's thinking was not confined to science, and he wrote much about the political state of the world as he saw it. A German by birth, Einstein witnessed the rise of Fascism in his native country and he remained a staunch opponent of extremism throughout his life. Although his scientific research led eventually to the development of nuclear weapons, Einstein opposed their use in 1945 and wrote, "I do not know how the Third World War will be fought, but I can tell you what they will use in the Fourth—rocks!"

1933
Einstein emigrates to the United States

1939
World War II breaks out. Einstein writes a letter to President Roosevelt warning of the possibility of Germany building an atomic bomb, and urging the U.S. to begin nuclear research

1940
Einstein becomes a U.S. citizen, but also retains his Swiss citizenship

APRIL 18, 1955
Einstein dies of an aortic aneurism, still working until his final hours

1999
Albert Einstein is named "Person of the Century" by *Time* magazine

THE SECOND WORLD WAR ≈ 1939–45

World War II was the largest conflict the world has ever seen, involving some 40 million combatants and causing more than 55 million deaths. Bitterness in Germany at the restrictions placed on it by the 1919 Treaty of Versailles contributed to Adolf Hitler's rise to power from 1933. His National Socialist (Nazi) regime engaged in rearmament, reoccupied the Rhineland, and then, in 1938, annexed both Austria and the German-speaking regions of Czechoslovakia.

OUTBREAK

France and the United Kingdom stood by in the face of these aggressive actions, but when the German army invaded Poland in September 1939, both countries finally declared war on Germany. The early phase of the war was dominated by "Blitzkrieg," rapid and devastating attacks by the Germans. They occupied Denmark and Norway in April 1940, and then invaded France in May, roundly defeating the French and British defenders.

THE BATTLE OF THE ATLANTIC

One of the most important campaigns of World War II was the Battle of the Atlantic, in which the German surface and submarine fleet tried to inflict catastrophic damage upon the convoys of merchant shipping transporting supplies vital to Britain's survival. Although the Germans managed to inflict heavy losses throughout the war, the British Royal Navy, and later the United States Navy as well, supported by land-based aircraft, ensured enough supplies filtered through. The ability of the Allies to read German naval signals, thanks to the breaking of the Enigma code system, also proved instrumental in the winning of the battle.

ABOVE: *A British public-information poster from World War II urging people to take care not to give away confidential information through careless talk.*

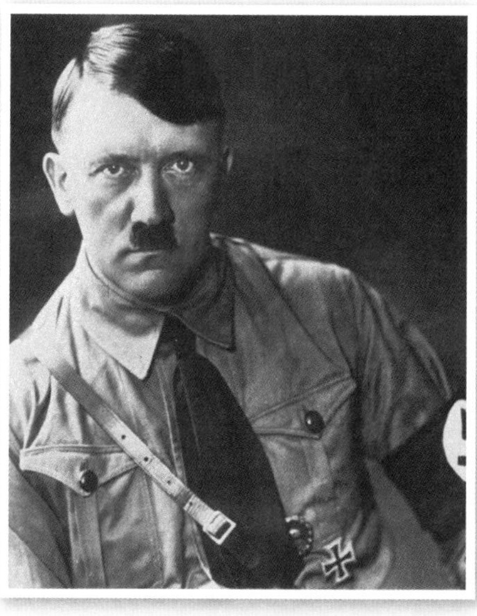

LEFT & RIGHT: *Determined foes, photographed in August–September 1939: Winston Churchill (left) when First Lord of the Admiralty in Britain, and Adolf Hitler (right), Chancellor of Germany.*

The United Kingdom was now isolated, though protected by the Channel and the British navy. The war's center of gravity switched to the Mediterranean, where an advance into Egypt by Italian forces (who had joined Germany in the "Axis" alliance in September 1940) was rapidly repulsed, leading to direct German intervention in this theater. A further Italian expedition against Greece

KEY DATES OF WORLD WAR II

SEPTEMBER 3, 1939
Great Britain and France declare war on Germany following the invasion of Poland

MAY 10, 1940
Germany invades the Low Countries and France (which surrenders on June 22)

JUNE 22, 1941
Operation "Barbarossa," German invasion of the Soviet Union

DECEMBER 7, 1941
Japanese surprise attack on Pearl Harbor, Hawaii launches the war in the Pacific

NOVEMBER 2, 1942
End of the Battle of El Alamein, the decisive battle of the Desert War

also provoked a German invasion of Greece and the Balkans in April 1941. Then Nazi Germany launched what was to become the major land campaign of World War II, when its armed forces attacked the Soviet Union in June 1941.

By late 1941, the Japanese had also resolved to instigate a war in the Pacific. They launched a surprise attack on the U.S. Pacific Fleet at Pearl Harbor, Hawaii in December, rapidly followed by assaults on British and other colonial possessions throughout Southeast Asia.

THE TURNING POINT

The entry of the United States into the war brought much-needed material aid to the United Kingdom and the Soviet Union. The turning point for the War in the Desert came with the Battle of El Alamein in November 1942, while on the Eastern Front, the German Sixth Army was cut off at Stalingrad the same month, finally surrendering in January 1943.

With the final defeat of German and Italian forces in North Africa, and the first Allied assault on Europe through the Italian mainland, the war in the east also turned. German forces were pushed back by the Soviet Red Army, and with the success of the Allied invasion of German-occupied France in June 1944, they finally buckled and the Nazi state collapsed after the Soviet capture of Berlin in May 1945.

In the Pacific, United States forces won important naval victories at the Coral Sea and Midway in mid-1942. They gradually pushed the Japanese back from their Pacific island possessions, with the Philippines being recaptured in early 1945. The cost, however, was high. A strategic bombing campaign against the Japanese mainland culminated in the dropping of the first atomic bombs in August 1945, on the cities of Hiroshima and Nagasaki, forcing the Japanese surrender and bringing World War II to an end.

LEFT: *The distinctive mushroom-shaped cloud forms over Hiroshima, Japan, after the first atomic bomb explodes on August 6, 1945.*

BELOW: *Allied forces land on Omaha Beach in Normandy, France, on June 10, 1944 to start the reconquest of Europe.*

THE ATOMIC BOMB

On August 6, 1945, the B-29 Superfortress *Enola Gay* dropped the first atomic bomb on the Japanese city of Hiroshima, killing some 90,000 people. This was the culmination of the Manhattan Project, a secret program inaugurated in autumn 1942 under the overall command of Brigadier General Leslie Groves and the scientific direction of Julius Robert Oppenheimer. The project brought together some 6,000 scientists in four major laboratories: Los Alamos, New Mexico; Oak Ridge, Tennessee; Richland, Washington; and Chalk River, Ontario. The project cost some $2 billion, and succeeded in creating a uranium weapon—"Little Boy"—that was dropped on Hiroshima, and a plutonium weapon—"Fat Man"—dropped on Nagasaki on August 9.

JULY 10, 1943
Operation "Husky," the Anglo-American invasion of Sicily

JUNE 6, 1944
D-Day: the Anglo-American invasion of occupied Europe begins on the north coast of France

MAY 8, 1945
VE (Victory in Europe) Day: the Allies formally accept the surrender of all German forces

AUGUST 6, 1945
The first atomic bomb, "Little Boy," is dropped on Hiroshima, Japan

AUGUST 15, 1945
VJ (Victory in Japan) Day: Japan accepts the terms of the Potsdam Declaration and surrenders, ending World War II

MAHATMA GANDHI ≈ 1869–1948

The man who would be revered by Indians as "the Father of the Nation" was a rarity among international political leaders—a man of peace who shunned violence and who advocated telling the truth. Born in 1869 in Porbandar in northeast India, in 1888 Gandhi traveled to London to study law. The young lawyer returned to India in 1891, but moved within two years to South Africa, which had a sizeable Indian community.

NON-VIOLENT PROTEST

There, he became a campaigner for civil rights, and in 1894 helped found the Natal Indian Conference, an organization designed to counter racial discrimination. He encouraged non-violent forms of protest, and, after seven years of lobbying against anti-Indian legislation passed in 1906, Gandhi finally secured the granting by the South African authorities of greater civil liberties to the Indian community.

Gandhi returned to India in 1915, where he became involved in the Indian National Congress (INC), a political party that was campaigning for Indian self-determination. In 1918, he incited a successful *satyagraha* (non-violent protest) against poor rural conditions and taxation in Champaran in northern India. Then, in 1919, Gandhi led a major *satyagraha* after the Amritsar Massacre, when an Indian crowd was fired on by the British, killing hundreds of people.

RIGHT: *Mohandas Karamchand Gandhi, photographed in London in 1931.*

BELOW: *Soldiers marshal some of the 5,000 people at Jallianwala Bagh in Amritsar on April 13, 1919 before the massacre that took place there.*

A MAN OF PRINCIPLE

During his career Gandhi lived by the principle of *satya* (truth), and encouraged honesty in all things. When he left for London, he promised his mother to abstain from meat, alcohol, and promiscuity. Gandhi remained a vegetarian and teetotaller all his life, and was loyal to his teenage bride, Kasturba. He favored simplicity in clothing and possessions, adopting the *khadi* as his daily attire. He embraced *brahmacharya* (spiritual and secular purity), and was a devout Hindu throughout his life. Above all, Gandhi abhorred violence, and this policy formed the basis of *satyagraha*—the tactic that shook the foundations of the British Empire. The title Mahatma means "great soul."

KEY DATES IN THE LIFE OF MAHATMA GANDHI

OCTOBER 2, 1869
Gandhi born in Porbandar. The day is now a national holiday in India

1894
Gandhi founds the Natal Indian Conference in South Africa

1915
He returns to India and joins the Indian National Congress, one of the main political parties

1918
Gandhi successfully leads the first Indian *satyagraha* in Champaran, northern India

1921
Gandhi launches his first campaign of non-cooperation with the British

In 1921, Gandhi became the leader of the INC, and promoted policies including non-cooperation with the British authorities, a boycott of non-Indian goods, and the wearing of homespun *khadi* rather than imported cloth. His objective was to encourage grassroots support for the independence movement. In March 1922, Gandhi was imprisoned for six years on a charge of sedition. He was released after just two years, by which time the INC was divided along religious grounds, leaving Gandhi the immense task of trying to heal the growing sectarian rift in India.

THE SALT MARCH

In 1928, Gandhi called on the British to make India a self-governing dominion, but the British ignored him. He then organized a new *satyagraha* against a British-imposed salt tax, and his Salt March in 1930 seriously undermined British authority in India. Gandhi was subsequently invited to negotiate with the British in return for a cessation of his campaign. He returned to active politics in 1938, and during World War II he launched a "Quit India" campaign, urging his fellow Indians to resume their campaign of civil disobedience. As a result Gandhi was imprisoned for two years from November 1942.

When the war finished, Gandhi ended his campaign, as the British had promised to grant Indian self-determination. He participated in negotiations, but was unable to prevent the partition of India into separate Hindu and Muslim states. In August 1947, India finally became an independent nation, as did Pakistan. The religious violence continued, and thousands of refugees crossed the border between the two new states. Gandhi embarked on a fast-unto-death in an attempt to end the discord, forcing Indian and Pakistani leaders to make peace with each other. However, feelings still ran high, and on the evening of January 30, 1949 Gandhi was assassinated by a Hindu fanatic. As Indian Prime Minister Nehru put it, "Bapu—the father of the nation—is no more."

RIGHT: *Thousands of people march in celebration on the day of India's independence, August 15, 1947.*

BELOW: *Gandhi, along with many supporters, takes part in the Salt March of March 12, 1930.*

THE SALT MARCH

On March 12, 1930 Gandhi led a *satyagraha* against a British tax on salt by walking from Ahmedabad to the coastal city of Dandi—a distance of 240 miles. He declared that he would defy the British by making his own salt when he got there. Thousands joined him, and his *satyagraha* evolved into a mass protest. On April 5, Gandhi reached his destination. He scooped up a handful of salt-encrusted mud, declaring, "With this I am shaking the foundations of the British Empire." His actions caught the attention of the world's press, and Gandhi became a figure of international repute.

MARCH–APRIL 1930
Gandhi wins worldwide recognition during the "Salt March"

AUGUST 1942
Gandhi launches his "Quit India" campaign to force the British to negotiate

AUGUST 14–15, 1947
India and Pakistan become independent nations; the dates are subsequently declared national holidays

JUNE 1948
Lord Mountbatten steps down as the last viceroy of India

JANUARY 30, 1949
Gandhi assassinated in New Delhi by Nathuram Godse

THE HOLOCAUST'S IMPACT — 1939–

In 1932, the Jewish population of Europe numbered around nine million people. Then, in January 1933, Adolf Hitler came to power in Germany, and his Nazi regime set about the systematic persecution, and later eradication, of the country's Jewish population—with far-reaching consequences.

This government-inspired anti-Semitism was based on Hitler's own views of Aryan supremacy; he saw the Jews as a threat to the racial purity of the German people. As the German Reich extended its reach into Austria and Czechoslovakia, anti-Jewish legislation was introduced into those countries.

Following the outbreak of the Second World War in 1939, the German army overran or gained control over large parts of Europe. Persecution now evolved into the mass murder of Europe's Jewish population.

ABOVE: *Inmates of the Nazi concentration and extermination camp at Auschwitz, photographed by Boris Borisov as the camp was liberated by the Russians in January 1945.*
RIGHT: *Haifa port, Palestine, April 19, 1947: a boat packed with 2,700 illegal Jewish immigrants waits for disembarkation; despite earlier clashes, the immigrants were eventually allowed to enter the country without resistance.*

THE BRITISH IN THE MIDDLE EAST

During the First World War (1914–18) the British campaigned against the Ottoman Turks in both Palestine and Mesopotamia, and by 1918 most of this region had come under British control. Mesopotamia became a British mandate, out of which, in August 1921, the Kingdom of Iraq was created. In 1932, the country was given its independence, although Britain retained an involvement in the region until 1947. Neighboring Iran had always been independent, but growing links with Germany forced the Allies to intervene in the country in 1941. By 1948, both Iraq and Iran were rich and independent oil-producing countries, governed by progressive pro-Western rulers.

KEY DATES OF THE HOLOCAUST AND ITS IMPACT

AUGUST 1920
Britain is given a United Nations mandate to govern much of the Middle East

AUGUST 1921
The Kingdom of Iraq, formerly part of the mandate of Mesopotamia, is founded by the British

JANUARY 1933
Hitler becomes German chancellor; institutionalized persecution of Jews

SEPTEMBER 1939
Outbreak of the Second World War: anti-Semitic policies spread across much of Europe

MAY 1945
Surrender of Nazi Germany—the full horror of the Holocaust is revealed

See the Belsen Concentration Camp Report in Envelope IV

THE MARSHALL PLAN IN THE MIDDLE EAST

In May 1948, the United States became the first foreign power to recognize Israel, and the two countries have maintained economic and political ties ever since. The post-war Marshall Plan (named after General George Marshall) saw the diversion of almost $13 billion of American funds to help underpin the economic recovery of war-torn Europe. Marshall was worried that a similar support for Israel would antagonize the Arabs and risk the flow of Middle Eastern oil. As a result, Israel received limited financial support from the United States, whose funds were also used to develop the economies of its oil-producing Arab neighbors.

ABOVE: *David Ben-Gurion, Chairman of the Executive Jewish Agency for Palestine, arrives in New York aboard the liner* Excambion *to campaign for support in November 1941.*
BELOW RIGHT: *In 1949, the then U.S. First Lady, Eleanor Roosevelt, holds up a poster of the UN's Universal Declaration of Human Rights, which had been adopted on December 10, 1948; December 10 was later declared Human Rights Day.*

The process was dubbed the "Final Solution to the Jewish question"; it later became known as the Holocaust, after the Greek word meaning "sacrifice by fire." By 1945, this had resulted in the killing of more than six million Jews—two-thirds of the entire population in Europe. Millions of others also fell victim to the Nazis, including homosexuals, Slavs, Romanies, the disabled, and left-wing political opponents.

THE FOUNDING OF ISRAEL

While these horrors were occurring in Europe, Jewish settlers were carving out a homeland in the British mandate of Palestine, site of the biblical land of Israel. Jewish immigrants had been arriving there since the late 19th century, encouraged by Zionists who called for the re-establishment of a Jewish state there. This *aliyah*, or immigration to the Holy Land, was accelerated after the end of the Second World War, as Holocaust survivors sought a new life in a Jewish homeland. British controls over immigration to Palestine limited this migration, and the incarceration of Holocaust survivors in detention centers only increased worldwide sympathy for the Zionist cause. Britain was to relinquish its Palestine mandate in 1948, by which time the Jewish settlers and their Palestinian neighbors were in open conflict. While politicians tried to find a solution, the violence escalated, and neighboring Arab states drew up plans to intervene as soon as the British left. In response, Jewish leaders, notably David Ben-Gurion, campaigned for support overseas and prepared for the inevitable war.

In November 1947, these Jewish leaders accepted a partition plan proposed by the United Nations, but the Arabs, wholly opposed to a Jewish state, unanimously rejected it. On May 14, 1948, the day before the British mandate ended, Ben-Gurion proclaimed the foundation of the State of Israel. The new country was immediately recognized by Britain and the United States, but the following day five Arab countries declared war. Although outnumbered, the fledgling Israeli army fought and defeated the Arab armies, and in early 1949 a ceasefire was agreed. The main losers were the Palestinians, many of whom lost their homes in the war or found themselves incorporated into neighboring Arab states.

HUMAN RIGHTS

On the world stage, the Holocaust engendered a resolve of "never again": a question of protecting not just the Jewish people but all human life. This was enshrined in the United Nations' Universal Declaration of Human Rights, adopted on December 10, 1948.

NOVEMBER 29, 1947
UN partition plan for territory of the Palestine mandate is rejected by Arab nations

MAY 14, 1948
Declaration of foundation of the State of Israel

MAY 15, 1948
Official end of British mandate and start of Arab–Israeli war (1948–49)

DECEMBER 10, 1948
United Nations General Assembly adopts the Universal Declaration of Human Rights

JULY 20, 1949
Syria ends hostilities with Israel, ending the first Arab–Israeli war

MAO ZEDONG ~ 1893–1976

Mao Zedong was born in Shaoshan, in the Chinese province of Hunan, on December 26, 1893. Throughout his formative years, he was keenly interested in political theory and Marxism, first learning about the communist thinker while working as a library assistant at Beijing University. In 1921, Mao attended the founding meeting of the Communist Party of China (or CPC) in Shanghai, and would argue for several years in favor of a violent revolution led by rural peasants.

THE LONG MARCH

Throughout the 1920s and 1930s Mao led an army of Communist revolutionaries against the Nationalist forces of Chiang Kai-shek. By October 1934, Mao's forces were forced into a retreat that became known as "The Long March," during which many of them perished. It was during this period that Mao emerged as the leader of Communist forces in China. He regrouped, recruited reinforcements, and launched a civil war against the Nationalists, winning a series of decisive victories in Manchuria in 1947–48. By October 1949, Mao had defeated Chiang Kai-shek's forces and he then became the leader of the newly founded People's Republic of China (P.R.C.).

As leader of the PRC, Mao introduced a series of controversial reforms, which had long-lasting effects. The first of these, in 1958, was the "Great Leap Forward," an economic plan to increase production and industrialize the nation using

LEFT: *Mao Zedong in January 1967, at the height of the Cultural Revolution, wearing the uniform of a Red Guard.*

THE CULT OF MAO

Mao created a "cult of personality" in order to cement his status as the nation's leader. His image became ubiquitous throughout China, often depicted as a benevolent and smiling father figure. Today, Mao's image adorns a vast array of consumer items such as coffee mugs and t-shirts, even in the West. In this way, perhaps ironically, Mao's influence continues to be felt decades after his death. He has become, in many ways, a symbol of the PRC itself. His body lies on permanent display in the Chairman Mao Memorial Hall in Tiananmen Square in Beijing.

KEY DATES IN THE LIFE OF MAO ZEDONG

DECEMBER 26, 1893
Mao Zedong is born in Shaoshan in Hunan province of China

OCTOBER 16, 1934–OCTOBER 19, 1935
Mao leads the Long March to escape Nationalist forces and gains support among the Communist Party members

1943
Mao becomes chairman of the Chinese Communist Party

OCTOBER 1, 1949
Mao declares the founding of the People's Republic of China from the Tiananmen Gate in Beijing

collectivist techniques. Under the program, people were ordered to form large communes, and work on huge infrastructure projects. All private food production was banned. Many new and unproven agricultural techniques were introduced, leaving millions of Chinese people to die of starvation.

THE CULTURAL REVOLUTION

The second policy, known as the "Cultural Revolution," was introduced in 1966, and focused on transforming society. Fearful that his power was threatened by factions within the Communist Party, Mao instigated a campaign to root out "counter-revolutionary" elements from society. Groups of young people known as the "Red Guards" were organized to overcome "bourgeois" groups. Millions of people were exiled to the countryside, where they were made to learn "right thinking."

Mao is widely seen domestically as being a unifying figure, who lifted China up from centuries of civil strife and humiliation at the hands of foreign powers. His political philosophy has become known as Maoism, the symbol of which is his "Little Red Book" (a collection of his sayings).

After Mao's death, China changed rapidly; economic reforms which relaxed the state's control on the economy led to an explosion of growth from the 1980s. Modern China is now a very different country from that which Mao led, but Mao's influence is undeniable, and he is still celebrated and revered as the man who made China great.

LEFT: *Crowds pass under a portrait of Mao in April 1989 on Beijing's Tiananmen Square. Two months later this was to be the scene of the brutal crushing of student protests.*

BELOW LEFT: *A propaganda poster entitled "Heavenly Thunderstorm Opens Up a New Universe" features Mao wielding a calligraphy brush and inciting young people to action.*

BELOW: *Mao Zedong's "Little Red Book," which comprises 427 quotes divided into 33 chapters.*

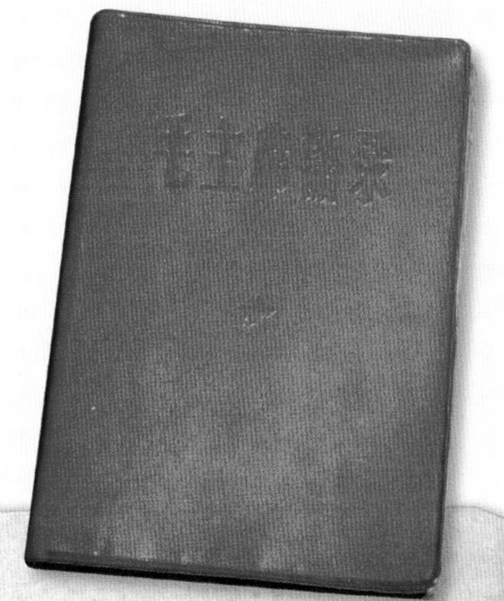

MAO'S LITTLE RED BOOK

Officially known by the title *Quotations from Chairman Mao Zedong*, this book contains a collection of excerpts from Mao's speeches and published works. It was the most printed book of the 20th century, with over five billion copies issued. It became an essential possession for any conscientious Chinese citizen. The book covers a variety of subjects, from the nature of class struggle, and proper revolutionary conduct, to the role of women in society.

DECEMBER 1949
Chiang Kai-shek's Nationalist forces are defeated, and flee to Taiwan

JANUARY 1958
The Great Leap Forward begins, with the intention of increasing production

1966
Mao launches the Cultural Revolution, challenging "bourgeois" thinking

FEBRUARY 1972
Mao meets with U.S. President Nixon, beginning a process of normalizing relations between the two countries

SEPTEMBER 9, 1976
Mao Zedong dies, aged 82, and is laid to rest in Beijing

THE KOREAN WAR — 1950–53

The Korean Peninsula had been occupied by Japan throughout World War II, and after that country's defeat in 1945, the Potsdam Conference of July–August decided that the country should be divided between the Americans and Soviets along the 38th Parallel. The Korean people themselves had no say on the matter, and they soon began to protest against this arrangement, particularly in the American-administered south of the country. There were many industrial strikes and some police officials were murdered.

INVASION

In 1948, strongly nationalist leaders came to power in both parts of Korea, and the divisions between the two sides quickly hardened into one between Communist north and anti-Communist south. After the withdrawal of U.S. troops in 1949, the South Koreans were ill equipped to resist northern Communist aggression. On June 25, 1950, following months of skirmishes along the 38th Parallel, North Korea (now the Democratic People's Republic of Korea, or D.P.R.K.) invaded South Korea (now the Republic of Korea or R.O.K.).

President Truman acted swiftly to support the R.O.K. forces, arguing strongly that Communism must be contained. American and United Nations troops soon joined the fight against the invading forces, but by August they had been pushed back to the southern port of Pusan and controlled only 10 percent of the country. However, as the Battle of Pusan continued, the United States gradually built up and strengthened its forces, and conducted interdiction sorties against enemy logistics networks. On September 15, the Americans counter-attacked, staging an amphibious invasion at Inchon. Soon, they were pushing the D.P.R.K. forces back across the 38th Parallel and into D.P.R.K. territory.

Some worried that advancing too close to the border of China would provoke that country to enter the war, but the United States commander, General MacArthur, was undeterred, determined to defeat Communism in Korea once and for all. As UN forces approached the Yalu River, China did indeed intervene in the conflict, with thousands of "volunteers" (in fact highly trained military personnel) joining the fight. Faced with these reinforcements, the UN forces were pushed back to the 38th Parallel, and the war settled into a static conflict characterized by trench warfare.

THE TRUMAN DOCTRINE

On July 27, 1953, both sides signed a ceasefire, which effectively ended the war. An armistice established the 38th Parallel as the border between the two countries,

ABOVE LEFT: *South Korean soldiers drag a North Korean from his hiding place on the Pohang front, September 1950.*
RIGHT: *General Douglas MacArthur at Yang Yang in North Korea, April 1951; behind the driver can be seen Major General Doyle O. Hickey of the UN forces.*

GENERAL DOUGLAS MACARTHUR (1880–1964)

General MacArthur led the United Nations forces in the Korean War until 1951. Previously, he had been a leading general in the Pacific campaign of World War II. He was considered a national hero in America, and his "gung-ho" attitude gained him many admirers. He accepted Japan's surrender on September 2, 1945, and oversaw the U.S. occupation of that country from 1945 until 1951. During the Korean War, MacArthur attracted controversy when he publicly advocated using tactical nuclear weapons against the Chinese. Alarmed at this recklessness, President Truman dismissed him on April 11, 1951.

KEY DATES LEADING UP TO AND INCLUDING THE KOREAN WAR

SEPTEMBER 9, 1945
The U.S. accepts the Japanese surrender in Korea

AUGUST 15, 1948
The Republic of Korea is proclaimed. Syngman Rhee is elected as its first president

JUNE 29, 1949
Last U.S. troops leave South Korea; skirmishes along the 38th Parallel

JUNE 25, 1950
D.P.R.K. forces cross the 38th Parallel and invade the R.O.K. without warning

JUNE 29, 1950
The R.O.K. capital, Seoul, falls, and bridges across the Han River are destroyed. Many of the R.O.K.'s best forces trapped on the northern side

ABOVE: *Marilyn Monroe sings for the troops in Korea, February 1954, an understandably great boost to morale.*
RIGHT: *Turkish United Nations forces searching newly captured Chinese prisoners in Korea, December 1950.*

but this time with a 2.5-mile-wide demilitarized zone as a buffer between the two belligerents. No peace treaty was ever signed, and to this day the D.P.R.K. and R.O.K. are technically still at war.

The Korean War was significant in being the first major armed conflict of the Cold War, and in many ways it was also a proxy war between the Soviet Union and the United States, with American politicians declaring a policy of "containment" by which they hoped to halt the spread of Communism globally. This policy is sometimes known as the "Truman Doctrine," named after the U.S. president who formulated it.

DEMILITARIZED ZONE (DMZ)

After the war, the area along the 38th Parallel was declared a demilitarized zone, in which neither country could place military forces. Just outside the DMZ, however, both countries have massed vast numbers of troops and armor, making it the most heavily militarized border in the world. As the two countries are still technically at war, a constant watch is maintained for signs of renewed enemy aggression. The border also serves as means to intimidate, and there is intense competition to have the highest flagpole and the largest flag. North Korea has even built idealized "propaganda" villages, hoping to convince their enemy that life is better in the North.

JULY 12, 1950
The U.S. Eighth Army takes command of ground operations in Korea

SEPTEMBER 15, 1950
American marines land at Inchon; fighting destroys the city of Inchon

APRIL 11, 1951
Truman dismisses MacArthur for openly disagreeing with his methods of conducting the war

JANUARY 20, 1953
Dwight D. Eisenhower becomes U.S. president, and immediately seeks a swift end to the war

JULY 27, 1953
A ceasefire is signed, ending any open armed conflict, but a peace treaty is never agreed upon

THE CUBAN REVOLUTION ≈ 1953–59

The Cuban Revolution had its roots in the Cuban elections of 1952, during which the U.S.-sponsored Fulgencio Batista seized power and in doing so lost the sympathy of important elements of the Cuban populace. Fidel Castro and his brother Raul were among those disenfranchised by Batista's power grab, and the brothers began plotting the dictator's downfall.

THE CASTROS

Needing weapons and ammunition to support their revolution, the brothers planned an attack on the remote Moncada barracks in July 1953. Their hopes that an element of surprise would compensate for their lack of numbers and arms proved ill founded, and federal soldiers captured and killed the majority of the Castros' men. The brothers themselves initially escaped, but were soon captured and put on public trial. Fidel Castro, a trained lawyer, sought to turn the trial into a forum in which to denounce Batista's power seizure, but was nevertheless sentenced to 15 years' imprisonment.

Just two years later, the Batista government bowed to international pressure to release political prisoners, including the Castros, who headed to Mexico to regroup. There they formed the new "26th of July Movement." They also met the Cuban exile Camilo Cienfuegos and the Argentine radical Ernesto "Che" Guevara, and the new group began to evolve a plot to return to Cuba.

RIGHT: *Che Guevara gives a press conference in 1955, the year that he first met the Castro brothers and became involved with the Cuban revolutionary movement.*

BELOW: *Fidel Castro (center), his brother Raul (kneeling) and members of the guerrilla army in the jungle, probably in Mexico in June 1957.*

CHE GUEVARA
(1928–67)

Born on June 14, 1928, Argentine Marxist Ernesto "Che" Guevara was Fidel Castro's charismatic second in command. His romanticized image, epitomized in the Alberto Korda portrait *Guerrillero Heroico*, made him a hero of the popular imagination. Che's radical ideology was born during his travels throughout Latin America as a young medical student, and he became involved in social reform in Guatemala before meeting Raul and Fidel Castro in Mexico City. After the Revolution, he was involved in repelling the Bay of Pigs Invasion as well as in the acquisition of the missiles that provoked the Cuban Missile Crisis of 1962. A prolific writer and diarist, Guevara's book *The Motorcycle Diaries* remains a bestseller today.

KEY DATES OF THE CUBAN REVOLUTION AND CHE GUEVARA'S LIFE

JUNE 14, 1928
The Argentine Marxist revolutionary Ernesto "Che" Guevara is born

MARCH 10, 1952
General Fulgencio Batista overthrows Cuban President Carlos Prìo Socarrás

JULY 26, 1953
Assault on Moncada barracks in Santiago de Cuba

MAY 1955
Fidel Castro released from prison

NOVEMBER 25, 1956
Granma yacht sets sail from Mexico carrying 82 rebels and armaments

THE *GRANMA* YACHT

Built in 1943 and bought by young lawyer Fidel Castro for $40,000, the yacht *Granma* secured its place in history with its arrival in Cuba on December 2, 1956, setting in motion a chain of events that would culminate in the overthrow of Batista's regime. Designed for a capacity of 25, the yacht was packed with 82 rebels together with two canons, 35 sniper rifles, 55 assault rifles, three machine-guns and 50 pistols. Stocks of ammunition were scant, as were food and water for the seven-day, 1,240-mile journey from Tuxpan, Mexico, to Las Coloradas on the southeast coast of Cuba. Che Guevara and Fidel Castro were amongst the seasick, hungry men who stumbled ashore on December 2.

On November 25, the rebels set sail for Cuba on board the tiny yacht *Granma*. Reaching the mangrove swamps of Las Coloradas, their cause almost died then and there. Betrayed by their own guide, the landing met with an ambush and air attacks in which all but a handful of revolutionaries were killed. The survivors—including Cienfuegos, the Castros, and Guevara—made it to the highlands of the Sierra Maestra. There, they regrouped, replenished their supplies of weapons and ammunition, and swelled their ranks, gaining publicity from foreign journalists and by carrying out guerrilla assaults on military targets.

SUPPORT

Entrenched in the mountains, the 26th of July Movement grew in strength and soon won the support of other rebel groups in Cuba's towns and cities, one of which almost succeeded in assassinating Batista. In summer 1958, the dictator decided to flush out the rebels and sent a sizeable military contingent to the mountains to hunt the Castros down. His actions backfired, and many soldiers defected to join the Castros. By the end of the year, victory for the rebels was within sight. Leaving their mountain hideouts, Cienfuegos and Guevara swept across Cuba's plains in December 1958, capturing a string of towns and villages and being welcomed as liberators. Cienfuegos captured the garrison of Yaguajay on December 30; meanwhile, Guevara and 300 rebels defeated a much larger military force in the city of Santa Clara.

With defeat seeming inevitable, Batista fled. Cienfuegos and Guevara entered Havana in triumph on January 2, 1959; Fidel Castro joined them there six days later, celebrating with the citizens of each town and village he passed through. All traces of the Batista regime—and of any rival rebel groups—were eliminated as Raul Castro and Guevara brought to trial and executed the "war criminals" of the old regime.

ABOVE: *The Plaza de la Revolución in Havana, Cuba is one of the largest city squares in the world, and has been the scene of several addresses to the Cuban people by Fidel Castro.*

LEFT: *The Moncada barracks in Santiago de Cuba, attacked on July 26, 1953 at the start of the battle against Batista.*

DECEMBER 2, 1956
Yacht *Granma* lands at Las Coloradas on the southeast coast of Cuba

DECEMBER 28–30, 1958
Victory for the rebels over the government forces of President Batista at Santa Clara

JANUARY 1, 1959
Batista flees the country and eventually finds refuge in Portugal

JANUARY 8, 1959
Castro enters Havana, having spent six days celebrating with Cuban citizens

OCTOBER 9, 1967
Che Guevara dies in Bolivia after being captured by government forces

THE ROCK 'N' ROLL ERA  1950S–70S

Phillips's studio. Over the coming years, the Presley sensation took the world by storm: from gospel ballads to pounding rock, between 1956 and 1963 his every record was a hit.

NEW FACES

The 1960s brought a new direction for rock 'n' roll in America, with the likes of Smokey Robinson and the Miracles, the Temptations, and Diana Ross and the Supremes introducing what would become the "Motown" sound. Meanwhile, in the United Kingdom, Carl Perkins and Elvis inspired the coming together of perhaps the most famous four-piece act in musical history: the Beatles. Their fame soon spread beyond the British Isles, with first Europe then America falling for their innovative music, compelling stage personalities, and trend-setting haircuts. A spate of Beatles-influenced groups followed: the Searchers, the Yardbirds, the Kinks, and the Rolling Stones.

LEFT: *British teenagers in London dance to rock 'n' roll in September 1959 after the arrival of the U.S. movie* Rock Around the Clock.

BELOW: *Elvis, photographed in Memphis, Tennessee, 1956.*

Rock 'n' Roll took the international music scene by storm. The phrase was coined in 1951 by Cleveland, Ohio disc jockey Alan Freed, whose radio show *Moondog Rock 'n' Roll Party* began broadcasting black music to white teenagers in that year. The same year brought the release of Ike Turner's "Rocket 88," the first rock 'n' roll record, while the first jukebox playing 45 r.p.m. records appeared on the market. Within four years, the sale of 45 r.p.m. records had overtaken that of 78s.

THE ORIGINS

Early rock 'n' roll music was a fusion of rhythm and blues, soul, jazz, gospel music, and country and western. It took the youth of America by storm, bringing some of the immediacy and sexuality of so-called "race music" to the nation's white heartlands, and it epitomized the age-old rebellion of teenagers against their parents. With its solid rhythm, heavy beats, and defiant lyrics, the new music inspired new kinds of dancing and performing that survive to this day.

The first rock 'n' roll stars included Chuck Berry, Jerry Lee Lewis, Little Richard, and Carl Perkins, and each new star brought a new twist to the evolving genre, whether in terms of showmanship or musical influence. In 1952, Sam Phillips founded the iconic Sun Records with the declaration, "If I could find a white man who sings with the Negro feel, I'll make a million dollars." Within the next year, rock 'n' roll's brightest star was born in Mississippi, when truck driver Elvis Presley made his first recordings in

KEY DATES IN THE ROCK 'N' ROLL ERA

1951
Ohio disc jockey Alan Freed coins the expression "Rock 'n' Roll"

1952
Sam Phillips founds Sun Records in Memphis, Tennessee

1953
Leo Fender invents the Stratocaster electric guitar, which is favored by many bands

1954
Bill Haley's "Rock Around the Clock" is the first rock song used in a movie soundtrack

1955
Sales of 45 r.p.m. records overtake 78s, paving the way for the era of singles charts

See a party invitation for the Beatles' Magical Mystery Tour in Envelope IV

THE CAVERN CLUB

In the early years of the 1960s, the Cavern Club in Liverpool rose to prominence as one of the most famous nightclubs in the U.K., if not the world. The Beatles first played there in January 1961 (although some of the band's members had played the venue earlier as "The Quarrymen"). Over the next two years, the club became the center of the evolving Merseybeat sound, with regular performances from the Beatles themselves—the band played their last Cavern gig on August 3, 1963—as well as bands including Gerry and the Pacemakers and the Swinging Blue Jeans.

Taking the genre back toward its rebellious roots, the Rolling Stones put the "rock" into rock 'n' roll, bringing a dramatic new vigor and anger to the '60s musical scene.

By the end of the decade, musical recording techniques and the psychedelic influence of the swelling drug culture ushered in a spate of long, complex songs of an often abstract nature, from bands including the Doors, the Jimi Hendrix Experience, and the Grateful Dead. The Beatles, too, took this path, producing the landmark *Sgt. Pepper's Lonely Hearts Club Band* album in the summer of 1967.

Throughout the following decade, rock 'n' roll continued to evolve, taking on influences from folk music, country music, and jazz music, culminating in the "new wave" music of the Clash, the Police, and Elvis Costello.

ABOVE: *The Beatles'* Sgt. Pepper's Lonely Hearts Club Band, *chosen as one of the greatest albums of all time by, among others,* Rolling Stone *(2003) and* Time *(2006) magazines.* BELOW LEFT: *The "fab four" Beatles (from left): George Harrison, John Lennon (back), Paul McCartney (front), and Ringo Starr.*

GRACELAND

Elvis Presley was born on January 8, 1935 in a modest two-room house in Tupelo, Mississippi. His childhood years were spent there in relative poverty, but his most famous home remains his Graceland mansion in Memphis, Tennessee, which he purchased in 1957 for around $100,000. The 23-room mansion underwent numerous modifications during Elvis's 20-year occupancy. He added a fieldstone wall surrounding the grounds, a wrought-iron music-themed gate, a swimming pool, a racquetball court, a memorial garden dedicated to his twin brother who died at birth, and the "Jungle Room," converted into a recording studio in 1976 for the albums *From Elvis Presley Boulevard, Memphis, Tennessee* and *Moody Blue*.

1956
Elvis releases his first film, *Love Me Tender*, providing fans with both songs and charisma

1957
Buddy Holly records "That'll Be the Day," a quintessential rock 'n' roll track

1960
Dance craze "The Twist" sweeps across the world, encapsulating the freedom of the new decade

SUMMER 1967
The Beatles release the landmark album *Sgt. Pepper's Lonely Hearts Club Band*

AUGUST 16, 1977
Elvis dies at Graceland, his mansion in Tennessee, an enduring place of pilgrimage for fans

THE COLD WAR ≈ 1945–91

LEFT: *The Soviet Union's annual May Day parade crosses Moscow's Red Square in front of the Kremlin wall and Lenin's mausoleum, May 1964.*
BELOW: *The Berlin Wall separated families and communities when it was constructed, and many people did not see relatives or friends until it was brought down in 1989.*

THE BERLIN WALL

From 1960 to 1989, Berlin was divided by what became known as the Berlin Wall. This was a security measure put in place by the German Democratic Republic—the state the Soviet Union established in its zone of occupation in 1949—in order to prevent people moving from East to West Berlin. Family members became separated and those who worked in the West were cut off from their jobs. The wall soon became a potent symbol of the divisions that the Cold War was causing across the globe. It is estimated that between 100 and 200 people died attempting to escape across the Berlin Wall before mass protests in East Germany forced its opening in 1989.

The end of World War II ushered in a new world order. The Allies who had fought to free Europe from Nazi occupation now argued about its future. At a series of conferences at Yalta and Potsdam in 1945, the victorious Allies agreed on spheres of influence in Europe, while Germany and Austria were divided into zones of occupation. Eastern Germany fell to the Soviets, whilst the western zones (the future West Germany) were administered by the French, British, and Americans.

Yet Stalin, suspicious of Western designs, went far beyond what was agreed in the Potsdam Declaration, engineering the installation of Communist-controlled regimes throughout Eastern Europe through a mixture of propaganda and naked force.

THE IRON CURTAIN

In 1946, Churchill called the divide this created the "Iron Curtain," the most visible frontier in what was now a "Cold War" between the United States and the Soviet Union and their allies. The next four decades were characterized by constant political, military, and economic tensions between the West and East. Gradually, the ideological confrontation between the two sides became formalized, with the establishment by the Western powers of the North Atlantic Treaty Organization (NATO) in 1949 to defend themselves against perceived Soviet aggression and the founding of the Soviet bloc's counter-alliance, the Warsaw Pact, in 1955.

In the U.S. the investigations of the infamous House Un-American Activities Committee and Senator Joseph McCarthy from 1950 to 1954 epitomized the paranoia and mistrust that characterized political attitudes during this time. In the Soviet Union the ideological witch-

KEY DATES OF THE COLD WAR

MAY 1945
Soviet troops occupy Berlin, marking the collapse of the Nazi regime and the beginning of Soviet dominance in Eastern Europe

AUGUST 1945
First-ever detonation of a combat nuclear weapon, over Hiroshima, Japan

APRIL 1949
North Atlantic Treaty Organization (NATO) is formed, creating an alliance of Western powers

SEPTEMBER 1949
The Soviet Union detonates its first nuclear weapon

1950–53
Korean War is fought, ending in an uneasy stalemate that has long-lasting implications for the future stability of the region

hunts were much more brutal, with millions of people being sent to *gulags*—work camps with appalling conditions where huge numbers died.

THE NUCLEAR ARMS RACE

The detonation of the first nuclear weapon over Japan in August 1945 had signaled that any future conflict could be far more destructive than the one that had just ended. The new world superpowers—the United States and the Soviet Union—entered into an arms race, with each country attempting to achieve a clear superiority in nuclear weapons. On October 14, 1962, U.S. reconnaissance discovered missile silos being constructed in Cuba, a Soviet-allied country just 100 miles from American soil. After a naval blockade and intense talks between U.S. President Kennedy and Soviet Premier Khrushchev, the crisis was eventually defused after ten days, when an agreement was reached that the missiles would be removed in return for an agreement by the United States not to invade Cuba. The world had narrowly averted a nuclear war.

Although the United States and the Soviet Union never did fight a "hot war" in central Europe, they did wage several "proxy wars," fought against third parties allied to one power or the other. The most important of these were the Korean War of 1950–53, the Vietnam War of 1965–75, and the Soviet–Afghan War of 1979–89. By 1990, however, the reformist *perestroika* ("restructuring") policies of Mikhail Gorbachev in the Soviet Union had inaugurated a new era of calmer relations with the West. The Cold War was over.

BELOW LEFT: *U.S. President Kennedy and Soviet premier Khrushchev chat, apparently amicably, in Vienna, Austria, after a summit meeting in June 1961.*
BELOW: *An American U-2 reconnaissance plane, during the 1950s.*

ESPIONAGE

Throughout the Cold War the U.S. and the U.S.S.R. engaged in constant espionage and counter-espionage against the other. Intelligence agencies such as the CIA and KGB became synonymous with clandestine activity aimed at gathering intelligence. Both powers also used technology to gather information, including spy planes and satellites. Occasionally these activities came out into the open and caused enormous tension, as when the U-2 spy plane piloted by Gary Powers was shot down over the U.S.S.R. in 1960.

OCTOBER 4, 1957
The world's first artificial satellite, *Sputnik*, is launched by the Soviet Union, causing paranoia in the U.S.

AUGUST 1961
The border between East and West Berlin is closed by East German forces, and the Berlin Wall is constructed

OCTOBER 1962
The Cuban Missile Crisis grips the world for several weeks, causing widespread fear of a nuclear war

1965–75
Vietnam War is fought, causing domestic strife in the U.S. and ending in victory for the North Vietnamese

DECEMBER 1979–FEBRUARY 1989
Soviet occupation of Afghanistan. The U.S. supplies Afghan militias with weapons to fight the Soviets

INDEPENDENCE IN AFRICA — 1960–75

In February 1960, British Prime Minister Harold Macmillan addressed the South African parliament, and spoke about African self-determination. He said, "The wind of change is blowing through this continent and whether we like it or not, this growth of national consciousness is a political fact. We must all accept it as a fact, and our national policies must take account of it." His speech acknowledged that, while much of Africa was still under European rule, these colonies would soon be granted their independence.

ABOVE: *British Prime Minister Harold Macmillan shakes hands with Sir Abubakar Balewa, President of Nigeria, in London in September 1962.*

THE FEW

The speech was given to mark the 50th anniversary of South African independence, but in 1960 that country was one of just a handful of independent African states. Before South Africa, only Liberia on the West African coast and Ethiopia were fully independent. Egypt gained its partial independence from Britain in 1922, and after 1952 the government there adopted a fervently anti-British policy. When Egypt nationalized the Suez Canal in 1956, Britain and France invaded the country, only to be forced to withdraw due to international pressure. It was clear that these European powers now lacked the political will to retain their African possessions.

In 1951, Libya was granted its independence from Britain, followed five years later by Sudan. After fighting a colonial rearguard action, Spain ceded control of Morocco in 1956, and France gave Tunisia its independence in the same year. Two years later, in 1958, the French West African colony of Guinea broke away. Similarly, in 1957 the British Gold Coast was granted independence as the Republic of Ghana.

THE MANY

After the "wind of change" speech there was a rush towards independence among African states. In April 1960, French Togoland became Togo, while later the same year French West Africa was divided into several smaller independent states—Mali, Senegal, Benin, Niger, and Mauritania. That August, French Equatorial Africa was divided into the states of Chad, the Central African Republic, Gabon, and Congo. At the same time, the French also granted independence to two smaller West African states: Ivory Coast and Upper Volta (now Burkina Faso).

THE WAR FOR ALGERIA

The most violent struggle for independence in Africa took place in Algeria, where the French attempted to retain control of their North African colony in the face of a widespread popular uprising that lasted from 1954 until 1960. While terrorist acts were carried out in the capital, Algiers, itself, the National Liberation Front (FLN) also waged a bitter guerrilla war in the mountainous interior of the colony, forcing the French to deploy considerable military resources in order to maintain control. Both sides were accused of atrocities and of torture, but the war became increasingly unpopular in France, and so in July 1962 Algeria was finally granted its independence.

BELOW: *Jomo Kenyatta (center) is sworn in as the Republic of Kenya's first president, watched by his wife Njina (left) and Chief Justice Sir John Ainley (right), in Nairobi, Kenya, in December 1964.*

KEY DATES FOR INDEPENDENCE IN AFRICA

1952–58
Mau Mau uprising in British East Africa (Kenya); it fails, but hastens independence

OCTOBER–NOVEMBER 1956
The Suez Crisis—Britain and France invade Egypt to force it to re-open the Suez Canal

FEBRUARY 1960
British Prime Minister Macmillan makes "wind of change" speech

APRIL 1960
France begins divesting itself of its central African possessions

JUNE 1960
Congo is granted independence: start of the Crisis

WAR IN THE CONGO 1960–65

While most African states gained their independence peaceably, the creation of the Republic of the Congo in June 1960 marked the start of a conflict which would last for six years, ending only in 1965 when Joseph Mobutu took power. The fighting began as a military coup, but it soon evolved into a war for control of the breakaway province of Katanga. The United Nations was forced to intervene, by which time the war had turned into a conflict between rival warlords, backed by European mercenaries. It is estimated that this brutal conflict cost the lives of around 100,000 civilians.

ABOVE: *U.S. President John F. Kennedy with Major General Joseph Mobutu, commander-in-chief of the Congolese armed forces, during a visit by the latter to Washington, D.C., in 1963.*

Britain was just as eager to divest itself of its imperial burden. In April 1960, Somaliland became Somalia and in October, Nigeria, a country which had been the most thriving colony in West Africa, was granted its independence. The following spring, Britain granted independence to Sierra Leone. Other British colonies would follow—British East Africa became Uganda in 1962, Tanganyika became Tanzania in 1964, and Kenya won its independence in December 1963 in the aftermath of the Mau Mau rebellion. Another imperial player was Belgium, but when the Belgian Congo became the Democratic Republic of Congo in June 1960, a bitter civil war began that would rage till 1965. Rwanda and Burundi were granted their independence from Belgium in 1962.

ABOVE: *The Mediterranean end of the Suez Canal, at Port Said, Egypt, in November 1956. British and French troops have just forced Egypt to re-open the canal, and ships that were sunk by the Egyptians to block its entrance are being removed to clear the channel.*

By 1965, the majority of Africa was independent. Only the Portuguese clung on to their colonial possessions, and the last of these—Mozambique and Angola—won their independence in 1975. Unfortunately, independent nationhood rarely led directly to peace and prosperity. For many of these African states, the years following independence would be marked by tribal and civil wars, deprivation, and genocide. In large parts of Africa, these hardships are still being faced today.

OCTOBER 1960
Nigeria, the most populous country in Africa, gains independence from Britain

JULY 1962
After years of terrorism and popular uprising, Algeria gains independence from France

DECEMBER 1963
Kenya becomes independent, with Jomo Kenyatta as president

NOVEMBER 1965
Joseph Mobutu seizes power in the Congo, ending the war there

NOVEMBER 1965
Rhodesia, under Ian Smith, unilaterally declares independence from Britain

MARTIN LUTHER KING JR. ⸺ 1929–68

Martin Luther King Jr. was born in 1929 and grew up in the Deep South, a region of America with a history scarred by slavery and racial segregation. An intelligent and deeply religious man, he attended college at the early age of 15 and went on to study theology, receiving his doctorate in 1955. He was inspired by early civil rights leaders, such as Howard Thurman, who knew King's father and was a trusted mentor. King also looked up to Mahatma Gandhi, and was to adopt his teachings of non-violent resistance in his own struggle for equality in the U.S.

JIM CROW LAWS

The Jim Crow Laws were a series of laws enacted by southern states and local authorities after the end of the American Civil War in 1865 to segregate public facilities and services according to race. Though supposedly blacks and whites were "separate but equal," in reality, the treatment of black Americans was far inferior to that which whites received. The laws resulted in severe social, educational, and economic disadvantages for blacks for generations. The abolition of these laws was the main focus of King's efforts for many years.

He also helped to found the Southern Christian Leadership Conference (SCLC) in 1957, and became its president, serving in that role until his death.

BOYCOTTS & THREATS

King was instrumental in organizing the Montgomery Bus Boycott in Alabama, a boycott of all city buses by black citizens as a protest against "Jim Crow" laws that segregated bus seating. The campaign was inspired by the actions of Rosa Parks, who refused to give up her seat for a white man, and was consequently arrested. The boycott lasted for 382 days and ended in success with the U.S. Supreme Court ruling in Browder v. Gayle that ended racial segregation on all public buses in Montgomery. During the campaign, King was arrested, threatened, and had his house bombed.

In the years to come, King was to live with a fear of violence every day, as he escalated the campaign for civil rights. He adopted a strategy of provoking local authorities to crack down harshly on protests and marches, thus drawing national media attention to the injustices being carried out in the South and garnering public sympathy and support for his cause. The main issues at hand were the right to vote and the desegregation of public places. King would deliberately choose locations and times that would provoke dramatic confrontations with the authorities, in an effort to garner maximum public attention. These would often turn violent, which was counter-productive for the upholders of the status quo as they were seen as perpetuating injustice through force, while King's supporters practiced non-violent protest.

ABOVE: *In Fort Worth, Texas, in October 1956, women picket a church that has just been sold to a black congregation, for fear that black people may move into the area.*
LEFT: *A young Martin Luther King Jr. in May 1956.*

KEY DATES IN THE LIFE OF MARTIN LUTHER KING JR.

JANUARY 15, 1929
King is born to parents Reverend Martin Luther King Sr. and Alberta Williams King

1944
King graduates from Booker T. Washington High School and is admitted to Morehouse College at age 15

FEBRUARY 25, 1948
King is ordained to the Baptist ministry at the age of 19

1953
Marries Coretta Scott and settles in Montgomery, Alabama

1955
Joins the Montgomery bus boycott after Rosa Parks is arrested on December 1

RIGHT: *In the center of Washington, D.C., Martin Luther King Jr. greets the crowds at the civil rights movement's "March on Washington," August 28, 1963.*

"I HAVE A DREAM..."

In 1963, King led the "March on Washington," a huge event where thousands gathered on the National Mall to hear him speak. It was intended to force the federal government to focus on their concerns by holding the protest at the very heart of the nation's capital. The "I have a dream" speech King gave there is considered one of the greatest pieces of oratory in American history. Many of the issues King was advocating were addressed in the Civil Rights Act of 1964 and the Voting Rights Act of 1965, but King continued to campaign for fair treatment throughout the 1960s, and was a vocal opponent of the Vietnam War.

On April 4, 1968, King was shot while standing on the balcony of the Lorraine Motel in Memphis, Tennessee. He died shortly afterwards, and the news of his death sparked a wave of riots in over 100 U.S. cities. Today, Martin Luther King is celebrated as one of the most influential figures in the nation's history, and Martin Luther King Jr. Day is observed on the third Monday of January each year.

ABOVE: *Rosa Parks is fingerprinted in Montgomery, Alabama, in February 1956, after her arrest for organizing a one-day boycott of the town's buses. Parks had been involved in the civil rights movement since 1943.*

THE BIRMINGHAM CAMPAIGN

The Birmingham Campaign was organized by the SCLC in the spring of 1963, and resulted in some of the worst violence of the civil rights movement. There was widespread police brutality, not only against protesters, but also against bystanders, using high-pressure hoses and attack dogs. These actions, instigated by Eugene "Bull" Connor, the Commissioner of Public Safety, backfired when images of the violence were published in the national media, provoking Americans to examine the issue of segregation in the South. Eventually, the protests caused such widespread confrontation that city authorities reluctantly agreed to end official segregation and discrimination. Martin Luther King's tactics had worked effectively, and as a result, a bi-racial committee was established to supverise the desegregation of the city's public schools.

1957
Helps form the Southern Christian Leadership Conference (SCLC) to campaign against segregation and achieve civil rights

APRIL 1963
The Birmingham Campaign is launched, which draws significant national attention to the civil rights cause

JULY 2, 1964
King attends the signing ceremony of the Civil Rights Act of 1964 at the White House

1965
The Voting Rights Act is signed into law

APRIL 4, 1968
King is fatally shot while standing on the balcony of the Lorraine Motel in Memphis, Tennessee

THE FIRST MAN ON THE MOON — 1969

On July 16, 1969, three United States astronauts set out on their historic voyage to the Moon. Their objective: to "perform a manned lunar landing and return." Neil Armstrong, commander, Michael Collins, command module pilot, and Edwin "Buzz" Aldrin Jr., lunar module pilot, were blasted off from Cape Kennedy at 9:32 a.m. EDT on board the Apollo 11 spacecraft to begin their eight-day lunar adventure.

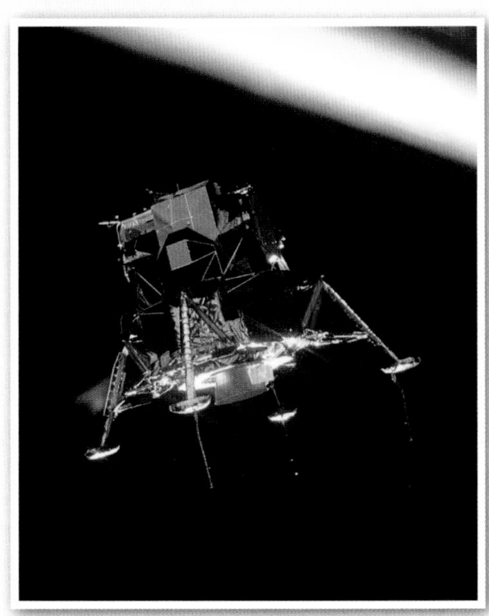

LAUNCH

Apollo 11, consisting of lunar module *Eagle* and command module *Columbia*, was launched into orbit of the Earth by a Saturn V rocket. One and a half Earth orbits later, the third stage of the rocket re-fired to blast Apollo out of orbit and on track to the Moon, with *Columbia* detaching from the Saturn V soon afterwards to reconnect nose-to-nose with lunar module *Eagle*, stored inside the rocket. The two elements separated from the Saturn V for the final stage of the astronauts' journey to the Moon.

On July 19, Apollo 11 entered into the Moon's orbit, and 24 hours later Armstrong and Aldrin separated *Eagle* from *Columbia* to head down to the Moon's surface. Landing at *Mare Tranquillitatis* (the Sea of Tranquillity,) Armstrong sent back the report, "The *Eagle* has landed." Less than six hours later, he would speak the historic words, "one small step for man, one giant leap for mankind," as he stepped down on to the Moon. Prior to stepping out of the lunar module, Armstrong had set up the television camera that would record his arrival.

ON THE MOON

As soon as they reached the Moon's surface, the two astronauts prepared the lunar module for re-launch in case of disaster contingencies, and they quickly stowed samples of the lunar surface in order to ensure that their mission would not return empty-handed. In the course of their mission, Armstrong and Aldrin collected 48 pounds of moon rocks, including basalts that testing revealed to be around 3.7 billion years old. Before leaving the Moon's surface, they also deployed a solar wind composition experiment, took panoramic photographs of the landing site and lunar horizon,

ABOVE LEFT: *Apollo 11 is launched from the Kennedy Space Center, Florida, by the Saturn V rocket.*

ABOVE RIGHT: *The lunar module* Eagle *bears Neil Armstrong and Buzz Aldrin towards the surface of the Moon; photographed from the command module by Michael Collins.*

LANDING SITE

Mare Tranquillitatis, or the "Sea of Tranquillity," is an area of the lunar surface located at 0.67 degrees North (latitude), 23.47 degrees East (longitude) and some 25 miles from the Moon's nearest highland region, the Kant Plateau. It was identified as a suitable landing site for Apollo 11 on account of the relative smoothness of its surface, but nevertheless the area is dotted with craters. In the final seconds before landing, Armstrong was forced to pilot the lunar module manually to avoid "West," a sharp-rimmed crater some 590 feet wide and 100 feet deep. The final landing of Apollo 11 was made in the southwestern sector of the debris-strewn *Mare Tranquillitatis*, 1,300 feet to the west of the crater.

KEY DATES IN THE SPACE RACE

1960
The U.S. Apollo program conceived, to be conducted by NASA

APRIL 12, 1961
Soviet cosmonaut Yuri Gagarin becomes the first man to fly in space

1966
Armstrong's first space flight as part of the Gemini program

JULY 16, 1969, 9:32 A.M.
Apollo 11 mission launched from the Kennedy Space Center in Florida

JULY 20, 1969, 4:20 P.M.
Lunar module touches down on the Moon on the west side of the landing ellipse

deployed a laser-ranging retroreflector and a passive seismic experiment package, and collected two core-tube samples of the lunar surface.

Less than 24 hours after landing on the Moon, after their scheduled meal and sleeping time, the two men blasted off to rejoin Collins, still orbiting with the *Columbia*. *Eagle* rejoined *Columbia* long enough for the astronauts to re-board the command module, and then the lunar module was cast adrift. Firing their rockets to break from the Moon's gravitational field, they set a course for Earth. Traveling at some 25,000 miles per hour, they made their way back through the Earth's atmosphere, successfully avoiding the dangers of burning up or bouncing back into space. The three men parachuted back down to the Earth's surface on July 24, landing in the Pacific Ocean southwest of Hawaii, to be retrieved shortly afterwards by the U.S.S. *Hornet*.

In their brief eight-day mission, the three men had made history. Since the Apollo 11 mission, ten more men have gone on to walk on the Moon. The most recent occasion was in 1972, when Eugene Cernan and Harrison Schmitt landed there with the Apollo 17 mission on December 11.

ABOVE RIGHT: *An official crew portrait taken a few months before the Moon voyage. Left to right: Neil Armstrong, Michael Collins, Edwin "Buzz" Aldrin.*

BELOW: *A view of the far side of the Moon, showing details of some of the craters scattered across its surface.*

NEIL ARMSTRONG

(1930–)

United States astronaut Neil Armstrong stepped into history on July 20, 1969 when he became the first man to set foot on the Moon. His love of flying developed at an early age, his first plane ride at the age of six leaving him hooked on aviation. The Korean War interrupted Armstrong's studies at Purdue University, and he flew 78 combat missions as a navy pilot between 1950 and 1952. He served as a civilian test pilot before becoming an astronaut in 1962, and four years later he and David R. Scott performed the first successful docking of two vehicles in space. Armstrong's involvement in the U.S. astronaut program lasted until 1970. His later career included posts with the University of Cincinnati and the vice-chairmanship of a presidential commission investigating the break-up of the space shuttle *Challenger*.

JULY 20, 1969, 10:56 P.M.
Armstrong steps on to the Moon, having set up a television camera to record the moment

JULY 20, 1969, 1:54 P.M.
Armstrong and Aldrin leave the Moon, having collected many samples

JULY 24, 1969, 12:51 P.M.
The astronauts return to Earth, splashing down in the Pacific Ocean

AUGUST 12, 1969
Televised post-flight press conference from the Manned Spacecraft Center, Houston, Texas

DECEMBER 11, 1972
Apollo 17 mission lands on the Moon—the most recent lunar landing

THE VIETNAM WAR ≈ 1960–75

The roots of the Vietnam War lay in the legacy of French colonialism. In the years following World War II, European colonies asserted their right to independence. In Vietnam this led to open warfare between the nationalist Viet Minh and the army of France, the colonial power. It was a conflict which the French finally lost, and Vietnam gained its independence in 1954.

The country divided into two: a Communist-controlled North; and the South under pro-Western, pro-capitalist leaders. As President Kennedy entered office in 1961, he was concerned about Communist expansion into South Vietnam, and sent military advisers and aid to the country to fight against insurgents.

ABOVE: *U.S. soldiers from the 1st Cavalry Division jump from a "Huey" or Bell UH-1 Iroquois helicopter to undertake a reconnaissance mission in July 1967.*

ESCALATION

The conflict escalated in 1964 with the Gulf of Tonkin Resolution, which gave the President power to declare war without the approval of Congress. This led to a rapid escalation of U.S. military involvement in Vietnam, and 1965 is generally seen as marking the beginning of the war proper. Over the next few years, thousands of U.S. troops were sent to the region, reaching a maximum of 553,000 in 1968.

The nature of combat in Vietnam was different from that which United States forces had encountered

MY LAI MASSACRE

One of the most notorious incidents of the Vietnam War was the massacre of civilians that occurred on March 16, 1968 in the hamlet of My Lai. Several hundred people were killed, often after having been abused and tortured. Details surrounding the event are sketchy, but when the massacre became public in 1969 there was an international outcry. In the subsequent investigations, Lieutenant William Calley was court-martialed and found guilty of ordering the massacre. The incident greatly reduced public support for what was an already unpopular war.

BELOW: *One of the iconic photos from the Vietnam War. Southwest of Saigon, children run from an accidental napalm attack by South Vietnamese aircraft. June 8, 1972.*

KEY DATES IN THE VIETNAM WAR

1954
French forces lose the battle of Dien Bien Phu. France grants Vietnam independence at the Geneva Conference, which splits Vietnam into two along the 17th parallel

1957
Communist insurgency begins in South Vietnam

AUGUST 1964
An alleged torpedo boat attack on U.S. naval forces in the Gulf of Tonkin leads the U.S. to declare war

1965
200,000 U.S. troops are sent to Vietnam

1968
Over 500,000 U.S. troops are now deployed in Vietnam

LEFT: *Outside the Pentagon, near Washington, D.C., troops in riot formation confront a massive anti-Vietnam War protest. Even at this relatively early stage of the war, in October 1967, anti-war feeling was widespread and determined.*

in past conflicts. In Vietnam, there was often no clear enemy to be engaged. When combat did occur, it was often through being ambushed, the North Vietnamese soldiers having perfected guerrilla warfare tactics against the French. It was frustratingly difficult to engage the enemy in open battle. In the dense terrain of Southeast Asia, the Americans' crushing advantage over the Vietnamese in air power was often ineffective. New weapons such as napalm and defoliants had mixed results, and often attracted controversy due to the indiscriminate nature of the damage they inflicted.

PUBLIC SUPPORT

While, initially, domestic U.S. public opinion was in favor of the war, before long it began to sour, and eventually there were widespread anti-war protests. This dissatisfaction was fueled by conscription, or "the draft," that compelled thousands of young men to serve in the military in a war they did not support. In general, most people did not really understand why the United States was involved in Vietnam, save for a vague notion that they were fighting Communism, and they were distressed by the large number of casualties.

In 1968, a withdrawal of U.S. forces from the region began. Without American support, the South Vietnamese military quickly succumbed to the North Vietnamese, and the war ended in 1975 with the last American personnel being evacuated from Saigon by helicopter just as the North Vietnamese army was closing in around the city.

BELOW: *South Vietnamese police chief General Nguyen Ngoc Loan executes Nguyen Van Lém, a member of the Vietcong, in Saigon in February 1968, during the Tet Offensive.*

THE TET OFFENSIVE

In the early morning hours of January 31, 1968, the North Vietnamese launched a major offensive against targets all across South Vietnam. In doing so they broke a two-day ceasefire that had been agreed in order to observe the Vietnamese New Year celebrations. Although the attack caught the Americans and South Vietnamese by surprise, it was a failure, as the conventional nature of the fighting gave an advantage to the Americans, who were better equipped and inflicted large numbers of casualties on the North Vietnamese forces. However, the attack succeeded in unnerving the American public, who had been led to believe that they were winning the war. Images of enemy forces storming the American Embassy in Saigon led many to reassess their opinion of the war.

JANUARY 31, 1968
The Tet Offensive is launched, resulting in heavy North Vietnamese casualties, but the attack succeeds in decreasing U.S. support for the war

MARCH 16, 1968
My Lai Massacre takes place in South Vietnam

1969
U.S. forces begin to be withdrawn from Vietnam in January; Ho Chi Minh dies, aged 79, in December

1973
A ceasefire is agreed in Paris, and all U.S. combat forces are withdrawn by March

1975
North Vietnamese forces invade South Vietnam and take control of Saigon, renaming it Ho Chi Minh City

THE WORLD WIDE WEB ~ 1989

In 1980, the British computer engineer Timothy Berners-Lee built Enquire, a personal database, for use by the European Organization for Nuclear Research (CERN) based in Geneva. In it, he used a system called hypertext, which linked each page of information with another. In effect, he was building the prototype for the World Wide Web, his revolutionary creation that he unveiled in 1989.

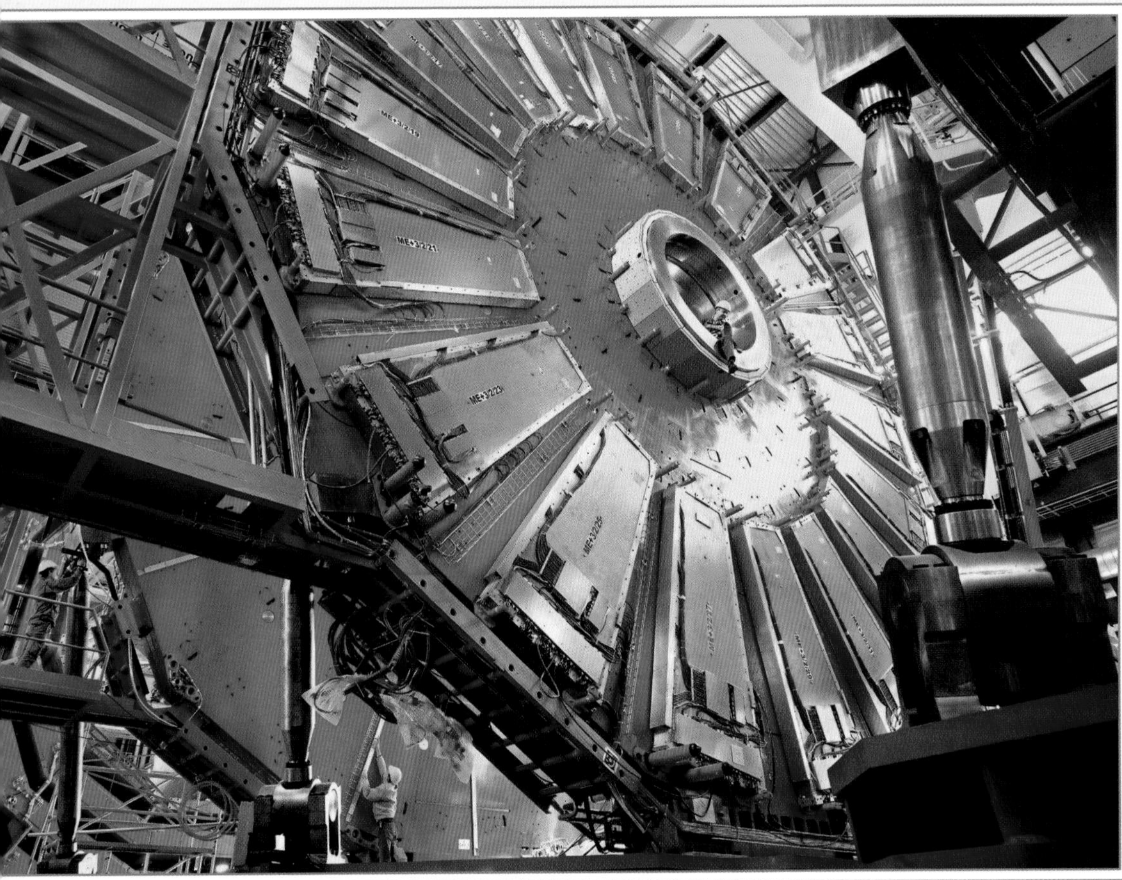

THE INTERNET AND THE WORLD WIDE WEB

These two terms are often confused. The Internet is a worldwide system of linked computer networks that use a shared communications system known as TCP/IP to communicate with each other. The Internet is still evolving and new technologies allow it to be used for telecommunications and broadcasting as well as the sharing of information and the sending of electronic mail (email). The World Wide Web is essentially a means of using the Internet to share information, drawing on Berners-Lee's hypertext to link documents together to create web sites, or to provide links from one source to another, creating a "web" of information.

ENQUIRE

Berners-Lee was brought up in London and educated at Oxford University in England. He graduated with a first-class degree in Physics in 1976, and become a freelance computer consultant specializing in software. In June 1980, he was hired by CERN to create a system to allow researchers to share their information. The work lasted six months and the result was Enquire. He returned to CERN four years later, this time to take up a full-time position. Since his development of Enquire he had considered ways of expanding the use of hypertext, and possibly even linking it to the Internet—the electronic portal that connected groups of computer networks around the world with each other using electronic signals.

Berners-Lee wanted to create a system like Enquire that allowed individuals to share information freely with each other, but which would have a global

ABOVE LEFT: *Construction of CERN's enormous Compact Muon Solenoid detector for studying particle physics. It was in the context of such research that Berners-Lee developed the World Wide Web to improve exchange of information.*
ABOVE: *Tim Berners-Lee, British inventor of the Web, who was knighted by Queen Elizabeth II in recognition of his services to technology.*

KEY DATES IN THE DEVELOPMENT AND PROLIFERATION OF THE WORLD WIDE WEB

1976
Berners-Lee graduates from Oxford University, where he studied Physics

1980
Enquire is developed, designed as a research tool for use by CERN

1984
Berners-Lee returns to CERN, to develop new ways of spreading his hypertext software

1989
Berners-Lee proposes the creation of the World Wide Web

1990
HTTP and URL are invented, allowing information transfer using the Internet

See Tim Berners-Lee's email explaining the idea of the Web in Envelope IV

THE WORLD WIDE WEB CONSORTIUM (W3C)

Berners-Lee became concerned about the direction the World Wide Web was taking, so in May 1994 he proposed the World Wide Web Consortium (W3C), an organization designed to help the Web operate smoothly, and to ensure it remains free of any commercial control. Later that year, W3C was established in the Massachusetts Institute of Technology (MIT). Berners-Lee wanted to make sure his invention would be freely available to everyone, and W3C helped guarantee this vision. Today, Berners-Lee and W3C help maintain Web standards and protocols, and W3C provides a forum for discussion on the future development of the World Wide Web.

reach. At the time, a CERN researcher could send a document to an overseas colleague using the Internet, but it had to conform to a format that was suitable for CERN's computers. In 1989, Berners-Lee proposed an information system that would create a web of information with documents linked to each other using hypertext. This evolved into the World Wide Web we all use today. In 1990, Berners-Lee developed Hypertext Transfer Protocol (HTTP)—a language computers could use to transmit hypertext-linked documents over the Internet. He also created a method of targeting specific Internet addresses, which became the URL (Uniform Resource Locator) used by web browsers today.

THE INTERNET

In 1991, Berners-Lee made his software and browser systems available on the Internet, and slowly computer enthusiasts, along with the existing Internet community, began to realize the full potential of these new tools. As the number of Web users grew, so too did the number of ways people found to share information. Soon, browsers were developed which could be used by almost all kinds of computers, and the web grew exponentially until it became an immense network of information, covering every facet of human knowledge and interest. Even more remarkably, Berners-Lee made his inventions freely available for all, and he therefore issued no patent, and claimed no royalties for his efforts.

In 1994, he established the World Wide Web Consortium (W3C), to safeguard the independence of the Word Wide Web, and to ensure its smooth working in the face of new technological developments. By the late 1990s, the Web had become a global tool, and in 1999 *Time* magazine named Berners-Lee as one of the 100 most important people of the century. In 2004, Queen Elizabeth knighted him, and today Berners-Lee still supervises W3C, while developing a new information-sharing system, dubbed the Semantic Web, designed to make access to information even easier.

ABOVE: *Massachusetts Institute of Technology (MIT,) in Cambridge, Massachusetts, home of the World Wide Web Consortium (W3C).*
RIGHT: *The NeXT computer, ca 1990, the machine used at CERN by Berners-Lee to devise the Web.*

1991
Berners-Lee makes his systems available on the Internet

1993
CERN announces that the World Wide Web will be free to everyone

1993
New browser systems permit the integration of text and graphics on the Web

1994
The World Wide Web Consortium (W3C) is created in Cambridge, Massachusetts

2010
It is estimated that over a quarter of the world's population uses the Web

PERESTROIKA & GLASNOST ≈ 1989

On June 12, 1987, in an historic speech given at the Brandenburg Gate to commemorate the 750th anniversary of the city of Berlin, Ronald Reagan called upon Mikhail Gorbachev—then General Secretary of the Communist Party of the Soviet Union—to tear down the Berlin Wall. "If you seek liberalization, come here to this gate. Mr. Gorbachev, open this gate. Mr. Gorbachev, tear down this wall!" he urged.

ABOVE: *Mikhail Gorbachev at a summit at the White House in Washington, D.C., in 1990. His open manner appealed to many in the West, but reaction was more mixed in Russia.*

MIKHAIL GORBACHEV

(1931–)

Born on March 2, 1931 to a peasant family, Mikhail Sergeyevich Gorbachev was the last head of state of the U.S.S.R., holding that post from 1988 until the country's collapse in 1991. He graduated from Moscow State University in 1955, and it was during his time at university that he became a member of the Communist Party of the Soviet Union (CPSU), rising through its ranks to become the organization's penultimate general secretary in 1985. Gorbachev's commitment to Soviet reform and willingness to negotiate with U.S. President Ronald Reagan contributed to the end of the Cold War, as well as bringing about the end of political supremacy for the CPSU and the dissolution of the U.S.S.R. Gorbachev received the Nobel Peace Prize in 1990.

LEFT: *The churches and palaces of the Kremlin, alongside the River Moskva in Moscow, Russia. Despite* glasnost, *the Kremlin's red walls retained their forbidding atmosphere.*

GORBACHEV'S VISION

Within less than three years, the tearing down of the Berlin Wall would become a reality, followed just two years later by the total collapse of the U.S.S.R. The terms *perestroika* and *glasnost* have become inextricably associated with this era of Soviet politics, although in fact the terms themselves were not new to Soviet rhetoric: both had been used by Stalin and his successors, while the word *glasnost* exists within the Soviet constitution of 1977. Under the leadership of Mikhail Gorbachev from 1985, however, the words took on new significance.

Perestroika in its broadest sense refers to restructuring, while *glasnost* means openness. It was Gorbachev's hope that through *glasnost*, the Soviet Union might achieve *perestroika*—and with it, a new-found degree of political and personal freedom for all of those living under the Soviet regime. The specific application of *perestroika* that Gorbachev had in mind extended to the introduction of genuinely contested elections and the democratization of the Communist Party. Economically, he saw it incorporating the legalization of cooperatives and semi-private businesses, and the abolition of state monopolies. In fact, he underestimated the power of the concept of *glasnost*, as it snowballed to expose criminality at all levels within the regime and the

KEY DATES IN THE ENDING OF THE COLD WAR

AUGUST 13, 1961
The border between East and West Berlin is closed

1984
Gorbachev highlights the importance of *perestroika* and *glasnost* in a key speech

1985
Gorbachev becomes General Secretary of the Communist Party of the Soviet Union

JUNE 12, 1987
Reagan challenges Gorbachev to tear down the Berlin Wall in a speech at the Brandenburg Gate

1988
Gorbachev becomes the last head of state of the U.S.S.R.

Communist Party, undermining public confidence in his government's ability to deliver on its promises of reform.

DEMOCRACY

Although Gorbachev's concept of *perestroika* was flawed, and his own political career suffered on account of this, it nevertheless allowed a process of liberation and democratization within the Eastern Bloc countries throughout the 1980s that would have been unimaginable just a decade earlier. His political decision that the Soviet Union should not interfere in the anti-Communist revolutions in other Warsaw Pact countries went a long way towards facilitating the fall of the Berlin Wall in 1989.

The actual breach in the wall was the culmination of a chain of events that began earlier that year. The removal of the border fence between Hungary and Austria on May 2 and the official opening of the border on October 10 allowed more than 13,000 East German tourists in Hungary to escape to the West. East German authorities quickly banned travel to Hungary, only to provoke a similar exodus through Czechoslovakia. This time, the travelers were allowed to leave, provoking protests within East Germany. Soon, the protesters' cry of "*wir wollen raus*" ("we want out") gave way to the chant "*wir bleiben hier*" ("we're staying here"). By November 4, over half a million East Berliners were protesting in the city's streets. Egon Krenz, head of the SED, the East German Communist party, took the decision on November 9 to permit East German refugees to exit directly into West Germany—including travel across the wall into West Berlin. News of this momentous decision reached the ears of the world within hours, and as 28 years of enforced partition came to an abrupt and unexpected end, celebrations broke out across Berlin.

THE BERLIN WALL: FACTS AND FIGURES

Stretching some 96 miles around West Berlin including 27 miles of inner-city borders, the Berlin Wall deviated from the political border between East and West only where rivers, canals and railway installations made this absolutely unavoidable. The earliest incarnation of the wall was a crude barbed-wire fence, but it soon evolved into a multi-layered security system featuring over 300 observation towers, more than 250 dog runs, 20 bunkers, and over 60 miles of anti-vehicle trenches. Up to 12 feet high in parts, the "face" of the wall rendered familiar by the world's media was the outer layer closest to the West Berlin side.

ABOVE: *A crowd gathers on the Brandenburg Gate of the newly breached Berlin Wall, November 10, 1989. The wall would be rapidly dismantled over the following weeks.*
LEFT: *Russian poster featuring Gorbachev and the words "Democracy Perestroika Glasnost," from the Museum of Political History in St. Petersburg, Russia.*

MAY 1989
Hungary opens its border with Austria, and East Germans use this route to escape to the West

NOVEMBER 9, 1989
The Berlin Wall is opened after protests by more than half a million people in East Berlin

OCTOBER 3, 1990
Reunification of Germany after a treaty is approved by West Germany and the G.D.R.

1990
Gorbachev is awarded the 70th Nobel Peace Prize

1991
Collapse of the U.S.S.R. and the formation of the C.I.S.

THE END OF APARTHEID 1990–94

South Africa's apartheid system, which discriminated against the majority non-white population of the country, came into being in 1948, when the Herenigde Nasionale Party (HNP) of D. F. Malan coined the term during the election campaign. The party came to power following the manipulation of constitutional boundaries, and the passing of the first apartheid laws swiftly followed.

ABOVE: *A street in the township of Alexandra, on the edge of Johannesburg, after a riot in 1992.*

ABOVE RIGHT: *Nelson Mandela addresses a crowded stadium in the Johannesburg township of Soweto on February 11, 1990, after his release from prison.*

SEGREGATION

The ethos and attitudes on which apartheid was founded can be traced back much further, however, to early 20th-century South Africa and the aftermath of the Boer War. Uneasy power-sharing between white South Africans of English descent and Afrikaners or Boers (the descendants of Dutch settlers) had characterized the political situation for years. The establishment of apartheid provided the HNP—which drew its support principally from the Afrikaner community—with a means of seizing control of the economic and social system in South Africa.

Initially aimed at segregating black and white South Africans, apartheid laws swiftly developed to encompass the separation of a third category of "colored" people, or those of mixed descent. Race laws affected every aspect of life, both social and

NELSON MANDELA
(1918–)

The first South African president to be elected in a fully representative democratic election, Nelson Rolihlahla Mandela is revered around the world for his contribution to the anti-apartheid cause. Born on July 18, 1918, prior to his presidency Mandela was leader of the African National Congress's (ANC's) armed wing, Umkhonto we Sizwe. He was imprisoned for 27 years on charges relating to his relentless campaigning against apartheid, and spent many of these years in the infamous Robben Island prison. His release on February 11, 1990 sparked celebrations around the world, and he served as president of South Africa from 1994 to 1999. In 2009, the UN General Assembly declared that his birthday would be known as Mandela Day, marking his contribution to world freedom.

KEY DATES IN THE LIFE OF NELSON MANDELA AND THE ENDING OF APARTHEID

FEBRUARY 18, 1918
Nelson Mandela born in the village of Mvezo, Transkei, South Africa

1948
Apartheid institutionalized following a general election

1950
Population Registration Act and Bantu Authorities Act are introduced

1951
HNP and Afrikaner Party merge to form the National Party

1953
Public Safety Act; Criminal Law Amendment Act

professional, as inter-racial marriage was prohibited and certain jobs were defined as "white only." The Population Registration Act of 1950 classified all citizens on the basis of their appearance and descent. To be categorized as white, both parents had to be white, and further considerations of "habits, education, and speech and deportment and demeanor" were taken into account. Black people were defined as those who belonged to, or could be assigned to, an African race or tribe, and colored people were those who fit neither category.

Under the Bantu Authorities Act of 1951, each black African was assigned citizenship of an African reserve or "homeland." Between 1976 and 1981, four such homelands were created, effectively denationalizing nine million South Africans. In becoming citizens of these homelands, they lost their rights of citizenship in South Africa. All blacks were required to carry a "pass book" to travel beyond the borders of their assigned "homelands," effectively making them aliens within their own country. The Public Safety Act and Criminal Law Amendment Act of 1953 further diminished the rights of black people, and when in March 1960 a group of blacks in Sharpeville refused to carry their passes, a state of emergency—which would last 156 days—was declared under the terms of these laws. The police opened fire on protesters, killing 167 and wounding 187.

PROTEST

Penalties for any political protest were severe, and large numbers, including the leading anti-apartheid activist Nelson Mandela, were imprisoned for long terms or banished from the country. Many more were sentenced to death or tortured.

Throughout the 1970s and 1980s, the international community began to mobilize against apartheid, vocalizing its discomfort and disgust at its inhumane practices. A period of extreme political violence in South Africa ensued, with black youth rising against "Bantu education" in the 1976 Soweto Uprising. Finally, in 1990 South African President F. W. de Klerk announced Mandela's release, and began the slow process of dismantling apartheid. The reform process was approved by a whites-only referendum in 1992, leading to South Africa's first truly democratic elections in 1994, which returned Mandela as president, with de Klerk and Thabo Mbeki as his deputies.

ABOVE RIGHT: *The platform of the railway station at Wellington, South Africa, with signs that clearly direct whites (or "Europeans") and non-whites to separate facilities of every kind, even telegraph offices.*

LEFT: *Supporters of Mandela's African National Congress gather at a rally before South Africa's first democratic election in 1994.*

GRAND APARTHEID AND PETTY APARTHEID

The practices and attitudes that made up apartheid—an Afrikaans word meaning "apartness"—can be divided into "grand apartheid" and "petty apartheid." Grand apartheid refers to government policies of 1960s and 1970s South Africa, which were designed to divide the country into "white South Africa" and African "homelands." Those relegated to the "homelands" were deprived of rights in "white South Africa," and effectively criminalized. Petty apartheid refers to the practices of the 1950s, when measures reminiscent of America's "Jim Crow" laws segregated residential areas and public spaces of all kinds, including schools, trains, buses, and parks, along racial lines, with the police imposing strict sanctions on any who contravened these rulings.

1960
Sharpeville Massacre, in which 69 people are killed by police during protests

JUNE 16, 1976
Soweto Uprising occurs after protests against the government's policies

FEBRUARY 11, 1990
Mandela walks free from Victor Verster prison, watched by millions around the world

1992
Anti-apartheid reform process approved by whites-only referendum

1994–99
Mandela's presidency of South Africa results from the first fully democratic elections

DNA & THE HUMAN GENOME ≈ 1952–

Deoxyribonucleic acid (DNA) is a macromolecule (or chain of molecules) that contains the key to life—the genetic code that governs the development of all living organisms. The existence of DNA was first suspected as early as 1869, but it was not until 1952 that geneticists first discovered that DNA was a genetic macromolecule.

The following year, the Anglo-American team of Francis Crick and James D. Watson discovered the "double-helix" structure of DNA. Simultaneously, two more British scientists—Rosalind Franklin and Raymond Gosling—produced the images of this "double helix" using x-ray technology. Franklin's Photo 51 provided the world with the first image of a DNA double helix. She died in 1958, but the remaining three scientists were jointly awarded the Nobel Prize for their ground-breaking research.

BELOW: *Francis Crick (left) and James D. Watson (right), photographed in 1993.*

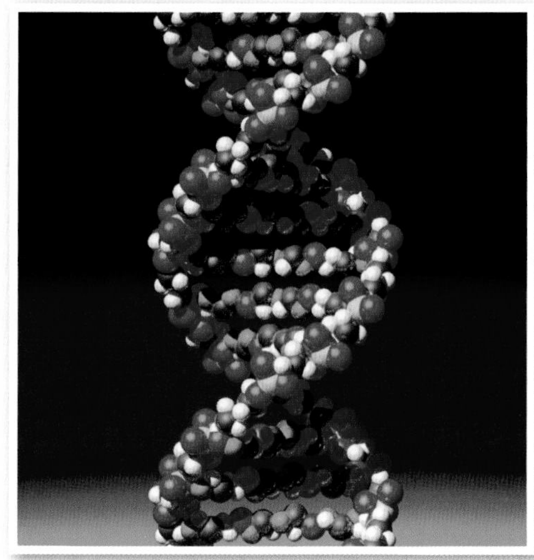

ABOVE: *A model of the DNA molecule, illustrating its intricate double-helix structure.*

MOLECULAR BIOLOGY

This pioneering work led to the development of molecular biology, as scientists attempted to understand the importance of DNA. This early research revealed that the DNA macromolecule was made up of two long polymers—repetitive sequences of molecules linked together by a chemical backbone. This DNA chromosome—the organized structure of DNA and proteins found in cells—forms a genetic code that carries the instructions which govern life. It was found that one part of a chromosome did not interact with the other parts, thereby preserving the integrity of the genetic information it contained. However, scientists proved that genetic crossover could take place, which raised the possibility that they might be able to alter chromosomes, and with them the genetic code. This offered incredible possibilities such as the elimination of hereditary defects. It also raised the prospect that organisms could be cloned or replicated.

Before any such experiments could take place, molecular biologists needed to map out the sequence of DNA, and to identify what the purpose of each part of these complex

KEY DATES OF DNA SEQUENCING

1953 Discovery of DNA double-helix structure by Crick and Watson, and Franklin and Gosling

1972 Development of recombinant DNA technology

1977 The first DNA genome is sequenced, identifying many important features necessary for the production of protein and RNA

1987 The automated DNA-sequencing machine is developed

1990 Large-scale DNA-sequencing research begins in the United States

macromolecules was. The aim was to identify the genome—the unique hereditary information contained in a DNA strand. Work on DNA sequencing began in the 1970s, but the limited technology available meant that progress was slow. In 1975, Frederick Sanger developed a method for DNA sequencing, and two years later he sequenced the genome of the bacteriophage or virus Phi X 174. This proved that DNA sequencing was possible. Other successes followed—in 1984 British researchers successfully sequenced Epstein-Barr, one of the most commonly encountered viruses found in humans. An automated sequencing device introduced in 1987 helped speed up the research.

GROUND BREAKING

In 1990, the U.S. National Institutes of Health began large-scale DNA sequencing, and the Human Genome Project was launched as part of an international effort to understand the sequence of human DNA. In 2000, a draft mapping of the human genome was published, and three years later the full detailed results were made public. This ground-breaking research will pave the way for further advances in medicine and biochemistry, and give scientists the tools they need to tackle disease and hereditary disorder. It is hoped that one day in the not-too-distant future the research might even help scientists discover a cure for cancer and other hitherto incurable diseases.

BELOW LEFT: *A DNA enzyme radiograph shows the order of nucleotides in a strand of DNA.*
BELOW: *Dolly the sheep, photographed in 1997.*

THE MORALS OF DNA SEQUENCING

The genetic code found contained in human DNA consists of approximately 23,000 genes, a quantity similar to the number of genes found in the DNA of other warm-blooded animals. These contain such identifying elements as racial identity, and discussion of the genetic basis of race has led to debates which are controversial on moral or ethical grounds. Some religious groups also oppose any form of genetic research, fearing that this scientific research could undermine religious belief. Scientists counter that, armed with a sound understanding of DNA composition, mankind is better able to help maintain the things that make us unique.

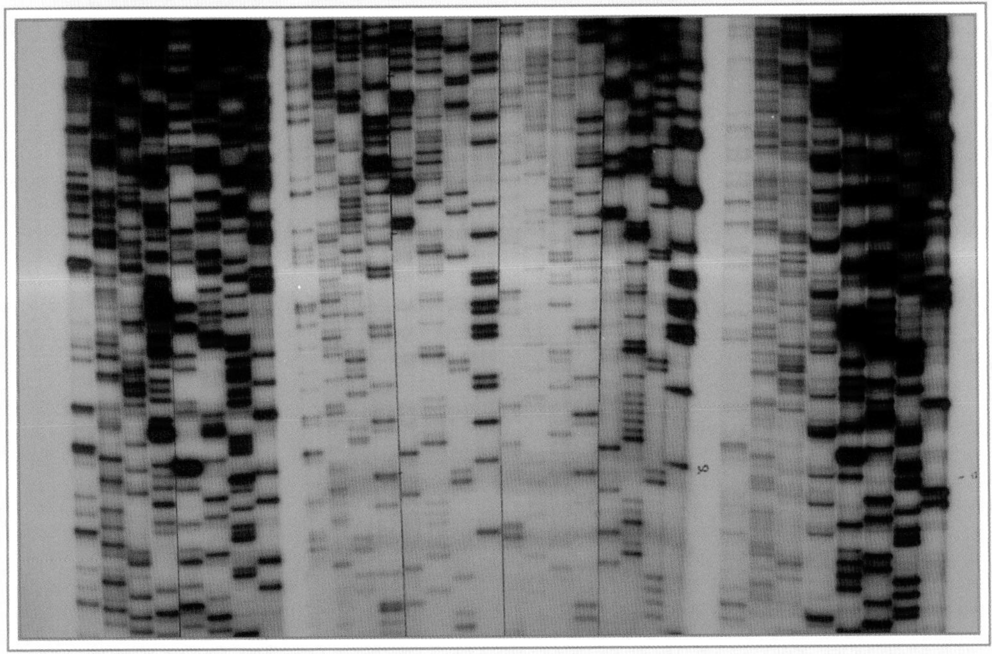

DOLLY THE SHEEP
(1996–2003)

In 1996, scientists from the Roslin Institute near Edinburgh, Scotland successfully cloned a sheep, which they named Dolly. She was created using a process of nuclear transfer whereby DNA from an unfertilized egg is injected into the DNA of the animal being cloned. The cloned cells are then placed inside the womb of an animal, which gives birth in the usual way. Dubbed the world's most famous sheep, Dolly lived for six years, dying from a cancer that was unrelated to her unusual form of birth. She also gave birth to two lambs, and demonstrated the feasibility of animal cloning.

1990
The Human Genome Project is launched with the aim of mapping the DNA sequence of human chromosomes

1995
The first genome of a free-living organism, that of bacterium *Haemophilis influenzae*, is mapped out

1996
Dolly the sheep cloned using a process known as nuclear transfer

2000
A draft map of human DNA sequencing is published, offering the first insight into the genetic code of human life

2003
The sequencing of the human genome is completed, marking the end of one of the 20th century's most ambitious scientific projects

THE 9/11 TERRORIST ATTACKS ≈ 2001

The terrorist attacks against America on September 11, 2001 shocked the world, and had far-reaching consequences for foreign policy and how Americans viewed their country's place in the world. The attacks were a coordinated series of acts against the United States instigated by the radical Muslim terrorist group al Qaeda. Although a major military participator in several wars throughout the 20th century, the United States had never before suffered such devastating outrages on its own soil.

OSAMA BIN LADEN AND AL QAEDA

Osama bin Laden is the man known to be the mastermind behind the September 11 attacks. As one of the founding members of the terrorist group al Qaeda, he planned the attacks and members of his organization carried them out. After initially denying involvement, in 2004 he claimed responsibility for the attacks. The United States is currently engaged in hunting down Osama bin Laden, who is widely believed to be hiding somewhere along the Afghanistan–Pakistan border.

HIJACKED

A total of 19 al Qaeda terrorists hijacked four passenger jets, intending to crash them into major landmarks and symbols of American power. Some of the most striking images of that day are of two of the airplanes crashing into the twin towers of the World Trade Center in New York. A third plane was flown into the Pentagon building in Arlington, Virginia, the headquarters of the Department of Defense. The last plane, United Flight 93, crashed into a field in

LEFT: *The second hijacked plane heads for the World Trade Center, which has already been hit by the first plane. The second impact is just moments away.*

ABOVE: *Osama bin Laden speaks in defiance of the U.S. on Al-Jazeera television, October 17, 2001.*

KEY DATES OF THE 9/11 TERRORIST ATTACKS AND BEYOND

SEPTEMBER 11, 2001: 8:45 A.M.
A hijacked passenger jet crashes into the north tower of the World Trade Center in New York City

9:03 A.M.
A second hijacked airliner crashes into the south tower of the World Trade Center

9:17 A.M.
The Federal Aviation Administration shuts down all New York City airports

9:43 A.M.
American Airlines Flight 77 crashes into the Pentagon

10:05 A.M.
The south tower of the World Trade Center collapses. Huge clouds of dust race down the surrounding streets

rural Pennsylvania, after it had altered course to head towards Washington, D.C. It is thought that the actions of the passengers and aircrew prevented the plane from reaching its final destination. There were no survivors from any of these aircraft.

The most devastating of these attacks were the ones against the World Trade Center. Within two hours of the planes hitting, both towers had collapsed, damaging nearby buildings and shrouding Manhattan in dust. An estimated 2,973 people died as a result of the attacks on September 11, 2001, not including the 19 hijackers. The majority of these were in New York. Before the twin towers collapsed, firefighters and police officers rushed into the burning buildings, hoping to rescue the thousands of people inside. Many perished when the towers collapsed, and the people of the New York City Fire Department became heroes in the eyes of New Yorkers.

THE WAR ON TERROR

Following the immediate shock of such severe damage and human casualties at the heart of American cultural and economic life, the United States government quickly reacted by launching the "War on Terror." This resulted on October 7 in Operation "Enduring Freedom," the invasion of Afghanistan. A coalition of nations took part in the invasion, which was a direct response to the attacks of September 11. The operation's rationale was to depose the Taliban, the fundamentalist Muslim group that had harbored al Qaeda and other terrorists, and capture or kill the man behind the attacks: Osama bin Laden. A decade later, the war in Afghanistan showed no sign of being concluded.

Domestically, America struggled to understand what these terrorist attacks meant. Many re-examined America's place in the world, and there was a new and disquieting sense of vulnerability. In order to prevent such events happening again, the United States government focused heavily on national security, creating a Department of Homeland Security, and passing the PATRIOT Act, which gave the government unprecedented powers to monitor suspected terrorists. In the years since September 11, 2001, there has been an increased focus on terrorism as the principal threat to the security of all Western nations. With the Cold War over, large-scale military conflicts between sovereign states have become increasingly unlikely, and nations around the world are instead adapting their defense policies to counter the threat of international terrorism.

RIGHT: *New buildings, including 7 World Trade Center (right), and memorial gardens have been proposed for the Manhattan site of the September 11 onslaught.*

BELOW: *Damage to the Pentagon (in Arlington, Virginia, near Washington, D.C.) caused by the September 11 attack.*

NEW WORLD TRADE CENTER

In the years following September 11, 2001, various plans have been made to rebuild the destroyed World Trade Center. In the immediate aftermath of the attacks, workers were occupied with clearing rubble and debris, a task which continued for eight months, 24 hours a day. Plans for the 16-acre site include the construction of six new towers, of which 7 World Trade Center has already been constructed (in 2006). A 1,776-foot tower called the Freedom Tower will eventually be built, and will be one of the tallest skyscrapers in the United States. The final site will also include a memorial garden for the victims of the 2001 attacks.

10:10 A.M.
United Airlines Flight 93 crashes in Somerset County, Pennsylvania, southeast of Pittsburgh, after passengers intervene against the terrorists

10:28 A.M.
The World Trade Center's north tower collapses, strewing further debris and dust

OCTOBER 7, 2001
Operation "Enduring Freedom" is launched and a coalition of nations invades Afghanistan

OCTOBER 26, 2001
President Bush signs the U.S. PATRIOT Act, which grants the government increased powers to monitor suspected terrorists

2006
A new tower, 7 World Trade Center, opens at the site of the destroyed World Trade Center in Manhattan

THE PLANET IN CRISIS

In 1920 the world population stood at an estimated 2,000 million (or two billion) people. By 1960 this had increased to 3,000 million. In 2010 the total had increased to 6,802 million people—a doubling of the world population in just half a century. Over the next decade this is set to climb further, with a projected world population of eight billion people by 2020. While the world population has been growing continually since the Middle Ages, a reasonably steady level of increase turned into an exponential curve in the years after the end of the Second World War.

ABOVE: *A boy stands on the cracked, baked mud of a dried-up lake bed, Lac Abbé, Djibouti, Africa, 2007.*
LEFT: *A polar bear on an iceberg on the islands of Svalbard, off northern Norway, in 2004. With ever-smaller ice caps, polar bears are increasingly endangered.*

SCARCITY OF RESOURCES

As early as 1783, scientists predicted that the population would eventually exceed food supply. Fortunately, the post-war population boom coincided with dramatic improvements in agricultural yield, helping to postpone a worldwide crisis for several decades. However, scientists now predict that by 2030 the growing demand for food, water, and energy will reach a critical level. Although birth rates have declined slightly in recent years, improvements in worldwide health care mean that now people live longer. The population explosion is particularly acute in the Indian subcontinent, the Far East, and in parts of Europe and Central America. In these areas it is becoming increasingly difficult to house the booming population without decreasing the arable land available for food production. While scientists are experimenting with ways to increase food production, the long-term prospects for our planet are grim.

CLIMATE CHANGE

A related problem is climate change. The impact of this teeming population on the environment has been profound. Increased land use, higher carbon dioxide levels, pollutants, the use of fossil fuels, and deforestation have all had an effect. In turn, these have cumulatively added to the threat posed by global warming. While climate change is measured over the course of thousands of years, global warming represents the increase in the average temperature of the air around us, and of the world's oceans. The human impact on the environment mentioned above

KEY DATES OF THE CRISIS IN WORLD POPULATION AND CLIMATE CHANGE

1988
Establishment of the Intergovernmental Panel on Climate Change to monitor global warming

1990
The first major report on global warming highlights the scale of the problem

1997
The Kyoto Protocol attempts to combat global warming

2005
The Kyoto Protocol takes effect—apart from the U.S., all industrial nations agree to reduce carbon emissions

2007
A temporary rise in global food prices causes widespread suffering and unrest

A FOOD CRISIS

The dramatic increase in world population means that the demand for food will increase, and unless a solution is found then food shortages will be inevitable, leading to mass starvation and unrest. A foretaste of this came in 2007–08, when increased oil prices, worldwide drought, a reduction in farming subsidies, and financial speculation led to a sharp increase in global food prices. Another factor is rising affluence in parts of Asia, where the growing population is increasingly demanding a more varied diet. This in turn caused food shortages in many developing nations. Was this a sample of what the future holds?

has been blamed for the increased level of greenhouse gases—the gases in the atmosphere that admit and absorb radiation from the sun. As a result solar radiation reaching the Earth's surface will increase in proportion to the increased level of greenhouse gases.

ABOVE RIGHT: *Riot police and protesters clash in Kathmandu, Nepal, in January 2008. A hike in the price of fuel and cooking gas led hundreds of people to join anti-government protests.*
BELOW: *Thousands of protesters throng to Copenhagen, Denmark, for the climate summit in December 2009, to persuade world governments to do more, and do it quickly.*

Scientists predict that an increase in global temperature caused by increased solar radiation will result in melting ice caps, rises in sea levels, reductions in the amount of arable land in the world, the extinction of some species, and increased instances of natural disasters such as flood or drought. Meanwhile politicians, environmentalists, industrialists, and scientists are still arguing about the potential impact of climate change and global warming on our planet. While most world governments have agreed to reduce carbon emissions, and so slow the build-up of greenhouse gases, a handful of the world's leading industrial powers have steadfastly refused to accept a binding limit on the emissions caused within their own borders. Unless an agreement can be reached quickly, the planet will endure the full impact of global warming over the coming decades.

COUNTERING GLOBAL WARMING

Today there is a general worldwide agreement that we face a global warming crisis, and international measures are planned to counter this threat to our planet. Climate change mitigation involves everything from seeking out environmentally friendly sources of energy to carbon sequestration—the storage of carbon emissions on or beneath the Earth's surface. Geoengineering involves finding scientific ways of reducing the build-up of greenhouse gasses and reversing the process of global warming. Apart from the limiting of carbon emissions, or schemes to increase the absorbing of solar radiation, no feasible solution has yet been found.

2008
The United Nations takes steps to avoid future global increases in food prices

2009
In Copenhagen the majority of world powers fail to reach agreement on the capping of carbon emissions

2010
The world population is estimated at more than 6.8 billion people

2030
By this date, scientists expect the planet to face a population and food crisis

2035
According to scientists' predictions, sea levels will have risen by over 16 feet since 2010

THE SPACE STATIONS ≈ 1984–

Ever since the heyday of space exploration in the 1960s and 1970s, countries have sought to place permanent structures in space in order to conduct scientific experiments, develop the technology for further, long-distance space exploration and even for military purposes. In the 1970s, the Soviet Union developed the Salyut series of manned and unmanned space stations, while in 1973 the United States space agency, NASA, launched Skylab.

ABOVE: *The International Space Station orbits the Earth, photographed from the shuttle* Atlantis *in November 2009.*
BELOW: *Launch of space shuttle* Atlantis, *September 2000.*

END OF THE SPACE RACE

In the 1980s, Soviet (later Russian) scientists built the Mir space station, which stayed in orbit for 15 years from 1986 through to 2001, despite a series of on-board accidents.

Both the United States and the Soviet Union had planned further space stations—Space Station Freedom for the Americans, announced by President Reagan in 1984, and Mir 2 for the Soviets. However, the collapse of the Eastern Bloc in 1989 removed the heat from the Space Race between the two former superpower adversaries of the Cold War, and led to a drop in funding for both programs and then their cancellation.

The new-found spirit of cooperation between the two great space powers led to increased American

THE SPACE SHUTTLE

The main workhorse of the ISS construction program has been the U.S. space shuttle. Designed and tested from the late 1960s onwards, the Space Transportation System (STS), as it is officially known, made its first launch on April 12, 1981. A total of five orbiters were built: *Columbia*, *Challenger*, *Discovery*, *Atlantis*, and *Endeavour*. Both *Challenger* and *Columbia* were destroyed in accidents (in 1986 and 2003), with the loss of all the astronauts on board. The shuttle program is nearing the end of its operational life, with the craft due to be retired once the ISS is complete.

KEY DATES OF SPACE EXPLORATION

OCTOBER 4, 1957
Launch of Soviet satellite Sputnik 1, the first man-made object to orbit the Earth

JULY 29, 1969
First manned lunar landing by Neil Armstrong, Michael Collins, and Edwin "Buzz" Aldrin Jr.

APRIL 19, 1971
Launch of first Salyut space station, from the Baikonur Cosmodrome, U.S.S.R.

MAY 14, 1973
Skylab, first U.S. space station, launched. It lasts until 1979

APRIL 12, 1981
Space shuttle *Columbia* undertakes first mission, commanded by John Young

RIGHT: *U.S. astronaut John "Danny" Olivas poses with two Russian Orlan spacesuits in the International Space Station while* Atlantis *was docked with the station, June 2007.*

involvement with the Russian Mir space station and plans were developed for the joint launch of a new space station, based around the work that had already been completed for the Mir 2 and Freedom projects.

COLLABORATION

The result of these collaborations was the International Space Station (ISS) program. The station was designed as a collaborative effort by NASA, the Russian Federal Space Agency (RKA), the Japan Aerospace Exploration Agency (JAXA), the Canadian Space Agency (CSA), and the European Space Agency (ESA). The first components of the station were launched in 1998, and missions to add further structures are still ongoing, with the last taking place in December 2011. All in all, the process will have taken over 45 separate space flights.

When finished, the station will consist of 16 different pressurized modules, covering roughly the same size as a soccer field. These modules consist of the living quarters, scientific laboratories, docking stations, and observation cupolas. Six permanent crew members occupy the station, serving six-month tours before being replaced by one of the regular supply missions undertaken by the U.S. space shuttle or Russian *Soyuz* craft.

The ISS has come in for some criticism from politicians, the press, and even from scientists for the enormous expense of the program; the craft is estimated to be the most costly man-made structure ever built, while it has also suffered considerable delays, and some have claimed that the scientific experiments conducted have lacked ambition. However, the ISS, which will remain in service until at least 2015 and possible longer, has proved to be a successful testing ground for many of the technologies required for more long-distance space travel and lunar bases, both of which are being considered by NASA as future options.

RIGHT: *Chinese astronaut Yang Liwei on his way to take part in China's first manned spaceflight. Jiuquan Satellite Launch Center, Gansu province, October 2003.*

THE FUTURE OF SPACE EXPLORATION

For so long dominated by the two Cold War superpowers, space exploration has become the domain in recent years for the new world powers, notably China and India, to such an extent that it is now possible to talk of an Asian "space race" comparable to that contested by the U.S. and Soviet Union during the Cold War. China launched a first manned space flight in 2003, while India has announced plans for such a flight by 2015. A number of other countries in the region, including South Korea, Indonesia, and Malaysia have also invested heavily in space programs in recent years.

JANUARY 28, 1986
Challenger shuttle disaster sees the loss of the orbiter and all seven astronauts

FEBRUARY 19, 1986
The Soviet Mir station is successfully launched after an initial attempt was aborted three days earlier

NOVEMBER 20, 1998
First module of the International Space Station launched

FEBRUARY 1, 2003
Columbia breaks up on re-entry with the loss of all the crew

DECEMBER 2011
Completion of the International Space Station, a joint operation among five space agencies

INDEX

CREDITS

PICTURE CREDITS

The publishers would like to thank the following sources for their kind permission to reproduce the pictures in this book.

Key: t=Top, b=Bottom, c=Centre, l=Left and r=Right

Akg-Images: /Erich Lessing: 8r, /North Wind Picture Archives: 99b

Alamy Images: /David Lyons: 22r

British Library: /©The Trustees of the British Museum: 15t

Carlton Books Ltd: 98b, 123t, 143t, /Royal Botanic Gardens, Kew: 110r

Corbis: 66r, 78l, 115r, 117t, 119b, 137l, /Peter Adams/JAI: 155t, /Alinari Archives: 50r, /Paul Almasy: 29t, 67l, /James L. Amos: 7t, 77l, /Art Archive: 50l, 56l, 89r, 93t, /Maher Attar: 176r, / Bettmann: 39r, 41l, 49t, 51l, 67r, 73b, 77r, 83br, 85t, 92r, 95l, 102l, 111t, 112l, 115t, 118l, 122l, 129br, 130r, 135 t, 138, 139bl, 140b, 140t, 144l, 149, 150, 152l, 153t, 154b, 156t, 158l, 160r, 162r, 163r, 166l, 166r, 167t, /Blue Lantern Studio: 59b, /Burstein Collection: 29b, 33b, 43b, /Car Culture: 128b, /Enrique Castro-Mendivil/Reuters: 38l, /Marc Charuel/Sygma: 19br, /Dean Conger: 9b, 36l, 158t, /Araldo de Luca: 9t, 51r, /Alessandro Della Bella/ Keystone: 86r /Digital Art: 175r, /Patrick Durand/Sygma: 25t, / Macduff Everton: 66l, /Fine Art Photographic Library: 64l, /The Gallery Collection: 37b, 63l, 68r, 72t, 72r, 80, 89l, 92l, 94r, 95t, 96b, 96t, /©The Gallery Collection/© Succession Picasso/DACS, London 2010: 131t, /Gianni Dagli Orti: 10t, 28l, 30r, 36r, 40, 101b, /Peter Ginter/Science Faction: 168l, /Robert Holmes: 31r, 169t, /Angelo Hornak: 71b, /Dave G. Houser: 57t, 65b, /Hulton-Deutsch Collection: 117b, 123b, 133tl, 134r, 153b, 160l, 161l, 161r, 173r, /John Farmar; Cordaiy Photo Library Ltd: 58l, /Wolfgang Kaehler: 12b, /Kelly-Mooney Photography: 11b, 23b, /Earl & Nazima Kowall: 34b, /Paul H. Kuiper: 63t, /Julian Kumar/Godong: 26, /Masatomo Kuriya: 176l, /Dorothea Lange/Bettmann: 141b, /Charles & Josette Lenars: 17t, 31b, /Liu Liqun: 43t, /Andrew McConnell/Robert Harding World Imagery: 178r, /Dan McCoy - Rainbow/Science Faction: 175l, /Lawrence Manning: 46r, /Francis G. Mayer: 94l, /Manfred Mehlig: 24l, /Mohamed Messara/epa: 35t, /Michael Ochs Archives: 156b, 162l, /Hank Morgan - Rainbow/ Science Faction: 168r, /Nabil Mounzer/epa: 35b, /NASA/Reuters: 180t, /National Archives - digital vers/Science Faction: 125t, /News Photo/Reuters: 19t, /Michael Nicholson: 69b, /Douglas Pearson: 71t, /Perrin Pierre/Sygma: 174, /Sergio Pitamitz/Robert Harding World: 103t, /David Pollack: 129t, /PoodlesRock: 48t, /Louie Psihoyos: 6, /Steven Puetzer: 6t, /William Radcliffe/Science Faction: 124t, /Roger Ressmeyer: 151t, /Reuters: 175r, /Robert Harding World Imagery: 11t, /Royal Ontario Museum: 33t, /David Samuel Robbins: 16l, /Money Sharma/epa: 70b, /Narendra Shrestha/epa: 179t, /Stapleton Collection: 42l, 54, 122r, /George Steinmetz: 18, /Hans Strand: 178l, /©Succession Picasso/DACS, London 2010: 130l, /Swim Ink: 151b, /Luca Tettoni: 16r, /Gustavo Tomsich: 74r, /David Turnley: 172l, /Peter Turnley: 158b, 170, 172r, 173l, / Underwood & Underwood: 53tl, 113l, 118r, 121l, 125b, 157b, / Yoan Valat/epa: 179b, /Vanni Archive: 47b, /Bill Vaughan/Sygma: 177l, /Werner Forman: 28r, 38r, 39l, /Stuart Westmorland: 109t, / Nik Wheeler: 14l, /Ralph White: 127t, 127b, /Roger Wood: 12t, 13r, 17b, /Adam Woolfitt: 88t, /Xinhua/Xinhua Photo: 181b

Getty Images: 177r, /SSPL: 90l, 169b

IStockphoto: /istock.com/Donald Erickson: 136b

NASA: /NASA Great Images in NASA Collection: 164r, /NASA Marshall Space Flight Center Collection: 165t, 165b, /NASA Marshall space Flight Center Collection: 164l

Picture Desk: /Bibliothèque de l'Arsenal Paris/Kharbine-Tapabor/ Coll. Jean Vigne: 48b, /Palace of Chihil Soutoun Isfahan/Gianni Dagli Orti: 79r, /Shandong Provincial Museum/Granger Collection: 19b, /Warner Brothers/The Kobal Collection: 139br

Private Collection: 60tr

Scala Archives: /Digital image, The Museum of Modern Art, New York/Scala florence/© Succession Picasso/DACS, London 2010: 131b,

The Bridgeman Art Library:
/British Museum, London, UK/The Emperor Kiang Hsi on Tour in the Southern Provinces, 1699 (pen, w/c and gouache on silk), Chinese School, (17th century): 87t, /Joseph-Nicolas Robert-Fleury / Louvre, Paris / Peter Willi: 75c, /Jan Matejko / Nicolaus Copernicus Museum: 60b, /© Oriental Museum, Durham University, UK/ Brush pot decorated in famille verte enamels, Chinese, Qing dynasty, K'ang Hsi period (1662-1722) (porcelain): 87b, /Dutch School, (17th century) / The Stapleton Collection: 81 t, /Private Collection / Archives Charmet/Battle of Boyaca (engraving): 103b, /Private Collection/Genghis Khan in battle, preceded by Gebe, one of his generals: 42r, /Private Collection / Peter Newark American Pictures/ Lewis & Clark on the Lower Columbia River, 1905 (oil on canvas), Russell, Charles Marion (1865-1926): 99t, /Private Collection / The Stapleton Collection/Kang Tsi (1662-1722) Manchu Emperor of China from 'Receuil des Estampes, Representant les Rangs et les Dignites, suivant le Costume de toutes les Natio: 86l, /Private Collection/Triumph of the Navigators (oil on canvas), Brooks, Robin (Contemporary Artist): 91t, /National Historical Park, Independence, Missouri, MO, USA /Portrait of William Clark, c.1807 (oil on board), Peale, Charles Willson (1741-1827): 98t

Topfoto.co.uk: 7b, 13b, 21b, 32r, 44l, 62, 63b, 73t, 81br, 100r, 105t, 114, 120r, 121r, 126b, 132b, 133b, 141tr, 142l, 146l, 148b, 152r, 157t, 180b, /AP: 167b, /©2006 Alinari: 68l, /Alinari: 27tr, / British Library / HIP: 27b, 32l, 44r, 45l, /Dinodia: 147r, /Fortean: 61l, /Fotoma: 106b, /The Granger Collection: 2, 10b, 21r, 24r, 37t, 41r, 48b, 49b, 52t, 52br, 53b, 57br, 58r, 59t, 61l, 64r, 65l, 69t, 70t, 75t, 76b, 78r, 79l, 81bl, 83bl, 83t, 84l, 85b, 91b, 99c, 100l, 102r, 104b, 105b, 107l, 107, 108r, 109b, 110l, 112r, 113r, 115l, 116t, 116b, 119t, 120l, 124b, 126t, 128l, 132tr, 135b, 136t, 139t, 159, 163l, /HIP: 13t, 14r, 55t, /HIP / The British Library: 22l, /IMAGNO/Austrian Archives: 93b, 154t, /The Image Works: 76r, /Lightroom Photos: 145b, /Lightroom Photos/NASA: 4-5, / National Pictures: 56tr, /©Photri: 181, /Print Collector / HIP: 20r, 108l, /Public Record Office /HIP: 45r, 111b, 144tr, /RIA Novosti: 53tr, 148t, /RSMPH/Eaglecrown: 171l, /Luisa Ricciarini: 25b, 34t, 46l, 47t, /Roger-Viollet: 8b, 30b, 82, 84r, 88b, 101t, 144br, 145t, / Spectrum/HIP: 23t, /UN: 149b, /UPP: 151c, /Ullsteinbild: 15b, 20c, 27tl, 55b, 74l, 90r, 97t, 132l, 134l, 137r, 142r, 143b, 146r, 147b, 155b, 171r, /© Ken Welsh: 106t, /Woodmansterne: 45l, / World History Archive: 97b, 104t

Every effort has been made to acknowledge correctly and contact the source and/or copyright holder of each picture and Carlton Books Limited apologises for any unintentional errors or omissions, which will be, corrected in future editions of this book.

MEMORABILIA CREDITS

Envelope 1: A: TopFoto.co.uk/Roger-Viollet; B: © The Trustees of the British Museum; C: Goettingen State and University Library: D: akg-images; E: © V & A Images, Victorian and Albert Museum. Envelope 2: A: National Archives, UK; B: The Linnean Society, London; C: National Archives, UK: D: Biblioteka Jagiellonska at the Uniwersytet Jagiellonski, Kraków, Poland; E: Centre Historique des Archives Nationales, France (MUS/AE/I/7-3). Envelope 3: A: Centre Historique des Archives Nationales, France (400/AP/7/24); B: Rare Books & Special Collections Division, The Library of Congress ; C: US National Archives; D: The National Library of Norway; E: Corbis/The Mariners' Museum. Envelope 4: A: Top; B: Corbis; C: Imperial War Museum, Department of Documents: D: tracks.co.uk; E: CERN.

PUBLISHING CREDITS

National Geographic Society:
John M. Fahey, Jr., President and Chief Executive Officer
Gilbert M. Grosvenor, Chairman of the Board
Tim T. Kelly, President, Global Media Group
John Q. Griffin, Executive Vice President; President, Publishing
Nina D. Hoffman, Executive Vice President; President, Book Publishing Group

Prepared by the Book Division
Barbara Brownell Grogan, Vice President and Editor in Chief
Marianne R. Koszorus, Director of Design
Susan Tyler Hitchcock, Senior Editor
Susan Straight, Project Editor
Melissa Farris, Design Consultant
R. Gary Colbert, Production Director
Jennifer A. Thornton, Managing Editor
Meredith C. Wilcox, Administrative Director, Illustrations

Manufacturing and Quality Management
Christopher A. Liedel, Chief Financial Officer
Phillip L. Schlosser, Vice President
Chris Brown, Technical Director
Nicole Elliott, Manager
Rachel Faulise, Manager

Carlton Books:
Editorial Manager: Vanessa Daubney
Art Directors: Darren Jordan & Sooky Choi
Additional design work: Sally Bond & Brian Flynn
Editors: Philip Parker, Catherine Rubinstein & Nicky Jeanes
Picture Researcher: Jenny Meredith
Production Controller: Rachel Burgess

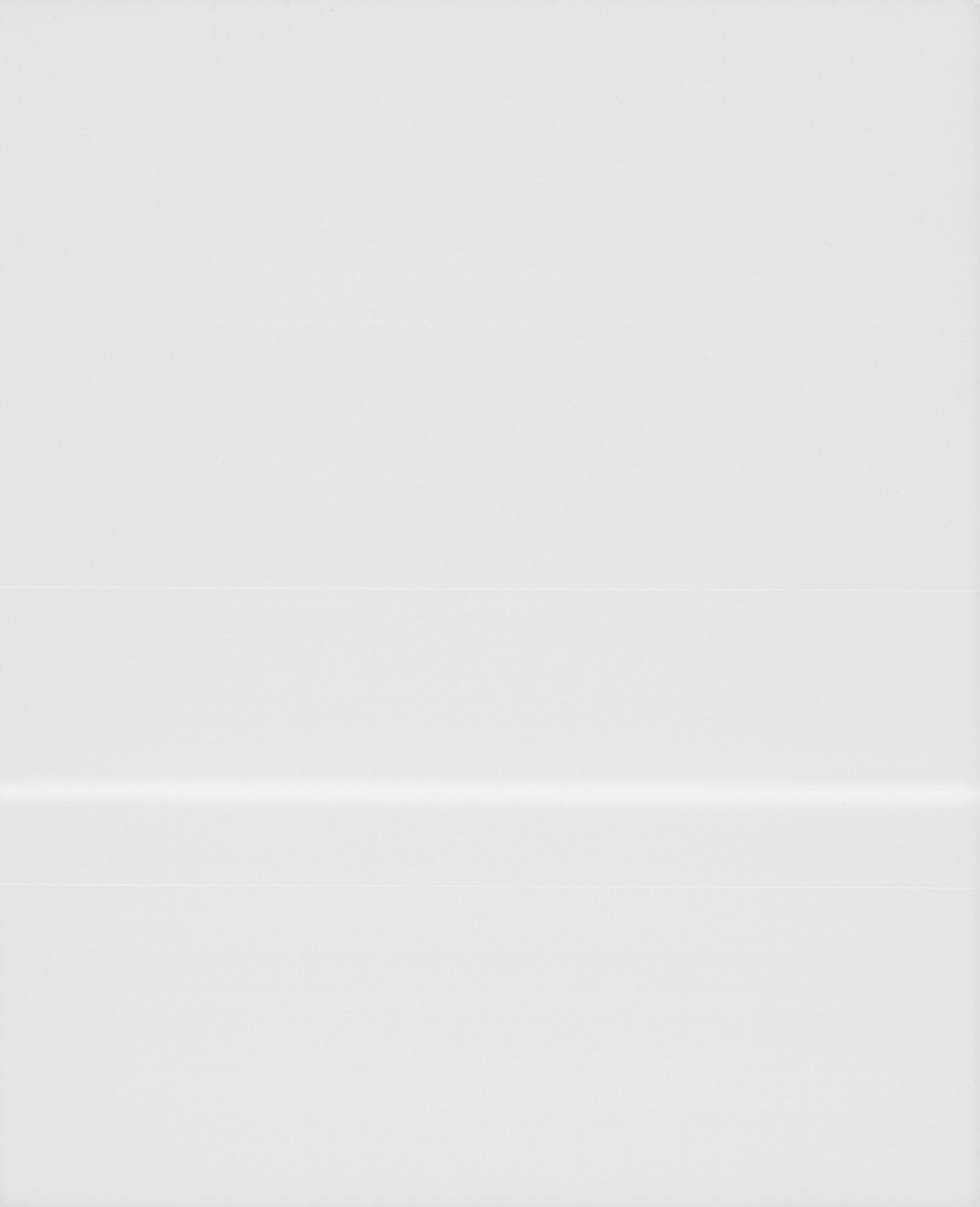